ENTREPRENEURSHIP IN A GLOBAL CONTEXT

This collection presents selected papers from the Fourth Annual Global Conference on Entrepreneurial Research, held in 1994 at INSEAD, France. Covering a wide selection of themes, methodological approaches and organization types, the papers aim to provide global perspectives on a variety of possible approaches to entrepreneurial research.

Employing a multidisciplinary approach, the papers cover all aspects of current Entrepreneurship theory in multinationals, economics, organizational sociology, marketing, leadership and finance. Other issues discussed include gender and networking, strategies in entrepreneurial growth, job satisfaction and franchising. A number of case studies highlight specific examples of entrepreneurship around the world, including the reform of state-owned enterprises in China and Vietnam, regional business creation in Quebec and the Italian tannery industry.

The first volume dealing with international entrepreneurship to draw on both eastern and western perspectives, this will be of interest to students and researchers in international business and related areas.

Sue Birley is Director of Research and Professor at the Management School, Imperial College, London. **Ian C. MacMillan** is Executive Director of the Sol. C. Snider Entrepreneurial Centre and the George W. Taylor Professor of Entrepreneurial Studies at the Wharton School at the University of Pennsylvania.

ROUTLEDGE STUDIES IN INTERNATIONAL BUSINESS AND THE WORLD ECONOMY

ENTREPRENEURSHIP IN A GLOBAL CONTEXT

*Edited by Sue Birley
and Ian C. MacMillan*

London and New York

First published 1997
by Routledge
11 New Fetter Lane, London EC4P 4EE

Simultaneously published in the USA and Canada
by Routledge
29 West 35th Street, New York, NY 10001

© 1997 Sue Birley and Ian C. MacMillan

Typeset in Garamond by
Florencetype Ltd, Stoodleigh, Devon

Printed and bound in Great Britain by
Mackays of Chatham, Kent

British Library Cataloguing in Publication Data
A catalogue record for this book is available from the British Library

Library of Congress Cataloging in Publication Data
A catalogue record for this book has been requested

ISBN 0–415–13132–4

CONTENTS

CONTENTS

FIGURES

FIGURES

TABLES

CONTRIBUTORS

Howard E. Aldrich is Kenan Professor of Sociology, Director of the Industrial Relations Curriculum, Director of the Sociology Graduate Studies Program, and Adjunct Professor of Business at the University of North Carolina, Chapel Hill, USA.

Alexander Ardishvili, Carlson Center for Entrepreneurial Studies, Carlson School of Management, University of Minnesota, USA.

Saugata Banerjee is Assistant Professor of Finance, Koc University, Istanbul, Turkey.

Sue Birley, Management School, Imperial College, London.

Max Boisot, E.S.A.D.E., Barcelona, Spain.

Amanda Brickman Elam is a second-year graduate student in Sociology at the University of North Carolina, Chapel Hill.

William D. Bygrave is the Frederic C. Hamilton Professor for Free Enterprise and Director of the Center for Entrepreneurial Studies at Babson College, Maryland, Visiting Professor at INSEAD (the European Institute of Business Administration) and Special Professor at the University of Nottingham.

Richard N. Cardozo, Carlson Center for Entrepreneurial Studies, Carlson School of Management, University of Minnesota, USA.

Paola Dubini, Universita Bocconi, Milan, Italy.

David Forlani, University of Minnesota, USA.

William B. Gartner is the Director of the Center for the Study of Enterprise and a Professor in the Department of Management, College of Business Administration, San Francisco State University.

Rita Gunther McGrath is Assistant Professor in the Graduate School of Business at Columbia University. She received her PhD from the Wharton School of the University of Pennsylvania.

Thomas D. Kraemer, Wharton School of the University of Pennsylvania, USA.

Umberto Lago, Universita Bocconi, Milan, Italy.

Benoît F. Leleux is assistant professor in the Department of Finance at Babson College, Maryland, USA. He obtained his PhD at INSEAD, where he specialized in both Corporate and Entrepreneurial Finance and is still a visiting professor.

Ian C. MacMillan is George W. Taylor Professor of Entrepreneurial Studies in the Department of Management of the Wharton School of University of Pennsylvania. He is Executive Director of the Sol C. Snider Entrepreneurial Center.

Shuichi Matsuda, Waseda University, Japan.

John W. Mullins, University of Denver, USA.

Atul A. Nerkar is a doctoral candidate in the Department of Management at the Wharton School of the University of Pennsylvania. He is also a Research Associate at the Sol C. Snider Entrepreneurial Center of the Wharton School.

Pat Ray Reese received her PhD in Sociology from the University of North Carolina, Chapel Hill, in 1992. She is currently a Pharmaeconomic Manager, International Research Department, in Glaxo-Wellcome Research and Development, North Carolina.

Gilles Roy, H.E.C., Montreal, Canada.

Paul Severn, Carlson Center for Entrepreneurial Studies, Carlson School of Management, University of Minnesota, USA.

Scott A. Shane, Georgia Institute of Technology, USA.

Itaru Skirakura, Waseda University, Japan.

Anne Sickels, Carlson Center for Entrepreneurial Studies, Carlson School of Management, University of Minnesota, USA.

Steven Spinelli Jr, Center for Entrepreurial Studies at Boston College.

Jean-Marie Toulouse, H.E.C., Montreal, Canada.

Luc Vallée, H.E.C., Montreal, Canada.

S. Venkataraman is Warren H. Bruggeman, '46 and Pauline Urban Bruggeman Distinguished Chair at the Lally School of Management and Technology of Rensselaer Polytechnic Institute. He is also the editor of *Journal of Business Venturing*.

INTRODUCTION

As you will discover in the following volume of research, the Fourth Annual Global Conference on Entrepreneurship Research, held in 1994 at INSEAD, France, included a wide selection of themes, methodological approaches, fields and organization types. In this, it reflects our aims to provide young scholars with a global perspective on a variety of possible approaches in entrepreneurship research.

Another objective of this conference is to give these young scholars an opportunity to present their ongoing research to positive, supportive, helpful senior researchers, and to benefit from their critiques in improving the papers for publication. The feedback on papers has been constructive and most of them have been rewritten in accordance with suggestions.

A serious issue arose when the large increase in the number of papers submitted to the conference made it impossible to include all of them in the proceedings. The participants were therefore asked to vote for those papers they wanted to see published in order of preference. The papers that did not make the cutoff are instead published as abstracts.

The main body of the book therefore consists of those papers that received the votes to be published in full. Abstracts of the other papers are to be found at the end of the volume.

We hope to continue to participate in entrepreneurship research that remains multi-disciplinary in spirit, multi-method in measurement and fascinating in its results.

Sue Birley
Ian C. MacMillan
1995

1

STRONG TIES, WEAK TIES, AND STRANGERS

Do women owners differ from men in their use of networking to obtain assistance?

Howard E. Aldrich, Amanda Brickman Elam and Pat Ray Reese

INTRODUCTION

The growing number of woman-owned businesses has sparked debate on how men and women business owners differ and, more specifically, on the strength of the gender-based disadvantages women business owners face (Brush 1992). Such questions are critical to policy-makers, educators and potential entrepreneurs. Answers to these questions may provide guidelines for training and support programs designed to meet the needs of new business owners. Do women business owners have special needs? How different are their experiences?

Despite past evidence suggesting that male and female entrepreneurs share similar personality traits and demographic profiles, a growing body of research suggests that women entrepreneurs differ from men on some key dimensions. Brush (1992: 16) noted that: 'significant differences have been found in reasons for business start-up/acquisition, timing and circumstances of start-up, educational background, work experience and business skills. More differences are apparent in business goals, management styles, business characteristics and growth rates. These variations suggest that women perceive and approach business ownership differently than men.' Many studies have not been comparative, however, as they examined only men or women but not both, and many have not examined details of the resource mobilization process that lies at the heart of business operations.

In this chapter we examine the impact that gender-based differences in networking behavior have on the ability of men and women entrepreneurs to mobilize the support and resources they need for the survival and growth of new businesses. We believe that business networking is critical to the success of new ventures, and thus we present a framework for understanding network relations between owners and key resource providers. Within the context of this framework, we review some current research and its implications for the success of women-owned businesses. We ask why some of the findings from past research do not correspond to current data describing the actual survival chances of women-owned businesses. After presenting our findings, we consider their implications for policies and programs designed to meet the needs of new business owners.

IMPORTANCE OF NETWORKS

New businesses are founded as a result of motivated entrepreneurs gaining access to resources and finding niches in opportunity structures. From the beginning, social networks are crucial assets for business owners struggling to make a place for themselves in competitive markets. Networking allows them to enlarge their span of action, save time and gain access to resources and opportunities otherwise unavailable. From start-up to stability, the structure of owners' networks affects the life chances of their businesses (Aldrich and Zimmer 1986; Zimmer and Aldrich 1987).

Even though many studies have found very similar psychological profiles and 'traits' for men and women entrepreneurs, this does not necessarily translate into similar patterns of social networking (Chaganti 1986; Goffee and Scase 1985; Hertz 1986; Sexton and Bowman-Upton 1990). Men have more opportunities for meeting higher status individuals (other males) than do women (Aldrich 1989). Because women are subject to occupational and voluntary organizational sex segregation, we might expect limits on women's access to business resources. Work experience and education may partially reduce organizational sex segregation, but marital status and childcare responsibilities may isolate women and increase their separation from business opportunities (McPherson and Smith-Lovin 1986). The social and institutional forces that shape networking opportunities may thus make matters very difficult for individual women entrepreneurs.

Do women differ systematically from men in how they use networks to obtain resources and assistance for their businesses? In particular, are men business owners more systematic and instrumental in network building than women? Answering these questions calls for a comprehensive framework.

NETWORK FRAMEWORK

Entrepreneurs are embedded in networks of social relationships, some of which are personal, such as ties to family, friends and neighbors, and others which are business related, such as ties to customers, vendors and creditors. Social relations are, to varying extents, purposive: some arise because of accidental or unplanned encounters with individuals, some are created via

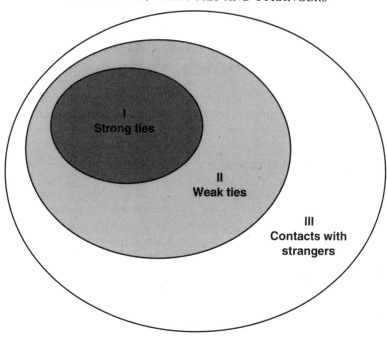

Figure 1.1 Framework of network relationships

organizational memberships, and others emerge as planned interactions to obtain access to specific information. In this sense, then, all entrepreneurs must construct networks of social relations in the process of obtaining resources for their firms.

We find it helpful to organize the types of relationships that make up a person's total set of relations into three circles, according to the strength of a tie, as shown in Figure 1.1 (see Granovetter 1985).

The inner circle (I) represents a business owner's advisor circle and includes a fairly small set of strong tie relationships. Strong tie relationships are usually of long duration and are based on a principle of implicit reciprocity. Individuals tend to make heavy investments in this type of relationship, requiring fairly frequent contact with the other person. Strong ties are typically more reliable than other ties and involve trust and emotional closeness.

The next circle (II), working outwards, involves weak tie relationships. These relationships are of much shorter duration and involve a lower frequency of contact. Weak ties are less reliable and more ambiguous and uncertain than strong ties. They often fade into dormancy, only to be revived when assistance is required.

The third outer circle (III) represents those relationships entered into for pragmatic purposes and may be best described as 'contacts' rather than as ties. Pragmatic contacts usually occur with strangers, or individuals with whom no prior ties have existed. These contacts are typically fleeting in duration and require little or no emotional involvement. We have only limited understanding of the value and importance of these pragmatic ties with strangers. In fact, very little is known about how they are established.

We proposed this three-part framework to help clarify the types of relationships that comprise a business network. In reality, however, the lines between these circles are not so easily defined. The differences between strong ties (Circle I) and weak ties (Circle II) are the easiest to distinguish. Differences between weak ties – which may involve infrequent contacts with other who are barely known – versus contacts with strangers – who are completely unknown – are a little more difficult to recognize. Consequently, most current research addresses strong ties, few studies touch on weak ties, and none really focus on contacts with strangers (Circle III).

CURRENT RESEARCH – HOW DOES IT FIT?

Even though men and women owners may be similar in many respects, some studies suggest that key differences still remain. For example, Sexton and Bowman-Upton (1990), searching for possible disadvantages of women entrepreneurs, found that men and women business owners differed on only two of nine psychological traits relevant to entrepreneurship. According to their results, women business owners scored lower on risk taking and endurance (energy level). Their findings may indicate that women business owners, when faced with limited abilities to develop strong tie networks through the usual channels (Circle I), may be less inclined to seek out the resources and information they require from strangers (Circle III).

Studies examining strong tie relations have found that women business owners are indeed embedded in different social relations than men. Aldrich *et al.* (1989) found significant differences in the sex composition of networks for men and women entrepreneurs in the USA and Italy. They suggested that structural constraints found in the workplace, in marriage and family roles, and in organized social life restricted the social networks of women business owners. Women-owned businesses are typically much smaller and limited to particular sectors of the economy, namely retail and services, as well as the lower status portions of the job market. Essentially, women appear to be left out of the informal, strong tie networks that provide men entrepreneurs with access to the resources and support needed for success and survival. Women entrepreneurs are thus left with the challenge of meeting their own needs through formal, weak tie channels.

Men simply do not include women in their business advisor circles. In a study of Circle I ties in five industrial nations in the late 1980s, Aldrich and Sakano (1995) found that only 10 percent of the people mentioned by men as being relied upon for advice and assistance were women. By contrast, approximately 40 percent of the advisor networks of women business owners were women. Thus, men were involved in mainly same-sex networks, dealing almost entirely with other men, whereas women were involved in mainly cross-sex networks, dealing mostly with men but also with a high proportion of women.

Signs of a higher proportion of cross-sex ties in women's than in men's networks was interpreted by Aldrich and Sakano (1995: 25) as indicating that 'women are seldom found in the personal strong-tie networks of all owners, probably because of women's place in the existing distribution of economic resources and power in these nations.' Furthermore, they found that cross-sex ties were of a shorter duration than same-sex ties and that women entrepreneurs were twice as likely as men to have used a broker or third party to meet more powerful (men) network members. Based on these results, we could conclude that women business owners must rely on other strategies of network building, involving weaker ties, to gain the resources and support they need.

According to Brush (1992), women's domestic responsibilities and limited mobility chances at work, together with other institutional factors such as sexism and patterns of childhood socialization (Gilligan 1982), combine to produce a different way of approaching business ownership. Building on work by Aldrich (1989) and others, Brush (1992: 16) suggested a new perspective on women entrepreneurs – the integrated perspective – which posits that 'women perceive their businesses as "cooperative networks of relationships" rather than separate economic units. In this conception, business relationships are integrated rather than separated from family, societal and personal relationships.' If women experience their personal reality as a seamless web of interconnected social relationships spanning work, family and other domains, whereas men view reality in separate and autonomous domains, then it seems likely that women would be less comfortable if they had to rely on weak ties and contacts with strangers.

In summary, past research indicates that the effects of structural constraints and gendered socialization may force women to rely more on relationships with weak ties and contact with strangers. Such relations could have two consequences:

- reluctance to seek out assistance from these relationships;
- fewer resources and less support from their networks than men.

However, these implications have not been put to an empirical test.

Implications

Strong tie networks are critical to the success of small business. Small business owners are in a difficult position in modern economies and strong ties of intimate friendship can provide social support than enables owners to weather crises and hardship. Strong tie relations of long duration are cemented by loyalty and trust and stand as a bulwark against an owner's being exploited by people out only for short-term gain. Past research suggests that women business owners are 'out of the loop.' Women are constrained by structural factors as well as by socialization. Not only do they apparently fall outside of the famed 'old boy's network,' but the business reality they face, or the more integrated approach they take to business, may further constrain their ability to succeed.

Given the importance of strong tie networks to the success of new ventures and women's exclusion from men's advisor networks, we might infer that women business owners have special needs. Based on prevailing evidence, policy-makers might conclude that programs should be designed to educate and support women business owners differently from men. Before jumping to any conclusions, however, we should examine these implications in the context of the actual success of women-owned businesses, relative to those of men. In particular, we need to look more closely at weak ties and contacts with strangers, to determine whether the pattern of gender disadvantage in strong ties carries over into other areas of women owners' social relations.

WHAT'S MISSING?

In their panel study of small businesses in Indiana, Kalleberg and Leicht (1991) actually found that, all things being equal, businesses run by women were just as likely to succeed as those run by men. They acknowledged that some gender differences do exist, that some factors seem to operate more favorably for one gender than the other, and that women do appear to face barriers originating from socialization practices, education experiences, family roles and weaker networks. Nonetheless, it appeared that women-owned businesses were generally able to survive and succeed, in spite of these gender barriers. Reese and Aldrich (1995), in their panel study of business survival in the Research Triangle Park Area of North Carolina, came to a similar conclusion.

These findings seem to contradict the dire implications of the research and theorizing we reviewed earlier. What produces such contradictions? Much of the research in the past has primarily considered the value and importance of strong tie circles, rather than weak ties or stranger contacts. Despite the indicated gender barriers and disadvantages, women entrepreneurs appear to be succeeding. Are women business owners, in fact, capable of mobilizing the necessary resources and support through their social relationships in Circle II and Circle III? Our results suggest that, indeed, this is the case.

STUDY OVERVIEW

Using data from a two-wave panel study on the networks of potential and active entrepreneurs in the Research Triangle Park Area of North Carolina, USA, we considered how women entrepreneurs compare to men in three areas: the process of acquiring information and assistance, relations with the people who supplied the assistance, and the cost and quality of assistance obtained. In this chapter we restrict our data analysis to the 217 entrepreneurs (157 men and 60 women) who were business owners at our initial contact in 1990 and whom we were able to interview again in 1992. We sampled most of them from the membership lists of organizations we found in the Research Triangle Area.

We wanted to study individuals in the early stages of organizational formation, as well as established organizations with a transaction history, and so in an exploratory phase of our project we located voluntary and non-profit organizations of interest to entrepreneurs in the Research Triangle Area of North Carolina. This area includes Raleigh, Durham, Cary, and Chapel Hill, and is well known because of the more than forty large firms and research institutes located in the Research Triangle Park, including IBM, Northern Telecom, Glaxo-Wellcome, BASF, the Environmental Protection Agency, Research Triangle Institute, and the SAS Institute.

Organizations differed in sex composition, purpose and membership interests, but they all focused on entrepreneurial or business activity:

1   the Council for Entrepreneurial Development (CED), based in Durham, included both entrepreneurs and service providers as members;
2   six networking organizations, all of which included both entrepreneurs and employees;
3   participants at Wake Tech Small Business Center classes, including entrepreneurs in very early stages of business start-up;
4   the National Association of Women Business owners (NAWBO), which is restricted to women entrepreneurs.

Our initial sampling list was constructed from members of those organizations. We added another subsample, randomly selected from business start-ups, to use as a reference. This sample was selected from new businesses that filed registration forms in Wake County, which includes Raleigh.

We collected the initial (Time 1) data in two phases. Phase I was a short questionnaire, which could be completed in about five minutes: Phase II involved in-depth, 30- to 40-minute telephone interviews that included structured and open-ended questions. We collected the Time 1 questionnaires and conducted interviews during a nine-month period in 1990 and 1991.

Combining all subsamples, we distributed 659 questionnaires and received 444 in a usable format, for an average response rate of 67 percent, as shown in Table 1.1. Response rates across the subsamples ranged from 41 percent to 78 percent. We conducted a total of 353 telephone interviews, yielding completed interviews for 54 percent of those who received questionnaires and 80 percent of those who returned a questionnaire.

Our response rates compare favorably with other efforts to study entrepreneurs. Birley *et al.* (1990), using records similar to those we used in the business sample, achieved a 24 percent response rate; Cooper and Dunkelberg (1987) reported a 29 percent return; Aldrich *et al.* (1987) achieved less than a 41 percent return in a study of CED members; and Kalleberg (1986), using phone interviews which traditionally have a higher response rate than questionnaires, reported response rates between 55 percent and 68 percent, although he excluded non-working phone numbers in his calculation, whereas our rates include such cases as non-responses. Our response rates and tests of non-response bias (Reese 1992) increase our confidence in our findings.

Table 1.1 Sample size and response rates

	Time 1			Time 2		
	Question-naire	Follow-up phone interviews	Question-naire	Questionnaire and phone interview		
Sample source	Number distributed	% returned	Percent of return completing interview	Number mailed	Fully completed %	Partially completed %	Combined completion %
CED members	339	76	82	250	53	37	90
Networking organization members	67	78	83	49	43	43	86
Wake Tech students	78	68	79	52	25	58	83
Business sample	150	41	64	61	39	45	84
NAWBO sample	25	76	84	19	63	32	95
Total percent	—	67	80	—	64	24	88
Total number	659	444*	353	431*	203	177	380

Note: *The difference between the 444 questionnaires returned at Time 1 and the 431 respondents followed up at Time 2 is due to people who refused to participate further at the end of Time 1 or who were lost to the sample during interviewing for Time 1 for other reasons.

In June and July of 1992 we contacted respondents who had returned questionnaires two years earlier. Of the 444 returned questionnaires, we removed 13 cases from the Time 2 sample for a variety of reasons: six respondents had moved between the first and second phase of the Time 1 data collection and could not be tracked two years earlier, four questionnaires contained large amounts of missing data, and two people had explicitly notified us that they did not want to participate in any future studies. We mailed questionnaires to the remaining sample of 431.

We used a two-phase approach much like our Time 1 contact: we began with a short questionnaire and conducted short follow-up telephone interviews. We repeated several of our networking measures: we asked about the entrepreneur's business, whether they had made specific changes in their business, their use of resources, information about their business strategy and environment, their reasons for starting the business, and their business performance, as well as information on new businesses that entrepreneurs had begun in the two years since our initial contact.

We had a very good response from our second round of contacts, as shown in the four right-hand columns of Table 1.1. Of the 431 mailed questionnaires, we received questionnaires from 246 entrepreneurs and completed a short follow-up interview with 175 of them. We collected full information on an additional 28 respondents by asking the questionnaire and interview questions during a long telephone interview. Thus, we have extensive data on 64 percent of the sample and complete or partial information on 88 percent of the Time 1 participants.

Because few researchers have attempted this kind of panel study of entrepreneurs, we have little to compare with our response rates. Kalleberg and Leicht (1991), in the second wave of their panel study of small businesses in Indiana, completed interviews with 70 percent of their original businesses. They obtained information that 34 companies were out of business, giving them information about 78 percent of their original sample. For our study, collecting information on 88 percent of the sample respondents after a two-year period of time gives us increased confidence in our results. In this chapter we restrict our data analysis to the 217 entrepreneurs who were business owners at our initial contact in 1990 and whom we were able to interview again in 1992.

Sample characteristics

We first checked that the 27 percent of our sample that are women did not differ in fundamental ways from the men. Otherwise, the simple tables we present might show sex differences because subsample compositions differ drastically, rather than because women are using networks in different ways from men. The age, business age and industry distributions for men and women owners in our sample do not differ significantly, as shown in Table

1.2. About two-thirds of both groups are between the ages of 35 and 54, as we would expect from previous research on entrepreneurship, and almost none are under 25. Only about one in nine are over 55.

Age of the owner's current business was measured in 1990, and so the surviving businesses in our second wave of interviewing are about two years older, on average, than the business ages shown in Table 1.2. In 1990, almost one-third of the women and men had been in their current business less than two years, reflecting our success in finding businesses in their formative period. About 59 percent of the men and 51 percent of the women had been in business less than four years. In a previous paper (Reese and Aldrich 1995), we showed that the youngest businesses were the least likely to survive as active firms over the two-year study period: only 65 percent of those under one year old were still active in 1992, compared to 84 percent of those between three and four years old.

Most businesses were in the services sector, especially business and professional services. In our previous paper (Reese and Aldrich 1995), we found that survival rates varied slightly across industries, with retail firms the least likely to survive and finance, insurance, and real estate firms the most fortunate. For our purposes, the most important point to note is that the industry distribution does not differ significantly by sex. As we described in the section on research design, our main goal in sampling was to increase the number of women owners and to obtain a representative sample, not to produce a quota by industry. Nothing was done in our sampling plan to equalize numbers of firms by industries. Thus, our finding that there is no sex difference in the industry distributions suggests that men and women appear to have equal access to initial business opportunities in the Research Triangle.

The women owners in our sample have completed significantly fewer advanced degrees than the men, but both groups are fairly well-educated. Only about 10 percent of either group stopped their education with a high school degree, and 40 percent of the men and 29 percent of the women earned a post-graduate degree of some kind. One in eight of the men have a PhD or MD, compared to one in fourteen of the women. The high level of technical qualification of our sample reflects the industrial base of the Research Triangle, with many knowledge-intensive firms (such as Glaxo and IBM) as well as three major research universities, plus smaller colleges and universities. As we will show in our subsequent analyses, the more advanced educational qualifications of the men do not seem to have given them any substantial advantages over the women.

FINDINGS

In our analyses, we present information in graphic form. Full information on all analyses and more details on the study are available from the senior author.

Table 1.2 Personal and business characteristics of sample at Time 1 (1990)

Owner's age (yrs)	Sex of owner		Business age (yrs)	Sex of owner	
	Men	Women		Men	Women
Under 24	1	2	0–1.9	32	33
25–34	20	24	2–2.9	13	10
35–44	41	42	3–3.9	14	8
45–54	28	21	4–9.9	30	32
55+	11	11	10+	11	17
Total percent	101	100	Total percent	100	100
(N)	(229)	(84)	(N)	(230)	(84)
	$X^2 = 2.62$, N.S.			$X^2 = 4.20$, N.S.	

Industry	Sex		Business education	Sex	
	Men	Women		Men	Women
Construction	4	6	High school	9	11
Manufacturing	12	12	College (2 yr)	7	23
Transportation	2	4	College (4 yr)	44	37
Wholesale	4	4	MA, MS,		
Retail	8	12	MBA, JD	28	22
Finance, ins, RE	9	8	PhD, MD	12	7
Services	60	54			
Other	1	1			
Total percent	100	101	Total percent	100	100
(N)	(227)	(84)	(N)	(229)	(83)
	$X^2 = 3.35$, N.S.			$X^2 = 18.18$, p=.001	

The process of acquiring assistance

One implication of the critical literature on sex differences is that women might be less pro-active in pursuing opportunities than men, as their autonomy is constrained because they view business activity as integrated into the rest of their lives. A sociological perspective would argue that, regardless of their personal views, women's embeddedness in a network of obligations and responsibilities could limit their freedom of action. Men, by contrast, are said to see their businesses as independent from the rest of their lives and thus are free to follow opportunities wherever they may lead. Moreover, institutional arrangements permit such action. Our findings do not support these expectations, as shown in Figure 1.2.

We asked owners if, during the past year, they had asked for four different kinds of assistance: legal, financial or accounting, business loans or business financing, and advice from someone with experience in the same line of work. Legal and financial or accounting advice are consulting services usually provided by professionals, and business loans are almost always provided by banks, insurance companies, or other institutions. By contrast, advice from

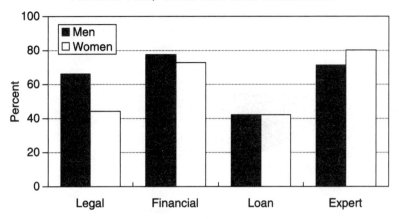

Figure 1.2 Percentage of owners who asked for assistance in obtaining four resources, by sex. Question: 'During the past year, have you asked for . . .?'

an 'expert' is more informal in nature. Thus, we have a range of types of assistance sought as well as possible types of providers. Nonetheless, entrepreneurs also need many other types of resources and our research is thus limited in its generalizability to the specific range that we were able to study.

In Figure 1.2, we show in bar graphs the percentage of men and women owners who reported they sought each type of assistance. In three of these four areas, we found no significant difference between men and women in the proportion asking for advice: about three-quarters of all owners asked for financial or expert advice, and about two-fifths asked for assistance with business loans. The only significant difference was in legal assistance. About 66 percent of the men, but only 44 percent of the women, had asked for legal assistance.

We explored this difference further by asking owners why they had asked for legal help and found no significant differences between men and women. As one might imagine, owners sought legal assistance for a variety of reasons and so we created a six-category scheme to code their responses. We found no significant gender differences in the reasons offered for seeking legal assistance. Men were no more likely to be involved in being sued, or suing someone, than were women owners. Similarly, very small proportions of both groups had sought legal assistance for creating incorporation papers or partnership agreements.

We also asked how many different people owners had sought out for assistance, testing the hypothesis that perhaps women had been more restrictive in their search than men. Again, however, in all of the four areas, we found no significant differences in the number of people contacted. Most owners had gone to only one or two people for legal, financial, and loan assistance, with men more active than women only in seeking loan assistance. Both groups were more active in seeking advice from someone in the

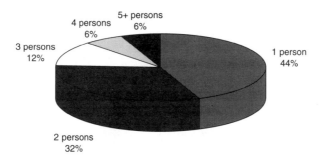

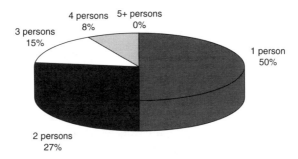

Figure 1.3 Number of lawyers who were contacted, by sex

same line of business, as about two-fifths sought assistance from five persons or more.

Because fewer women had sought legal advice than men, as shown in Figure 1.2, we looked more closely at those women who had searched for lawyers, comparing them with men who had sought legal advice. As shown in Figure 1.3, a detailed picture of the scope of the search engaged in by each group revealed very similar behaviors – women were essentially just as active as men in trying to find a lawyer to handle their business affairs. Thus, neither in the reasons they sought assistance nor in the intensity of their search – once they had decided on seeking legal assistance – did women owners differ from men.

We also looked more closely for possible difference as to why men and women owners were seeking assistance in obtaining business loans or business financing. We found no significant difference between men and women in the reasons they offered: about 20 percent of each group were concerned about their cash flow, another 20 percent were applying for a loan, and about one-quarter needed expansion capital. Indeed, the similarity in specific reasons mentioned was remarkable across the two groups.

Our results show that women were as active as men in networking activities in three of four critical areas: seeking financial, business loan, and expert assistance for their businesses. Only in the realm of seeking legal assistance were men more active and, even then, women owners who decided to seek such advice pursued as many leads as did men. The reasons they reported for seeking assistance were also indistinguishable.

The nature of relationships: who do owners seek out for assistance?

Instead of positing a difference in levels of networking activity, theories of sex differences sometimes assume that women seek assistance through different channels than men. Brush's (1992) 'integrative model,' for example, implied that women would be more likely to turn to family and friends than to work associates. If women are less opportunistic and prone to risk-taking, as some theories have suggested, then they may be less likely to seek assistance from strangers – people with whom they have no pre-existing tie (Sexton and Bowman-Upton 1990). To investigate this proposition, we asked owners about the last person they had contacted regarding a particular resource: 'Do you have a relationship with him/her, other than a consultant one – is he/she a family member, friend, a work associate or a member of the same organization?' Our results are displayed in Figure 1.4.

Three results stand out in Figure 1.4, which classifies the 'other' person by the primary relation identified: stranger, family member, friend, or business associate. First, women do not differ significantly from men in the proportion who sought assistance from strangers, ranging from a low of 25 percent of the men and 29 percent of the women seeking 'experts' to a high of 87 percent of the women and 88 percent of the men seeking business loan advice. Second, neither women nor men relied on family members for assistance for the four resources we asked about – in spite of Brush's (1992) arguments about business women living a more integrated life, women entrepreneurs show no greater inclination than men to ask family members for help. Instead, men and women apparently turned to people with the necessary qualifications, rather than relying on blood ties. Third, the overall pattern of relations is essentially the same for women and men – none of the differences in Figure 1.4 are statistically significant.

For legal and financial assistance, slightly less than half the owners turned to persons with whom they had a prior relationship. Almost no one turned to family members. Instead, they sought assistance from friends, work associates and people with whom they shared an organizational affiliation. Almost nine in ten owners of both sexes went to an accountant for financial assistance and all owners went to lawyers for legal advice, suggesting that most had no family members or friends in these professions.

About 42 percent of both groups sought assistance with business loans and almost all of them asked advice from people they did not know

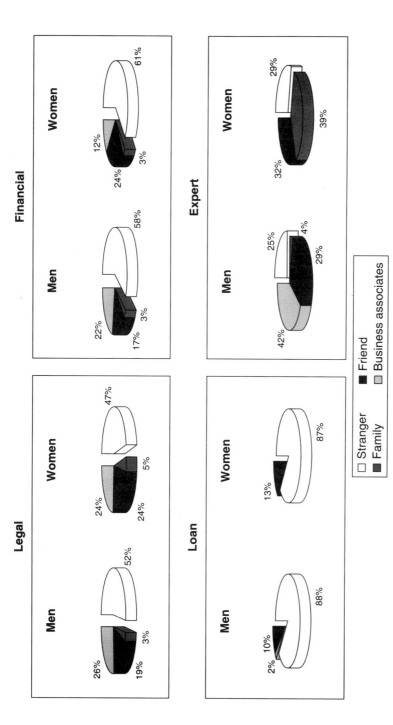

Figure 1.4 Owner's relationship to the last person they contacted for assistance, by sex. 'Percent who had specific type of relation to person contacted'.

previously. Only about one in ten made use of an existing non-consultative relationship to obtain assistance with business financing. Slightly more women than men, proportionately, used a bank loan officer for assistance, but the difference is not statistically significant.

Network ties played the biggest role in providing a channel for owners to seek advice from someone with experience in their own line of business. Only 25 percent of men and 29 percent of women owners turned to experienced persons with whom they had no prior ties. A slightly higher proportion of men than women sought advice from persons they had business relationships with, including competitors. Friends played a more important role in providing expert assistance than in any other domain, as 29 percent of men and 39 percent of women sought advice from them. About one-quarter of the friends were also identified as having some type of business relationship with the owner.

Clearly, when seeking assistance in obtaining crucial business assistance, men and women use similar channels: friends and business associates. Neither group relies on family members and neither shows a reluctance to seek out new persons with whom no pre-existing non-consultative tie has been established (i.e. the strangers we have placed in Circle III of our framework).

Cross-sex contacts

Might there still be a sex bias in the relationships relied upon by women owners? We investigated this possibility by asking owners the sex of the last person they had asked for assistance. In Figure 1.5 we show the percentage of men and women to whom the owners talked within each of the four domains. Men turned overwhelmingly to other men for assistance – for three of the four resources, three-quarters or more of the persons men asked for advice were men. Women also turned mostly to men for assistance, although not to the same extent as did male owners. In all four cases, the proportion of women asked for advice by women is higher than the percentage of women asked for advice by men, but in only two cases – loans and expert advice – is the difference statistically significant.

We noticed that the resource for which women owners turned most frequently to other women was business loan assistance and we also noticed that both men and women turned mostly to strangers for such advice. We speculated about whether women sought advice from other women more frequently when they had a pre-existing relation with the other party. Therefore, to test this idea, for each resource we examined whether having a prior relation affected the likelihood that a woman would be asked for assistance.

For men owners, the proportion of persons asked for advice who were women did not depend on whether a prior relation existed. For women owners, however, when they had no prior ties to the person from whom they sought legal assistance, all ten advisors were men. By contrast, 45 percent of the 14 persons they turned to because they already had a prior relation were women. Prior relations made no difference for financial assistance and too few cases were available of prior relations concerning loan assistance to allow an analysis. For expert advice, there is a hint of an association, but it is not statistically significant: 46 percent of the 24 persons to whom women owners turned and with whom they had a prior relation were other women, whereas of the strangers from who they sought advice, only 20 percent (two out of ten) were women.

Thus, although men and women draw on the same types of social relations when seeking assistance and turn to the same organizational representatives when required (accountants, bank loan officers), women appear to seek out other women when it is possible. Note, however, that this same-sex bias is highly resource specific; when women owners rely on prior ties they are much more likely to ask a woman for advice than otherwise. For advice about business loans, women may perceive that other women have experienced more turn-downs in loan applications than men, and thus they want information from the most relevant population. For legal assistance, women seeking advice who did not know any lawyers with the required expertise ended up with only men as advisors. When they knew someone already in that domain, it was much more likely that they chose a woman advisor (although most were still men).

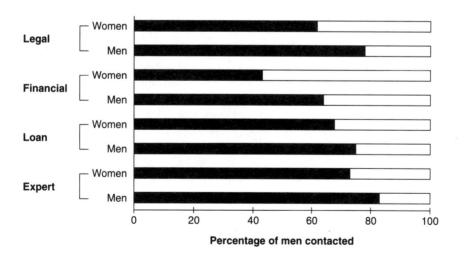

Figure 1.5 Percentage of owners who contacted a man to obtain specific assistance, by sex

17

Paying for the assistance obtained

We study networks in part because we believe that they take some business relations 'out of the marketplace,' allowing entrepreneurs to obtain resources without depleting their hard-earned capital. The 'old boy network' is said to favor men and disadvantage women. If true, then men using their network ties ought to secure favors not available to women. Thus, we investigated the extent to which women owners were as successful in obtaining assistance at below market rates as men.

We asked owners, 'Did you pay the market rate for the assistance you obtained?' Our results are shown in Figure 1.6.

Owners' abilities to avoid paying the market rate for advice differed dramatically by which resource they sought. Most paid market rates for legal and financial/accounting advice and many paid it for loan assistance, but almost no one paid the going rate for advice from others in their line of business. In two cases – financial and expert advice – women fared no better than men, having to pay the same rates as men. However, in the other two cases – legal and loan advice – women did better than men.

In every case, as we would expect, owners who had some type of prior relation with the provider were much less likely to pay market rates than other owners (analysis not shown). As we showed in Figure 1.4, women owners were as likely to have prior relations with advice providers as men, and so they benefited in equal measure from such relations. The most extreme case is expert advice: only 7 percent of owners with a prior relation to their advisor provider paid market rates, compared to 23 percent of those who went to strangers.

Quality of the assistance obtained and its consequences

Do women obtain the same quality advice as men? We asked owners to rate the quality of the advice they obtained on a scale from 0 to 100, a procedure that our respondents found easy to carry out. In essence, we were asking for a 'report card' on their service providers. Most were quite favorable, as shown in the average ratings they reported: 81.2 for legal assistance, 82.4 for financial assistance, 70.4 for loan assistance, and 79.4 for experts' advice.

In Figure 1.7, we show the ratings separately for men and women. In three of the four cases, women rated quality nearly identically to men. Only in the case of financial/accounting advice did women rate the advice they obtained significantly less favorably than men, although the difference is not large (8 points on a 100-point scale).

Another indicator of assistance quality is whether the assistance or advice received changed business practices. We asked owners to tell us whether they had changed the way they do business as a result of the assistance they obtained, and the results are displayed in Figure 1.8. in most cases, owners

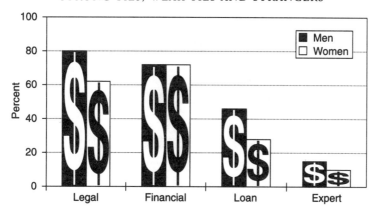

Figure 1.6 Percentage of owners who paid market rate for the assistance they obtained, by sex

did not change the way they did business, based on the assistance they received. Women were as unlikely to change as men in three of the four cases, but they differed from men in the way they used financial advice. Only one-fifth said they had changed the way they did business because of the financial advice they received, compared to about one-third of the men in our sample.

Curiously enough, the advice with the most powerful influence on business operations is that obtained from others in the same industry at below market rates. For women, advice from experts was the assistance most often sought, as shown in Figure 1.2; for men, it was the second most frequent type of assistance sought. Women owners conducted their most extensive search for assistance while looking for experts. Most owners – men and women – were able to find someone they knew, whether as a friend or work associate, who could provide expert advice, thus increasing the likelihood that they would not have to pay market rates for the assistance. Programs that bring established owners together with prospective owners should thus be a high priority for any economic development policies aiming to raise business founding and survival rates.

We have found that women do not seem to be disadvantaged by not being part of an 'old boys' network' when it comes to assistance that can be obtained from strangers or from experts known to them. Women seemed to benefit slightly more from their networks, as measured by being able to pay less than market rates for legal and loan assistance. They apparently received the same quality advice as men, regardless of what they paid, and they were no more likely to use the advice they received than men. We thus found no evidence that the material results of women's networking differ in any substantial ways from those for men. Both groups were able to find ways to obtain high-quality assistance at market rates for legal, business loan, and

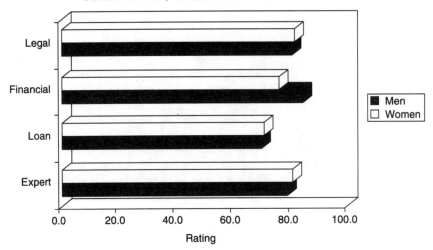

Figure 1.7 Owners' ratings of the quality of the assistance they obtained, on a scale of 0 to 100, by sex

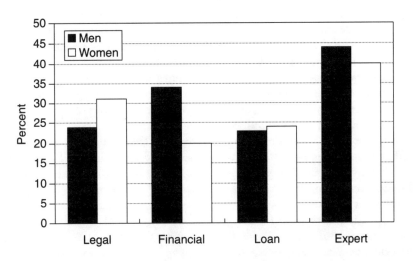

Figure 1.8 Percentage of owners who say that they changed their business practices as a result of the assistance they obtained, by sex

financial/accounting information, and high-quality assistance from other people in the same line of work at below market rates.

CONCLUSION AND RECOMMENDATIONS

From start-up to stability, the structure of owners' networks affects the life chances of their businesses, and thus studies of entrepreneurial networking have mushroomed in the past decade. Previous studies have told us a great deal about the personality and demographic characteristics of women owners, but few have focused on the comparative question we addressed: Do women differ systematically from men in how they use networks to obtain resources and assistance for their businesses? We reviewed some arguments for why women's networking might differ from men's, and used the previous literature to generate some guiding principles for our analysis.

Based on a two-wave panel study of 217 business owners in the Research Triangle Area of North Carolina, we conclude that women entrepreneurs are as active as men in networking to obtain assistance and as successful as men in obtaining high-quality assistance, some of which they obtain at below market rates.

Summary of findings

We examined entrepreneurs' networking activities in pursuit of four resources: seeking legal, financial, business loan, and expert assistance for their businesses. Our results show that women were as active as men in networking activities in three of these four critical domains. Only in the realm of seeking legal assistance were men more active and, even then, women owners who decided to seek such advice pursued as many leads as did men.

When entrepreneurs set off in pursuit of people who could help them, we found that men and women used similar channels: friends and business associates. Neither relied on family members and neither showed a reluctance to seek out assistance from strangers. Indeed, for some resources, especially business loan assistance, most entrepreneurs did not use pre-existing channels. Nonetheless, for the advice that ultimately paid the most dividends for owners – assistance from people already experienced in the entrepreneur's line of work – pre-existing ties were the main channel of resource acquisition. From other research we have conducted, we suspect such ties would fall into Circle II of our framework – weak ties, rather than strong ties.

Although men and women drew on the same types of social relations when seeking assistance and turned to the same organizational representatives when required (accountants, bank loan officers), women appeared to seek out other women when it was possible. Same-sex bias was highly resource specific and when women owners relied on prior ties, they were much more likely to ask a woman for advice than otherwise. For legal assistance, women seeking advice who did not know any lawyers with the expertise they needed ended up with only men as advisors. When they knew someone already in that domain, it was more likely that they chose a woman lawyer (although most lawyers were still men).

In our assessment of the quality of assistance obtained via networking, we found that rather than being disadvantaged by not being part of an 'old boys' network,' women seemed to benefit slightly more from their networks, as measured by being able to pay less than market rates for legal and loan assistance. However, they apparently received the same quality advice as men, regardless of what they paid, and they were no more likely to use the advice they received than men. Both groups were able to find ways to obtain high-quality assistance.

We must be cautious in generalizing from our findings to the more general problem of resource mobilization facing all entrepreneurs. Entrepreneurs use networking to obtain customers, technology, suppliers, physical resources, financial resources, managerial and psychological support, and personnel. Entrepreneurs are almost always cash constrained when founding their firms and during any growth phases they experience. Thus, they make extensive use of networks instead of cash and seek cooperative arrangements whenever possible to get around their cash constraints. We have not investigated these other extremely important uses of networking and future research should certainly do so. We are especially interested in resources that are highly specialized or not commercially available, and therefore harder to obtain. Based on our results so far, we believe that the burden of proof has now shifted to those persons who assert that women entrepreneurs do seek assistance via different channels than men.

Implications

We thus find scant evidence that the results of women's networking – in patterns or in outcomes – differ in any substantial ways from those for men. Some structuralist theories posit that, regardless of their personal views, women's embeddedness in a network of obligations and responsibilities limits their freedom of action. Some personality and gender role theories posit that women might be less pro-active in pursuing opportunities than men, because they view business activity as wholistically integrated into the rest of their life. Some theories of sex differences in networking posit not a difference in activity, but rather a difference in the channels through which women, as opposed to men, seek assistance. Because of their pre-existing network ties, women are seen as more likely to turn to family and friends than to work associates.

Our results do not support the predictions of these theories. Instead, they support a view of women's networking as only marginally different from men's, with the main difference being that women are more likely than men to turn to other women for some of the assistance they need. As in earlier studies, we found evidence for a sex bias in the composition of women's networks, but not in how they use them.

The entrepreneurship field's interest in networks has arisen in part because business strategists have asserted that personal networking can take some business activities 'out of the marketplace,' allowing entrepreneurs to obtain resources without depleting their hard-earned capital. These 'old boy networks' were formerly said to favor men and disadvantage women, but our results do not support this view. Instead, women now appear to be as good at playing them as the old boys themselves.

What are the implications for new/small business education programs? We believe that these programs should focus on skills sets, along with general education on issues of diversity, rather than on specialized agendas for special needs groups. There are two reasons why we feel this is important.

First, part of the battle against gender barriers in the world of new ventures involves changing stereotyped assumptions and low expectations about the capabilities of women entrepreneurs. Obviously, women business owners are just as capable as men at finding the assistance and support that they require for success. Until women are recognized as equally capable, they will continue to encounter resistance and obstacles in today's marketplace. Women-owned businesses continue to be smaller in size and lower in measures of profitability (Kalleberg and Leicht 1991), perhaps because of barriers in what we have labeled Circle I networks – strong tie advisor networks. Our results show that women are competing effectively in Circles II and III, but sex differences will persist as long as key positions are blocked to women.

Second, in a culture where gender roles are changing rapidly and work-places are becoming more heterogeneous, education about the potential barriers to success will benefit men as well as women. Building on Kalleberg and Leicht (1991), Fischer et al. (1993) found that innate gender differences were irrelevant to business success and that access to education was not a problem for women business owners. The area in which women entrepreneurs suffer most is access to start-up and industry experience, and subsequent exclusion from men's strong tie advisor networks. Because both men and women entrepreneurs will benefit from education on how to build their careers to gain necessary work experience, programs should be structured around agendas that focus on the development of business management skills.

Furthermore, educating men as well as women on the disadvantages faced by particular groups is also more likely, we believe, to lead to greater opportunities and access for these groups. For example, women know that, despite full-time employment, they carry more of the domestic burden than do their male counterparts. But what good is only raising the consciousness of the lower status group when much of the power for change lies higher up (Calas and Smircich 1992)? Improved chances for women business owners will come when both men and women are taught the skills and information necessary to achieve success in new businesses and to promote equal opportunity in the marketplace.

ACKNOWLEDGEMENTS

We wish to thank Candida Brush, Neil C. Churchill, Umberto Lago and Nancy Langton for their excellent comments on earlier drafts of this chapter.

REFERENCES

Aldrich, H.E. (1989) 'Networking among women entrepreneurs', in O. Hagen, C. Rivchun and D. Sexton (eds) *Women Owned Businesses*, New York: Praeger: 103–32.

Aldrich, H.E., Reese, P.R. and Dubini, P. (1989) Women on the verge of a breakthrough? Networking among entrepreneurs in the United States and Italy, *Entrepreneurship and Regional Development* 1: 339–56.

Aldrich, H.E., Rosen, B. And Woodward, W. (1987) 'The impact of social networks on business foundings and profit', in N. Churchill, J. Hornaday, O.J. Krasner and K. Vesper (eds), *Frontiers of Entrepreneurship Research 1987*, Wellesley, MA: Babson College Center for Entrepreneurial Studies: 154–68.

Aldrich, H.E. and Sakano, T. (1995) 'Unbroken ties: how the personal networks of Japanese business owners compare to those in other nations', in Mark Fruin (ed.) *Networks and Markets: Pacific Rim Investigations*, New York: Oxford Press.

Aldrich, H.E. and Zimmer, C. (1986) 'Entrepreneurship through social networks', in D.L. Sexton and R.W. Smilor (eds) *The Art and Science of Entrepreneurship*, Cambridge, MA: Ballinger: 3–23.

Birley, S., Cromie, S. and Myers, A. (1990) *Entrepreneurial Networks: Their Creation and Development in Different Countries*, SWP 24/90, Bedford, UK: Cranfield School of Management.

Brush, C.G. (1992) 'Research on women business owners: past trends, a new perspective and future directions', *Entrepreneurship: Theory and Practice* 16: 5–30.

Calas, M. and Smircich, L. (1992) 'Using the "f" word: feminist theories and the social consequences of organizational research', in A.J. Mills and P. Tancred (eds) *Gendering Organizational Analysis*, Newbury Park, CA: Sage: 222–34.

Chaganti, R. (1986) 'Management in women-owned enterprises', *Journal of Small Business Management* 24: 18–29.

Cooper, A. and Dunkelberg, W. (1987) 'Old questions, new answers and methodological issues', *American Journal of Small Business* 11: 11–23.

Fischer, E.M., Reuber, A.R. and Dyke, L.S. (1993). 'A theoretical overview and extension of research on sex, gender, and entrepreneurship', *Journal of Business Venturing* 8: 151–68.

Gilligan, C. (1982) *In a Different Voice*, Cambridge, MA: Harvard.

Goffee, R. and Scase, R. (1985) *Women in Charge: The Experiences of Women Entrepreneurs*, London: Allen & Unwin.

Granovetter, M. (1985) 'The strength of weak ties', *American Journal of Sociology* 78: 1360–80.

Hertz, L. (1986) *The Business Amazons*, London: Deutsch.

Kalleberg, A. (1986) 'Entrepreneurship in the 1980s: a study of small business in Indiana', in G.D. Likecap (ed.), *Entrepreneurship and Innovation, Vol. I*, Greenwich, CT: JAI Press.

Kalleberg, A.L. and Leicht, K. (1991) 'Gender and organizational performance: determinants of small business survival and success', *Academy of Management Journal* 34: 136–61.

McPherson, J.M. and Smith-Lovin, L. (1986) 'Sex segregation in voluntary associations', *American Sociological Review* 51: 61–79.

Reese, P.R. (1992) *Entrepreneurial Networks and Resource Acquisition: Does Gender Make a Difference?*, PhD dissertation, University of North Carolina, Chapel Hill, NC.

Reese, P.R. and Aldrich, H.E. (1995) 'Entrepreneurial networks and business performance: a panel study of small and medium-sized firms in the Research Triangle', in S. Birley and I. McMillan (eds) *International Entrepreneurship*, London: Routledge.

Sexton, D.L. and Bowman-Upton, N. (1990) 'Female and male entrepreneurs: psychological characteristics and their role in gender-related discrimination', *Journal of Business Venturing* 5, January: 29–36.

Zimmer, C. and Aldrich, H.E. (1987) 'Resource mobilization through ethnic networks: kinship and friendship ties of shopkeepers in England', *Sociological Perspectives* 30(4), October: 422–55.

2

THE DETERMINATION OF OPTIMAL MARKETING EXPENDITURES

An application of option theory

Saugata Banerjee, William D. Bygrave and Benoît F. Leleux

INTRODUCTION

This chapter studies conceptually the situation of a firm, operating in two separate markets (a domestic, highly controlled market and a foreign, competitive market) and facing an uncertain level of demand for its products, and determines, with the help of contingent claims pricing theory, the optimal marketing expenditures that the firm should undertake in order to minimize the effects of the price uncertainty prevailing in its two markets.

Since the publication of Black and Scholes' (1973) work on valuation of contingent claims in general, and options in particular, the general theory has been applied to a wide variety of settings. Among these, some of the most representative examples include the valuation of firms, the valuation of depletable natural resources, the computation of optimum insurance premium for bank deposits, and the valuation of projects which imbed various option components, such as the right to delay the cash outlays, significantly to change the size of the investments, or to fold down if the project does not turn out as expected.

The common feature of all these models is that, in each instance, the assets or services rendered can be viewed either as a call option or as a put option on the underlying asset. Furthermore, all cases entail truncating the payoff function in such a way that the value to the holder of the option is an increasing function of the variance of return on the underlying asset. This may, at first sight, appear counterintuitive from a mean-variance analysis point of view, but what is crucial is that the holder of the derived instrument has the option to exercise the right inherent in the option, not the obligation, thus avoiding the possibility of a forced loss. Therefore, the increased variance serves to increase the possibility of higher payoffs without increasing the corresponding possibility of losses.

It will be shown that the situation examined in this chapter lends itself very well to the contingent claims framework, so that optimal use can be made of theoretical developments in that sector to analyze the company's strategic decision. The chapter is organized as follows. The second section (pp. 27–30) introduces the general scenario being investigated here. The third section (pp. 30–4) analyzes the marketing expense optimization problem in a discrete setting, looking successively at a simple binomial model and extending it in a second part of a multi-period setting. Section four (pp. 34–5) generalizes the model to a continuous time environment and derives the closed-form formula for the value to the firm of the option to sell in the domestic market. It is then shown that this analytical solution corresponds to the upper bound of the domestic marketing expenditure. A general conclusion ensues with possible avenues for further research and developments.

THE SCENARIO

The chapter investigates the situation of a hypothetical firm called Lokenath Chatterjee and Sons Pvt Ltd (LCS) located in India. The company manufactures precision tools. These precision tools are not end products but serve as input for the production of more sophisticated machines which are then sold on the machinery market (the Original Equipment Manufacturer's (OEM) market). The production facilities of LCS are located, for example, in Calcutta, India. It employs about 300 people, consisting of engineers, workmen and administrative staff. LCS is organized as a private limited company (corporation), with all shares of the company in the hands of members of the Chatterjee family.

LCS has two potential output markets: domestic and international. The domestic market, in India, consists mainly of government companies in the heavy machinery business and other public sector enterprises which are subsidized by the government. The rationale for the strong governmental intervention is that it is felt that India, being a developing country, vitally needs to develop its industrial base in order to insure high productivity. Given the importance of such an objective, the fate of the sector cannot be left completely in the hands of the free market forces, as this may cause unnecessary volatility and jeopardize the economic progress of the country.

The international market includes countries such as the USA, Australia and some European countries such as Belgium, Germany, England, Ireland, the Netherlands and Austria. In these countries the customer base consists mainly of automobile manufacturers and producers of heavy machinery. Almost all of the foreign sales are made to private sector companies and very little, if any, to government agencies. In the international market, LCS is represented by agents in each country, (i.e. it does not deal directly with the final user of its products). The contract to supply is between LCS and the agent.

The input market of LCS is completely domestic. All the labor it employs is local. Raw materials, the bulk of which consists of steel products, are obtained from the Indian steel plants. The only exception is in the case of the machineries, some of which are imported from the USA and Europe.

The main feature of the output markets is that they are completely segmented and there is no communication between them. In other words, the pricing and supply policies of LCS in the international market has no influence on the domestic market, and vice versa. Furthermore, the general conditions prevailing in each market have no bearing on the other. Although this might, at first, seem improbable, the strict import–export laws in India and governmental control over key industries together insure such a complete separation. To be more specific, in an effort to boost the domestic industrial development, the Indian government has banned the import of such tools as long as they are available within the country. Also, due to tax benefits on foreign exchange earnings, original producers of goods find it more viable to export their products directly, rather than going through a domestic agent. Therefore, it is not unreasonable to assume that differences in prices and products in the two markets cannot be arbitraged out. That is to say, first, that the firm can get away with charging different rates in the two markets. Second, owing to the considerable degree of government intervention in the domestic market, the business cycles in the two markets are not perfectly related. Consequently, it is not unrealistic to claim that the markets are separated for all intents and purposes.

The foreign market is characterized by high selling cost and high uncertainty of demand. Given the present conditions, this would appear as only natural: the high labour costs in the developed countries (as opposed to the low costs prevailing in India) push up the manufacturing costs, forcing the selling costs in the same direction. The uncertainty of demand is driven by two fundamental factors:

- An abundance of firms in the foreign markets. Therefore, competition implies that any upward movement in price is followed by a strong negative movement in demand.
- The foreign market is closer to a free market mechanism than India, (i.e. the market forces are allowed to play to a much greater extent before the government steps in to control the situation).

Of course, it might be argued that the free market mechanism causes the extraordinary profits to be closer to zero, thus having a negative influence on the price. But when one considers the joint effect of a higher cost of living (implying a higher cost of production) and the unfavorable exchange rate (for India), then the higher selling costs in the foreign market should not come as a surprise.

The domestic market, on the other hand, has a lower selling price, but a greater stability of demand than the foreign market. A lower selling price is due to a combination of two factors:

- A lower cost of production, stemming mainly from a lower cost of labor, and lower input costs due to government subsidies in the factor markets.
- Strict monopolistic and restricted trade practices (MRTP) laws forbidding excessive profits for such industries. So, although there may exist entry barriers in the precision tools industry in the form of very high initial investments, these cannot be transformed into extraordinary profits because of MRTP regulations.

The stability of demand is due to a lesser number of firms (since this is a specialized industry, and requires expertise and sophisticated machinery) and a regular, steady stream of demand from the government in its drive to industrialize the nation.

As mentioned before, LCS is represented in the international market by its agents who purchase the products from LCS. Therefore, the burden of advertising in the international market is on these agents and LCS does not need to directly consider this factor. However, to be able to sell in the domestic market, the firm needs to make some marketing expenses. These can be in the form of direct advertising of their products in the media (e.g. setting up stalls in the domestic trade fairs, or maintaining selling points in major industrial areas). As is generally experienced for marketing expenses, the effects of one-time marketing expenses typically is spread over several periods, though at each successive period the intensity of the effect decreases.

The cost of production of the output is stable in the sense that the break-even point is well below the current level of production. This implies that the major part of the cost is variable, or that the per-unit share of fixed cost of marginal output is very low. This allows one to consider the cost solely as a variable. The per-unit variable cost is constant. Since the factor market is domestic, the volatility of the foreign market does not affect this. Further, the firm has limited capacity of production.

Given this scenario, the firm wants to maximize profits. Since it is a private limited company, this profit maximization is nothing else but the translation of the traditional maximizing share value concept to a private concern. If the relevant maximization problem was defined and subsequently solved, it is obvious that the solution would be to dedicate the entire capacity to exports. That is, under traditional techniques, the volatility of the two markets would be ignored, and since price is higher in the foreign market, the entire production capacity would be dedicated to exports. The firm would have no incentive to invest in marketing its product in the domestic market.

This approach to the problem fails to account for the potential benefits and risks of internationally competitive markets. For example, the sudden occurrence of a recession in the foreign market (as is currently the case) may endanger the very survival of the firm, which would then be faced with seriously diminished demand or no demand at all for its products. Remember that the domestic market would also be closed to the firm because of the absence of marketing investments in India over the years of intense foreign promotion. It is clear that the firm would like to insure itself against the possibility of such a traumatic turnaround in activity, and its associated losses. The question then arises: how much should the firm spend in domestic marketing? A contingent claims approach is used in the next sections to derive an analytically tractable solution to the firm's problem.

THE MODEL IN DISCRETE SETTING

It is useful to begin with a brief overview of the theory of contingent claims pricing, and in particular option pricing. A European call (put) option gives the holder the option to buy (sell) the underlying security at a specified future date, called the maturity date, at some specified price, known as the exercise price. An American option provides its holder with basically the same rights, except for the fact that the option can now be exercised any time up to the maturity date. Since the owner has the right to exercise but is never obliged to do so, his/her loss on a position turned sour is at most equal to zero. In other words, when the position is unfavorable, the owner will elect not to exercise the option.

In order to insure such a payoff, the buyer of the option has to pay the seller (also called the option writer) a price which will adequately compensate the writer for this risk. This is the value of the option. It can be computed either in a discrete binomial framework, where the price of the asset follows a binomial process, or it can be computed in a continuous time framework. In this first part, the situation faced is examined in a discrete binomial framework.

A single-period binomial model

The single-period binomial model represents the simplest situation possible and is used as the basis from which later generalizations will build. Two time periods are assumed, noted $t = 0,1$. The firm, called LCS to stay within the scenario guidelines, produces only one product. It can sell this product in either of two markets, foreign and domestic, denoted by $[I = f,d]$ respectively. The foreign market has a selling price per unit of the product S_f. This selling price follows a binomial process. At $t = 1$, it takes on the value $u.S_f$ with probability q and with probability $(1 - q)$ it takes on the value $d.S_f$ with $u > 1 > d$. The cost of production is constant and equal to c per unit of output, with $d.S_f < c < u.S_f$. In the domestic market, the price per unit is S_d, with $c < S_d < u.S_f$. This price remains constant in both periods.

Accordingly, the per-unit profit, given by selling cost minus cost of production, also follows a binomial process with the same general parameters.

At time $t = 0$, the firm decides its production schedule and marketing policies. It can always sell its product in the foreign market, independently of its marketing decision since agents carry out the duty. However, to be able to sell in the domestic market, the firm needs to spend money in the form of marketing expenses. This section assumes that the effects of marketing expenditures will only be felt in the period in which they are incurred, so that no long-term effect is to be expected (effects do not carry forward). The question of interest then becomes: How much should the firm be willing to spend on marketing in the domestic country in order to keep open the possibility to sell there at all should the foreign, and currently more lucrative, market turn sour?

To answer this question, it is important to note that the situation of the firm here is analogous to having a put option to sell its product domestically. By spending a certain amount on domestic marketing, the firm effectively purchases the option to sell in the domestic market when the foreign market is not available (due for example to newly established trade barriers or unfavorable tariffs) or becomes uninteresting (if other producers become more competitive). To further outline the option component of the decision, it is interesting to look at the payoffs to the firm if it decides to invest in domestic marketing.

First of all, it is important to highlight the fact that the option discussed above is somewhat different from the traditional 'financial' option on shares of equity because the firm cannot purchase the product in the foreign market at the prevailing market price, as it would have been able to do in the case of shares.

When the foreign market is up (u), the firm will not exercise its option to sell in the domestic market because $S_d < u.S_f$ Thus, in the 'up' state, the payoff from the option to sell is zero. This can be expressed as the maximum of zero, and the difference in profits from selling in the two countries, which is $[(S_d - c) - (u.S_f - c)]$. But this is also equal to:

$$m_u = max \ [0, \ S_d - u.S_f]$$
$$m_u = 0 \qquad\qquad (1)$$

However, when the foreign market is down (d), the firm will sell in the domestic market because $S_d > d.S_f$. In this case, the payoff to the firm can again be expressed as the maximum of zero, and the difference in profits from selling in the two countries, which now is $[(S_d - c) - (d.S_f - c)]$. But this is equal to:

$$m_d = max \ [0, \ S_d - d.S_f]$$
$$m_d = S_d - d.S_f \qquad\qquad (2)$$

Therefore, observe that in order to eliminate the problem of having c in the payoff function, it is necessary to take the difference in the profits and not the absolute excess over the cost. Note that the payoff in the 'down' state can be interpreted as consisting of two parts:

1 profit from selling in the domestic market, $(S_d - c)$;
2 prevention of loss, or opportunity gain, from not having had to sell in the foreign market $(c.S_f - c)$.

With the above payoff functions, it is possible to derive the value to the firm of the option of being able to sell in the domestic market. To do this, the usual approach is to first construct a risk-free hedge portfolio, composed in this particular case of one unit of the product S_f and α units of a put option written against this unit of product. Using the fact that this portfolio is riskless, so that the return on it should be equal to the risk-free rate of return (r_f) at equilibrium, the value of the put option can be simply stated as:

$$m = [p.m_u + (1 - p)\, m_d] \, / \, (1 + r_f) \tag{3}$$

$$= [0 + (1 - p)(S_d - d.S_f)] \, / \, (1 + r_f) \tag{4}$$

$$= [u - (1 + r_f)] \, (S_d - d.S_f) \, / \, [(u - d)\,(1 + r_f)] \tag{5}$$

where

$$p = [(1 + r_f) - d] \, / \, (u - d) \tag{6}$$

is the hedging probability, which is the value q would have in equilibrium if investors were risk neutral.

Therefore, m is the value of the option to sell domestically, or the amount that the firm would be willing to pay for the opportunity, given the relative level of prices in the two countries. Thus, the first should spend m in domestic marketing expenses.

In the foregoing analysis, it was assumed that the firm would invest in domestic marketing expenses. For this assumption to hold, a number of necessary conditions have to hold.

1 Clearly, if $S_d < d.S_f$, then the firm would not spend anything on domestic marketing. That is because in both the good and bad states of nature (the 'up' and 'down' components in the previous discussion), the firm would be better off selling in the foreign market. But this possibility is eliminated by the assumptions made that $d.S_f < c$ and $c < S_d$. Together, these assumptions imply that $S_d > d.S_f$.
2 To invest in the marketing expense, the expected payoff to the firm of selling in the foreign market and investing in the option must be greater than the expected payoff of simply selling in the foreign market, i.e.

$$q(u.S_f - c) + (1 - q)(S_d - c) - m > q(u.S_f - c) - (1 - q)(c - d.S_f) \tag{7}$$

where the first two terms in the left hand side represent the expected payoff with the option (note that the second term reflects the fact that with the option, the firm would sell in the domestic market in the bad state), and the third term is the cost of the option itself. The right hand side is the payoff if the firm does not invest in domestic marketing. The condition can be simplified to:

$$m < (1 - q)(S_d - d \cdot S_f) \qquad (8)$$

Another condition for the firm to invest in marketing is that the expected payoff exceeds the payoff from producing in the domestic country alone, i.e.,

$$q(u.S_f - c) + (1 - q)(S_d - c) - m > S_d - c \qquad (9)$$

The left hand side is the previous condition. Note that the right hand side reflects the fact that the domestic market price is the same in all the possible states of nature. This can be further simplified into:

$$m < q (u \cdot S_f) + (1 - q)(d \cdot S_f) - S_d \qquad (10)$$

But this can also be expressed as:

$$m < q (u.S_f - S_d) - (1 - q)(S_d - d.S_f) \qquad (11)$$

Since m is already less than the second term on the right hand side by the previous condition, substituting this in the above equation gives:

$$m < q (u.S_f - S_d) / 2 \qquad (12)$$

Therefore, given the second condition, this is the additional constraint that has to be met.

Extension to the multi-period binomial model

The previous analysis can be extended to the multi-period framework. Under the same assumptions as before and with the additional assumption that the firm could sell its product only at the end of the horizon (multi-period), the result would not be very different from those in the previous framework. The main adjustment would be with respect to the probabilities of the states of nature, which could be computed using the binomial formula.

The situation would be rendered more interesting if the following features were introduced:

1 The firm is able to sell its product at the end of each period.
2 It is allowed to decide after each period, whether or not it wants to invest in marketing in the domestic market.
3 An investment in domestic marketing in any period has a persistence effect (i.e. some of the benefits of the investment are still enjoyed in a limited number of subsequent periods).

In this setting, it is the authors' conjecture that the firm would follow an investment cycle pattern, where it would invest every few periods. It should be remembered that all development has been conducted under the assumption that knowledge of the occurrence of a bad state in one period does not influence the firm's decision to invest or not in the next period. The solution to such a problem in a finite horizon could be obtained using backward induction. However, for an infinite horizon, it is not clear what solution would result.

THE MODEL IN CONTINUOUS TIME SETTINGS

Up to now, it is assumed that the firm operates in a discrete time framework. However, to make it more realistic, it is also interesting to extend the analysis to the case of a firm operating in a continuous time framework. In order to adapt the problem to this new setting, and remain analytically tractable, some additional assumptions are required.

First of all, it is necessary to assume that the price process in the foreign market follows a lognormal distribution process, i.e.,

$$dS_f = \mu_f S_f dt + \sigma_f S_f dw \tag{13}$$

where μ_f is the rate of increase in price of a security which is perfectly correlated with the price of the output in the foreign market, σ_f is the instantaneous standard deviation which measures the volatility of the security investigated, and w is a standard Weiner Process, a particular class of Brownian motion. Since costs are constant, prices following this process will imply that profits will also follow a similar process through time.

The price in the domestic market is still assumed to remain constant. Under these assumptions, using Black–Scholes option pricing formula and the put-call parity, the value of this put option (V_m) can be easily derived. Specifically, it is given by:

$$Vm = S_d e^{-rfT}[1 - N(d_2)] - S_f[1 - N(d_1)] \tag{14}$$

where

$$d_1 = [ln(S_f/S_d) + (r_f + \sigma^2/2)T] / [\sigma\sqrt{T}] \tag{15}$$

$$d_2 = d_1 - \sigma\sqrt{T} \tag{16}$$

It is interesting to look at the comparative statics implied by this formula.

- $\delta V_m/\delta S_f < 0$: the higher the foreign market price, the lower the value of the option to market domestically. Intuitively, foreign price increases make foreign markets comparatively more attractive than domestic markets. The firm gains more by selling abroad and would consequently value the option to sell domestically much less.

34

- $\delta V_m / \delta S_d > 0$: the higher the domestic market price, the higher the value of the option to market domestically. Again, this is rather intuitive since, with a higher domestic price, the domestic profit margin increases and makes the firm more willing to pay for the possible increased gains.
- $\delta V_m / \delta \sigma_f > 0$: the higher the volatility in the price process of the foreign market, the larger the value of the option to market domestically. Again, this can be related to the truncation of the payoff function obtained by purchasing the option to sell domestically. The greater the uncertainty of earning profits by selling in foreign markets, the more the firm is ready to pay to insure itself against such a loss.

A last extension of the model consists in introducing the possibility of the domestic market price being also stochastic. To stay within the scenario presented, the domestic market price is assumed to have a lower variance than its foreign counterpart. The domestic price follows an evolutionary process of the form:

$$dS_d = \mu_d S_d dt + \sigma_d S_d dw \qquad (17)$$

with $\mu_d < \mu_f$ and $\sigma_d < \sigma_f$.

The value of the option to sell in the domestic market is given by

$$V^*_m = S_d e^{-(rh - \mu d)T}[1 - N(d_2)] - S_f[1 - Nd_1)] \qquad (18)$$

where

$$d_1 = [lnS_f/S_d) + (r_h - \mu_d + \underline{\sigma}^2/2)T] / [\underline{\sigma} \sqrt{T}] \qquad (19)$$
$$d_2 = d_1 - \underline{\sigma} \sqrt{T} \qquad (20)$$
$$\underline{\sigma}^2 = \sigma^2_f - 2\rho_{fd} \sigma_f\sigma_d + \sigma^2_d \qquad (21)$$

where r_h is the expected real rate of return on a hedge security whose stochastic percentage changes are perfectly correlated with the stochastic component of the percentage changes in the domestic price, and ρ_{fd} is the instantaneous correlation between the foreign and domestic prices.

It is worthwhile to examine the exact interpretation of the value of the option to sell in the domestic country. It is precisely the maximum amount that the firm would be willing to spend on domestic marketing in order to sell each unit of output there. It should not be confused with the marketing response model which will specify how effective the money spent on marketing is. If the marketing response model indicates that to sell every unit the firm has to spend $m' > m$, then the firm will be spending more than the value it will derive from spending this money. The total level of marketing expense will of course be given by the capacity utilization of the firm for the foreign market. If it produces x units for the foreign market, then the maximum aggregate amount it should be willing to spend on domestic marketing that will insure it to sell x units in the home country when the foreign market is down, is $m.x$ units of domestic currency.

CONCLUSIONS

This chapter applies the contingent claims pricing approach to a real-life scenario where a firm has to decide how much it should spend on marketing in the domestic country, given the fact the domestic market is much less volatile than the foreign market. Another way of looking at this problem would be where the domestic marketing expense would be in the form of minimum supply necessary to be maintained in the home market in order to be able to sell a greater quantity at any future point in time. Then the solution of this problem would give the optimal output allocation between the foreign and domestic markets. The corresponding option price in that case would be the amount of loss that the firm would suffer by selling to the domestic market. Under more realistic conditions, where the firm would be an ongoing concern, the problem would be one of dynamic optimization. The current prices at each instant in time would be the state variables that would be used to solve for the optimal marketing expenses at each instant. Coupled with this, the decaying nature of the marketing expense effectiveness would require some adjustment in this problem.

The contribution of this chapter lies in the very real, practical application of the options theory to a problem currently being faced by hundreds of large and small enterprises like LCS. It also emphasizes the firm level implications of policy decisions aimed at improving the industrial standing of some newly developed countries. In the particular example developed here, the government's policy toward primary industrial concerns is being rerouted to serve as a hedge against the risk inherent in export-oriented growth. In this sense, this 'redirection' of the policy can be seen as a positive hijacking of governmental policies. In many other instances, the effect of such individually rational decisions may go against the overall objective of legislation. Future developments envisioned for this preliminary research include computer simulations of the pricing models under reasonable parameter values to get a better feeling for the real impact of the option component on marketing decisions. Also, other option components in typical venture capital investments, and the way they interact with each other, should be considered.

REFERENCES

Black, F. and Scholes, M. (1973) 'The pricing of options and corporate liabilities', *Journal of Political Economy* 81, May–June.

Fisher, S. (1978) 'Call option pricing when the exercise price is uncertain, and the valuation of index bonds', *Journal of Finance* March.

Margrabe, W. (1978) 'The value of an option to exchange one asset for another', *Journal of Finance* March.

Stulz, R. (1982) 'Options on the minimum or the maximum of two risky assets', *Journal of Financial Economics* 10.

3

UNFINISHED BUSINESS

Obstacles to entrepreneurship in the reform of state-owned enterprises in China and Vietnam

Max Boisot

INTRODUCTION

China presents a bit of a puzzle for would-be reformers of socialist and post-socialist economies. The economy has been growing at a steady 9 percent a year since the early 1980s – 13 percent in 1992 – yet nearly half of its state-owned enterprises (SOE), the flagships of its economy, are losing money and a further quarter are barely breaking even. Calculated on a purchasing power parity basis, China has become the world's third largest economy, and yet, in contrast to Central and Eastern Europe and to the Commonwealth of Independent States (CIS), the country has embarked on no massive programme of privatization of state-owned assets: modest experiments with stock ownership leave the state firmly in control. Moreover, the Chinese leadership is in no way committed to the replacement of a Marxist–Leninist regime by a market order; at most it is committed to combining the two. Western observers thus confront the paradoxical possibility that by the year 2010, if it maintains just two-thirds of its current rate of growth, China could have become the world's largest capitalist and Marxist–Leninist state. What is going on?

In spite of a number of attempts to find a middle way between them (Brus 1990; Kowalik 1987), the Marxist–Leninist and capitalist paradigms have long been assumed to be incompatible so that the only way to move from one to the other is to perform a 'paradigm shift' (Kuhn 1962) involving rapid and massive institutional and social change. It is believed that an economy could not withstand the incoherencies involved in operating under both systems at the same time so that the quicker it can be made to move over from one to the other, the better. The current difficulties that confront the 'big bang' approach in Central and Eastern Europe and in the CIS, as well as China's relative success in getting both types of economy to coexist, challenge these beliefs. One major source of difficulty in bringing about a rapid transition or paradigm switch is that attitudes do not necessarily change as rapidly as the environment to which they must respond and adapt. As Kuhn (1962) observed in discussing scientific change, adherents to a given paradigm rarely give it up simply because a new and better one appears on the horizon. The new paradigm takes root gradually as those in thrall to the old paradigm die off and a rising generation uncommitted to the old one opts for the new one. Kuhn may have exaggerated the tenacity with which the old paradigm is held on to by its adherents (Kuhn 1962; Lakatos and Musgrave 1970). Much will depend on their prior commitment to it. Where this commitment has been high even a willingness to espouse a new paradigm may be undermined by the presence of the old paradigm surviving as an implicit model at an unconscious level.

In this chapter, we argue that what we are witnessing in China is paradigm change as an intergenerational phenomenon rather than as a 'shift', that the old paradigm survives at an implicit level in the sector that benefited the most from it, the state-owned enterprise sector, and that the new paradigm is taking root in a new sector of small and medium-sized enterprises that were never committed to the old paradigm. Our focus will mainly be on those features of the old paradigm that continue to block the emergence of responsive entrepreneurial behaviour in state-owned enterprises.

We proceed as follows. In the next section we examine those features of the old paradigm, traceable to Marx's labour theory of value, that remain consequential for the behaviour of state-owned enterprises. In the third section we look at how these are expressed both in the managerial practices of SOEs and in the reform measures designed to modify these practices. Our examples will be drawn from both the Chinese and Vietnamese reform experience. In the fourth section we briefly discuss the implications of our analysis for the way policy-makers approach the problem of economic reform in socialist and post-socialist countries. A conclusion follows.

MARX'S THEORY OF VALUE

Marx has been labelled the last of the classical economists (Elster 1985). Although he was writing at the time when the marginalist revolution was making its appearance in the works of Jevons, Menger and Walras (Blaug 1978), his theory of value was in the lineage of Quesnay, Adam Smith and David Ricardo (Mirowski 1991; Vianello 1990).

In the classical tradition, Labour is the primary source of value. In the work of Ricardo and Marx, it becomes a measure of value as well as its source. According to Marx, therefore, the capitalist who appropriates part of this value on the grounds that a factor called 'capital' also has to be remunerated is deluding himself since capital in the form of equipment and machinery is nothing but 'congealed Labour' (Marx 1970), that is an accumulation of past Labour embedded in things. The capitalist pays Labour the amount necessary for its subsistence and reinvests the difference between this sum and that for which he can sell Labour's output. This difference is defined by Marx as the 'surplus value' and measures the rate at which capital exploits Labour. Such exploitation remains invisible to Labour because it occurs in the sphere of production rather than in the sphere of exchange.

Note that there is no fundamental incompatibility between a theory of value of this kind and a simple market process in which workers exchange their outputs directly with each other. The target of Marx's criticism was not the market process as such but capitalist accumulation in which, through the appropriation, reinvestment and accumulation of surplus value, the capitalist gradually concentrates in his own hands means of production which properly belong to Labour.

Another term for capitalist accumulation is entrepreneurial organization building, both intensive and extensive. If we take entrepreneurship in the neoclassical sense of the organization and coordination of factors of production, then organizational skills according to the Labour theory of value, of themselves, can create no value and thus have no legitimate claim on Labour's output (i.e. managing cannot be considered a factor of production). But we might go further and with the Austrians (Hayek 1949; Kirzner 1979) expand the scope of entrepreneurship to include the spotting of opportunities and the taking of risk. The Labour theory of value, however, grants no more legitimacy to the factor claims of opportunity spotting or risk taking than it does to those of organizing productive factors.

The entrepreneur can thus claim no legitimate role nor be remunerated in a world in which value is created by Labour and by Labour alone. He becomes an interloper who adds nothing to what is already produced by Labour. He is a free-rider on Labour's back – a case of Williamsonian opportunism from above (Williamson 1975). In practice, the entrepreneur only succeeds in appropriating surplus value insofar as he is able to move the conditions of exchange away from efficient markets and thus to counter the long run tendency for the rate of profit to fall. Economists call this rent seeking; managers, more easy on themselves perhaps, call it securing a competitive advantage (Porter 1985). According to the Labour theory of value, however, any value created by securing a competitive advantage belongs to Labour as a whole and not to the individual entrepreneur. It finds expression in the 'socially necessary Labour time' required to produce a good or a service (Eatwell 1990).

Underlying the Marxist perspective on value is a denial that knowledge or information *per se*, whether it is used to spot profitable new opportunities in the market or to secure effective organizational coordination, adds any value when it goes beyond what is strictly needed for the physical Labour process of direct production. Skilled Labour in the Marxist scheme, to be sure, gets paid more, but not because it happens to possess more knowledge. It gets paid more because it has expended more effort (i.e. Labour time) acquiring that knowledge (Mirowski 1991). Marx was one of the few economists in the nineteenth century to incorporate technical change explicitly into his thinking (Freeman and Perez 1988). Yet technical change only finds its way into his theory of value in the determination of 'socially necessary Labour time'. Once created, technical knowledge becomes a common inheritance of mankind which is illegitimately appropriated by entrepreneurs and turned into a source of competitive advantage – a device for further extracting surplus value from Labour in the teeth of a secular decline in the rate of profit.

If information has no value then neither does entrepreneurship nor organization. There is a sense in which Marx shares Williamson's assumption that 'in the beginning there were markets' (Williamson 1975) since if all transactions were to be funnelled through efficient markets (i.e. there was no lumpiness in factor markets, including those for information), the means of production would effectively remain in the hands of the workers and neither the entrepreneur as an opportunity spotter nor the entrepreneur as an organizational coordinator would have any role to play.

What is the firm therefore in the Marxist lexicon? Pretty much what it is in the neoclassical lexicon: a 'nexus of contracts' (Cheung 1983) symptomatic of market failure (Alchian and Demsetz 1972; Fama and Jensen 1983; Jensen and Meckling 1976). Neoclassical economists then proceed to ignore the firm by focusing on the perfectly competitive case. Marx, by contrast, like Joseph Schumpeter some seventy years later and the economic historian Fernand Braudel, sees in this departure from perfect competition the essence of the capitalist process (Schumpeter 1942; Braudel 1979). Schumpeter framed the issue in terms of innovation leading to competitive advantage; Marx in terms of worker exploitation and the appropriation of surplus value. For the latter, therefore, the firm is the handmaiden of monopoly capital.

Given the existence of firms, however, things can evolve in two directions. In the first, monopoly profits are competed away by market processes and the more efficiently these can be made to function, the more one can afford to ignore the firm as an alternative governance structure. The returns to entrepreneurship and organization over time tend to zero; the function of antitrust policy is to bring an economy as close as possible to such an 'efficient' state of affairs. In the second, the process of capitalist accumulation and organizational concentration is allowed to continue but at a certain point the capitalist is expropriated by the state, which, acting in the name of hitherto dispossessed workers, reclaims the available surplus values which are rightfully theirs. In the Leninist programme surplus value is not distributed, however, but reinvested by the state on behalf of the workers. In theory they are the owners of the firm, but the state now exercises its property rights on their behalf. Schumpeter believed capitalism to be evolving inexorably in this second direction, one in which the economy is in effect converted into a single giant enterprise (Schumpeter 1942). Organizational discontinuities, expressed through the separation of productive units from each other, now become internal to the system since these units fall under a unified governance structure and no longer compete with each other in external markets.

The neoclassical and the Marxist approaches constitute distinctive ways of denying the legitimacy of information as a potential source of value: the first, by making information ubiquitous in the economic system – the postulate of perfect information – eliminates by assumption any durable rent-generating asymmetries; the second, by internalizing all transactions within a single hierarchy, either eliminates rent-seeking opportunistic behaviour by entrepreneurs, or appropriates any rents generated on behalf of the workers. In the neoclassical scheme, therefore, organization is unnecessary because markets can do it all. In the Marxist scheme, by contrast, markets are unnecessary because a single organization can do it all. In both cases any competitive advantage bestowed by information asymmetries disappears.

The economic theory of socialism purported to show that in welfare terms these two schemes turn out to be equivalent (Barone 1935; Lange 1936–7; Lerner 1936). The move from plan to market amounts to an exercise in decentralization in which information asymmetries are eliminated by making information rapidly and widely available to competing agents. What gets decentralized is information on price–quantity relationships, that is to say, well-codified and abstract data. How the data came to be codified and abstracted in the first place – that is, the tentative process of hypothesis generation and testing through which prices are initially formed and uncertainty gradually eliminated – is not satisfactorily addressed by the theory.

Yet according to neo-Austrians such as Kirzner (1973, 1979) this is precisely where an entrepreneur adds value. In fact he does so in two distinct ways, only one of which is identified by Kirzner. Value is first added by an entrepreneur when he reduces uncertainty by moving certain classes of transactions towards greater codification and abstraction (Boisot 1986) – by structuring and articulating new ideas, embedding them in goods and services, and extending their application into new fields. His ability to extract rents from such value then gets gradually competed away with the diffusion of transactionally relevant information that must sooner or later take place.

But value is also added by an entrepreneur when he moves away from the certainties of well-formed prices and quantities that characterize competitive markets and towards more tacit and impacted forms of data processing associated with learning by doing. Impacted learning underpins what Williamson in an organization content has termed 'the Fundamental Transformation', the move from large numbers *ex ante* competitive bidding to small numbers *ex post* exchange relations (Williamson 1991). It is something more than a process of discovery as presented by Kirzner, for in addition to identifying what exists in a latent form in the data of experience, it involves imagining what is possible but does not yet exist (Hamel and Prahalad 1991; Shackle 1972). In short, learning by doing prepares the ground for the emergence of creative entrepreneurial insights.

It is the ability to manage the learning process as a whole (i.e. the generation of new ideas as well as their exploitation) that constitutes the essence of entrepreneurship. Consequently, where economic thinking on socialist reform is confined to a simple concept of decentralization, assumed to be operating in an information environment already suffused with well-codified, abstract and well-diffused data – the orientation currently in force in Eastern Europe, CIS and China – the value-generating role of creative thinking is occluded. The Labour theory of value as an implicit economic paradigm, therefore, is not fundamentally threatened by a decentralization to markets: for in efficient markets the search for competitive advantage remains indistinguishable from a zero-sum game in which the entrepreneur adds no value as such but seeks opportunistically to appropriate for himself what is rightfully another's, that is, surplus value acquired by 'honest toil' (i.e. Labour). The virtue of efficient markets resides in the fact that he cannot succeed. In markets which are near equilibrium and where to some extent he can succeed, it will not be for long – indeed it is because by his very actions he is deemed to contribute to the market equilibrating process that he is granted legitimacy by the neo-Austrians (Kirzner 1979). His is a self-liquidating role that disappears when equilibrium is reached.

Where the entrepreneurial contribution to the creation of new ideas and opportunities is overlooked or misunderstood – as seems to be the case in both reforming socialist economies as well as in many post-socialist ones – the Labour theory of value may be robust enough to survive, albeit in an implicit form, the negative selective forces of an emergent market environment. In socialist economies, the theory will then lurk hidden from view in the modified institutional and organizational practices of existing Marxist–Leninist systems as they attempt to feel their way towards a more decentralized economic order. We illustrate this in the next section.

THE LABOUR THEORY OF VALUE IN PRACTICE

As early as 1921 it had become apparent to Lenin that, following the economic ravages of war, communism would have to be diluted with some market processes if it was to be made palatable to a near-starving population (Brus 1990; Kowalick 1987). The New Economic Policy (NEP) which he then introduced, however, turned out to be but the first of a number of attempts to find a 'middle way' between a command and a market economy – one that was snuffed out by Stalin in 1929 as he introduced the first of the Soviet five-year plans (Carr 1966). In 1968, Hungary also made an attempt to give greater scope to markets within the institutional framework of central planning through the New Economic Mechanism (NEM) (Brus 1990; Kornai 1990). Yet in spite of contributing to some greater measure of economic flexibility it did not prevent the country's economy from stagnating until the late 1980s when the central planning apparatus was swept away altogether.

In 1978 it was China's turn. Moving gingerly towards some kind of a market system in agriculture by allowing individual households to sell above quota production on their own account, the country extended the experiment to the industrial state-owned sector in October 1984 (Nolan 1987). The details of this experiment are discussed in Boisot and Child (1988). Here we simply note that it was guided by no theoretical principle – Chinese pragmatism at its most manifest – and that although it acted as a powerful stimulus to economic growth, the corruption and inflation that it subsequently provoked were important contributors to the climate of discontent that led to the Tiananmen Square tragedy.

Since the collapse of communism in Eastern and Central Europe in 1989 – but before the disintegration of the Soviet empire in 1991 – another communist country has been moving closer to markets in search of a middle way: the People's Republic of Vietnam. As in the Chinese case, the predominance and superiority of Marxist–Leninist ideology is proclaimed even while some form of institutional accommodation – it goes by the name of *Doi Moi* – is sought with the ideological rival (i.e. markets).

A halfway position between plans and markets is an uncomfortable place to be for the manager of a state-owned enterprise (SOE) trying to make some sense of the institutional environment in which his firm is expected to survive (Lawrence and Vlachousticos 1990). Yet it is also an interesting location for researchers wanting to observe implicit models at work of the kind we are discussing. The SOE, therefore, will be the focus of our discussion.

There have been a number of studies of the socialist enterprise (Granick 1975; Lawrence and Vlachousticos 1990; Tidrick and Chen 1987; Warner 1987) but most are descriptive and make no explicit attempt to link back observed institutional practices to any specific set of prior ideological assumptions. The task we have set ourselves here is to relate a number of existing organizational features of SOEs to the Labour theory of value operating as an implicit model. The link is at its most visible in a regime of reform communism when, in a quest for greater efficiency, some of the more extraneous features of Marxist–Leninist ideology are likely to be shed, thus exposing the core. For this reason we shall focus on Vietnam and China rather than on the new post-communist systems of Central and Eastern Europe. In the latter case it is the ideological core itself that is being jettisoned so that while we might plausibly argue that the Labour theory of value is still operating, it does so, if at all, covertly, with fewer visible institutional manifestations accessible to study. It might also be added that, at the time of writing, with the exception of Cuba and North Korea, not much else is left of communism to focus on. Yet since our chosen countries still have a combined population of nearly 1.3 billion, we are not exactly dealing with a small sample.

The material that follows is drawn from field interviews of enterprise managers and from field observations conducted by the author spread over a period of six years – between 1983 and 1989 – in the case of China, and a single field visit carried out in 1991 in the case of Vietnam. The material is thus 'grounded' but does not claim to be the fruit of systematic data-driven research. To keep the discussion manageable we shall focus on features of organizational practice that are common to both countries, briefly touching on elements specific to each where appropriate.

In both Vietnam and China, enterprise managers are required first to produce and then to manage the firm's tangible productive assets in ways that are largely decoupled from each other. Measures of asset productivity such as 'return on investment' are little used and for the most part are not even known. The most important basis on which performance targets are set is the past: last year's growth in enterprise sales and profits plus a percentage that notionally reflects the country's rate of economic growth (Chen 1992). The performance of other enterprises in the same sector cannot be used as a reference point in setting targets since they are themselves also subject to the same formula. The firm's strategic environment therefore – the one it is called upon to respond to – is less the industrial sector that it operates in than the state bureaucracy that hovers above it and directs it (Boisot and Xing 1992).

In addition to meeting such externally and hierarchically imposed performance targets, enterprise managers in both countries are charged with preserving the value of the state's assets. These are all the unamortized physical assets that the firm uses to produce its output (i.e. the past labour still congealed in physical plant and equipment). Intangible assets such as intellectual property do not figure in this calculation since they are considered public goods not under the direct control of firms. Nor do assets such as goodwill since in a socialist system firms as a whole cannot be bought or sold on the open market. There exists no way, therefore, of valuing a state-owned firm independently of its physical assets and the only basis on which the latter can be valued is on a depreciated historical cost basis. To do otherwise would be to acknowledge the existence of another source of enterprise value besides accumulated and current labour: entrepreneurship and organization. Recent experiments with stockmarkets in China, first in Shenyang and more recently in Shanghai and Guanzhou, have butted up against the issue. Shares become wildly oversubscribed because no economically rational method of valuing firms is available (*Financial Times*, June 1992).

The organizational consequences of this self-inflicted inability to value a state-owned enterprise independently of its physical assets are subtle but far reaching. With the firm having no value other than that of its physical plant, equipment and inventory, managers enjoy no protection from stakeholder interference: no 'veil of incorporation' is capable of bestowing upon the firm an identifiable and independent governance structure that can keep stakeholders at bay. In Western economic practice, the only time that the value of a firm reduces to that of its tangible assets is in liquidation when it is transformed from a living, legal personality into a carcass. At all other times it is a 'going concern' with certain rights of independence in relation to shareholders. While the firm is alive shareholders have a right to dividends and to appoint a governing board at the firm's annual general meeting, but their involvement in enterprise activities stops there. They have no direct claims over the firm's assets until it ceases to function as a going concern.

State-owned enterprises in Vietnam and China may or may not be going concerns – in China, some 40 percent or more of SOEs are thought to be making a loss although the absence of market prices makes this figure hard to establish. In Vietnam the figure is almost certainly higher, but the institutional means for expressing corporate viability in any objective way are lacking. With the exception of exiguous and heavily controlled stock market experiments, there is no market for firms that might establish a value for them independently of their physical assets. Being in competition with the Labour theory of value any such alternative approach to valuation (i.e. bestowing a value on the organization) at present enjoys little institutional legitimacy.

Firm ownership, therefore, instead of being primarily expressed as a residual claim on an uncertain future income – obviously unnecessary in a socialist system since enterprise level uncertainty has been banished by the central plan (even if this has now become purely indicative) – shows up as a direct claim on the firm's physical assets, a fact which makes it much easier for owners – the state and its many representatives such as the supervising bureaux, the Commissions, the territorial authorities, etc. – to reach down into the firm and to make good their ownership claims in disruptive ways. There is no organizational value to be eroded by such interference, no 'going concern' to be kept going.

Reducing the value of the firm to that of its tangible assets has some interesting effects on enterprise behaviour. The Marxist firm is no less given to maximization than the 'representative firm' of neoclassical theory (Marshall 1947). But whereas the latter is required to manage the firm's asset base so as to maximize the net present value of shareholder income streams relative to those assets over the long-term – this, after all, is how the value of the firm itself is maximized – the former can only maximize the value of the enterprise by maximizing the size of its tangible asset base (i.e. the value of dead and living Labour it commands), irrespective of profits earned. The legitimate goals of the socialist firm thus mirror in their own way and for quite different reasons those less legitimate goals imputed to 'managerial capitalism' in market societies (Burnham 1960; Marris 1964; Penrose 1958). These latter goals have the effect of increasing sales, the asset base, and consequently the size of the firm so as to secure status and prestige for a managerial class, but often only by pushing the levels of those variables well beyond the point at which they can achieve any competitive return for shareholders.

Yet even if managers East and West aim to maximize the same variables, there remains an important difference in how far they can respectively do so. Western managers may not be maximizing long-run shareholder wealth as required by textbook theories of the firm, but they are still well advised to accept shareholder profit expectations as a constraint on their behavior, failing which they will be penalized. Shareholders can always sell out or vote the managers out of office. By contrast, no such penalties attach to the managers of socialist enterprises, since there is no way of measuring what increase in the value of the firm is effectively foregone by physical asset maximizing behavior. For this reason the 'investment hunger' described and discussed by Kornai (1990), finds fewer constraints on its expression among socialist managers than among Western ones.

A second consequence of the socialist firm's tangible asset orientation to value concerns depreciation and the right to dispose of assets at the end of their useful life. In the absence of an income-based approach to asset valuation it becomes hard to identify and measure any opportunity cost incurred by the continued use of an asset. There is thus no basis for distinguishing the economic life of an asset – its net productivity over time relative to competing alternatives – from its physical life, measured by the point at which it physically ceases to yield any useful services. To get rid of a machine, for example, before it has been fully depreciated on the grounds that more up-to-date and productive equipment is available is viewed by a state-owned firm's supervising bureau as an unwarranted reduction in the value of the enterprise, a reduction that must at all costs be resisted.

Bureaux supervising state-owned enterprises often also have their own reason for maintaining a large assets base under their control. First, in both China and Vietnam, firms pay the bureaux a capital charge based on their book value for the use of state assets. In both countries, moreover, bureaux have been known to continue to charge firms for the use of fully depreciated assets and even, in certain cases, to prevent firms from getting rid of such assets solely in order to extract further revenue from them. Clearly, the greater the amount of assets a supervising bureau can 'place' with its client firms, the more income it can extract from them in the form of capital charges. Such restrictions on the upgrading of assets can impose a considerable burden on enterprise managers. In Ho Chi Min City, for example, a Liquidation Board was recently set up by the People's Committee (the local authority) to consider petitions by SOE managers who wish to get rid of assets that have outlived their usefulness. The Liquidation Board is no soft touch, however: a firm, for example, would not be allowed to sell off a state asset, even if not utilized, merely in order to repay a bank loan falling due. Assets belong to the state and liabilities to the enterprise.

A second reason for the bureau's concern to maintain the asset base of firms under its control is that it is the recipient of most, if not all, of the depreciation funds these assets give rise to. Bureaux rarely replough these back directly into the firm that initially generated them and whatever proportion of the depreciation fund a firm is allowed to hold on to for itself must often be used for the routine maintenance of existing machinery and equipment before other applications will be considered. Typically, the bureau prefers to use such funds to expand its asset base rather than to renew it and may do this by creating new firms. The supervising bureau in this case takes on the role played by the 'general office' in the Chandlerian multidivisional firm (Chandler 1962), allocating scarce investment resources as would a capital market. But whereas the capital market allocates resources so as to maximize the overall productivity of assets, the industrial bureau does so in order to maximize the size of the tangible asset base under its control. The bureau, not the firm, acts as an investment centre and the enterprise manager is merely required to administer the asset base under his care. Since there is no concept of the firm as a going concern, some firms are thus gradually 'hollowed out' at the bureau's pleasure (i.e. they are required to operate with decreasingly productive assets) in order than new ones may be created elsewhere.

The result is a natural bias towards organizational aging in the state-owned sector: the replacement of tangible assets typically lags way behind their economic life and often behind their physical life as well. In the heavy industrial sector in Vietnam, for example, the average age of assets is twenty-five years and many items of equipment are forty to fifty years old. In one marble-cutting factory visited by the author in China, forty-year-old Russian machines which were already out of date when acquired were still running. A brand new building was going up next to the old plant that housed them and upon its completion the existing machines were due to be transferred to it: the firm had been allowed to put up a new building by its supervising bureau but not to get rid of its old machines.

The way that depreciation is handled in Vietnam and China distorts the cost of capital that confronts firms. Given that capital charges can be quite modest as a proportion of initial purchasing costs, but that the depreciation life imposed on fixed assets is much longer than in the West, new firms sporting new equipment are unduly favoured while older firms in urgent need of modernization can be crippled by the financial burden involved.

A third consequence of valuing firms on the basis of their physical assets alone concerns the reformulation of property rights entailed by the move towards markets. To whom, indeed, might accrue any returns to the kind of entrepreneurship that both Vietnam and China now profess to want to develop? Under pure Marxist–Leninist doctrine the problem hardly arises. Entrepreneurship officially does not exist and does not need to; where it does it is of a furtive, opportunistic kind (i.e. petty commodity trading) that operates at society's expense and must be discouraged. Yet today both markets and entrepreneurship are officially sanctioned in both countries. How are they to be fostered?

Both China and Vietnam, each in its own way, have devised formulae for dividing up profits between the state and the firm that, it is hoped, will act both as motivator of entrepreneurial effort and as an incentive to enterprise renewal. In both cases ownership claims by the state have acquired the character of a fixed tax obligation that allows surplus profit to be retained by the enterprise and applied to bonus payment for individual workers, welfare expenditures for the workforce as a whole and to any investment which the firm wishes to undertake (Boisot 1987).

Yet an enterprise's obligations towards the state are not a function of its *ex post* performance but of the state's planned need for revenue. It is therefore fixed *ex ante* and is often due whether a profit has effectively been earned by the firm or not. To such a tax obligation are added any that the local authority, acting as a tax farmer on behalf of the state, then chooses to add on its own account. In an important sense, therefore, in Vietnam and China, the state, by converting what used to be profit remittances due to itself as owner into a fixed tax payment due to itself as territorial authority, has shifted the residual risk-bearing function of ownership on to the enterprise's own Labour force. They receive what is left in the kitty once the state has helped itself.

Ideologically, such a reform of the state's relationship with the enterprise is more problematic than might at first sight appear. For if, on the one hand, it is merely giving belated effect to the slogan that the workers are 'masters of the enterprise', on the other, the status of that part of the profits left over for reinvestment once the state has helped itself – which in Western firms are the minimum funds needed to keep the business operating as a going concern – is quite ambiguous. Do they belong to the state or to the workforce? How are the returns to this part of the reinvested profits to be distinguished from others? In neither country did the author get any clear answers to these questions. In some firms it was claimed that the profit generated by reinvestment funds belonged to the workers of the enterprise, in others the state was thought to be the beneficiary. Confusion reigns.

The enterprise labour force, having precious little control over the residual risks it is called upon to bear by a firm's supervising bureau – with the reforms, the formal power of state supervising bureaux may not be what it was, but the evidence in both Vietnam and China is that their informal power in most cases remains as great as ever – displays an understandable preference for 'jam today' over 'jam tomorrow'. In ways reminiscent of the Yugoslav Labour-managed enterprise, it exerts great pressure on the so-called investment fund (Vanek 1975). With the state now having collected its dues and with no concept of the firm as a 'going concern' to restrain competing stakeholder claims, the constituency for building up this fund, where it exists at all, will be found principally within the managerial ranks. How strong a constituency is it? The answer is: not very. The relationship between a local authority acting through various industrial bureaux and the firms under its care is in many respects a feudal one: display your loyalty towards us through the various tribute payments we demand – profit taxes are only one form of tribute, many others also exist (Boisot and Xing 1992) – and we shall protect you from the turbulence which you are encountering in the reform environment (Boisot 1987, 1989).

The response of enterprise managers to such 'industrial feudalism' has been mixed. Those running profitable enterprises in reform-minded provinces such as Guangdong or Fujian have discovered that they can effectively face the turbulence unaided and have thus been able to some extent to dispense with the bureau's 'protection'. Others less favorably positioned – and they are not a negligible quantity – see little reason to question such a cosy arrangement. Their managers then join their workforce as bonus maximizers.

If so many state-owned enterprises are making losses, who foots the bill for industrial feudalism? The answer is the central government. In Vietnam state subsidies to loss-making enterprises have now been halted and this is proving to be a major source of pain for many of them. But in both Vietnam and China, officially or otherwise, credit creation has long been under local rather than central control. In pre-reform days credit creation was rigorously linked to the requirements of the five-year plan, but no longer. Local variants of Western lending criteria and credit control mechanisms have been set up in places, but have proved of dubious effectiveness. For how in practice is a firm's credit worthiness to be evaluated? More challengingly, how is repayment to be enforced: by foreclosing on state-owned assets? Local branches of the state bank find it difficult to resist the pressure of local authorities to lend to 'their' firms, even when these are in difficulty, so that if subsidies are not available, credit, more often than not, will take its place. The resulting deficits are retransmitted upwards to the state budget and where necessary made good through the printing presses. Inflation remains a persistent problem in both countries. An important cause is the lack of credible credit discipline imposed on local authorities. These in turn are continually having to absorb the consequences of the 'soft budget constraints' under which their firms operate.

The difficulties involved in making industrial enterprises autonomous governance entities in the absence of an adequate concept of value are well-illustrated by the functioning of the so-called Contract Management Responsibility System (CMRS) in China. The main thrust of the industrial reforms initiated by the Chinese leadership in October 1984 had been to foster managerial responsibility and initiative by putting more distance between state-owned enterprises and their supervisory bureaux. The resulting decentralization, although significant by earlier standards, stopped well short of a full-blown market process. 'The market will control the enterprise, but the state will control the market' was the slogan that expressed the full ambiguity of the intention. The idea behind the CMRS, which had been operating in selected firms on an experimental basis since 1981 (Chen 1992), was that the relationship between a firm and its supervisory bureau should have a voluntary contractual character in which physical targets were replaced by more general financial targets. The firm committed itself to achieving certain output levels on condition that the state (i.e. the supervisory bureau) secured the required quantity of inputs. Once the agreed levels of output were achieved, the firm was free to secure additional inputs for itself in the open market and to sell its extra output there. The role of the bureau was to secure from its firms by means of contracts the minimum performance needed to meet state requirements, beyond that it was not to interfere.

In practice the CMRS did not always work out that way. It was, in effect, little more than a Chinese variant of management by objectives (MBO), a tool of internal managements which, as in the West, only gives autonomy to organizational units that are able to demonstrate high performance and are thus able to improve their bargaining position when negotiating with hierarchical superiors. The key difference, however, between MBO as practised in the West and the Chinese CMRS, is that whereas in the former case superior performance can be taken as a measure of managerial ability to operate in a competitive market environment so that in some sense managerial autonomy is earned, in China superior performance usually merely reflects the particular circumstances in which a manager has been placed by the vagaries of the central planning system.

There is evidence in China of well-placed enterprise managers rejecting the performance targets that they are being invited 'voluntarily' to subscribe to by their supervisory bureau. The bulk of the evidence, however, points the other way, demonstrating instead just how far the fate of an SOE remains in the gift of its supervisory bureau. The key to the bureau's power remains the soft budget constraint. An enterprise manager, either unable to meet unrealistic production targets set by the bureau or unwilling to exert himself to achieve even realistic ones, comes back to the bureau to renegotiate them. In one Beijing firm studied by the author, following successful renegotiation with its supervisory bureau, the CMRS target was adjusted downward beyond what was needed to put the firm back in the black; it was in fact reset at a level that would allow the factory manager to pay the bonuses he had originally promised his workers if they reached a given profit level. In such circumstances the ability of firms to achieve autonomous governance, or even wanting to, seems remote.

In sum, although the evidence presented is anecdotal, it would appear that whereas socialist enterprise managers in Vietnam and China can secure some measure of organizational autonomy for themselves on the basis of their firm's superior performance, where such performance is absent their dependence on the bureau remains largely unimpaired. Yet, how is the managerial component of firm performance established in a centrally planned economic environment where external resource dependency is so high (Child and Markoczy 1993; Markoczy 1992; Pfeffer 1978) and the prevailing concept of economic value focuses so strongly on the preservation of physical assets?

The Labour theory of value orients managerial attention towards past expenditures and their preservation rather than towards future income streams and the alternative possibilities of action that might secure them. In market economies, managers are often torn between an administrative conception of their role (i.e. the stewardship of resources) and an entrepreneurial one. It is the essence of the managerial skill to strike the right balance between such conflicting requirements. In socialist economies, by contrast, the Labour theory of value operates as a hidden force that continuously biases the outcome of this balancing exercise in favour of administration. Yet it has only been by reducing value to cost that the old socialist dream, the 'administration of things rather than people' (Talmon 1952) has found fulfilment.

DISCUSSION

The focus on the preservation of what is and what has been over what might be is the antithesis of entrepreneurship, of the process of creative destruction described by Schumpeter (Schumpeter 1934). It is present in those parts of Western firms where the administrative perspective has taken hold and where the main concern is with costs and cost control – hence the past – rather than with revenue generation. But whereas in the Western enterprise, market competition ensures that the cost and the revenue perspectives balance each other out – failing which a firm may not survive – in socialist state-owned enterprises the cost perspective continues to be the only one on offer. Where value is created by the expenditure of effort alone the entrepreneur has no function; he can generate no value. In a world from which environmental uncertainty has been banished by omniscient and omnidirectional planning, the returns to uncertainty reduction brought about by entrepreneurial action must by definition be zero. By its capacity to enact an appropriate environment for firms (Weick 1979), the state creates a framework of certainty for managerial operations that make managerial risk-taking superfluous.

Entrepreneurial competition is destructive of such certainty partly because it is destructive of the asset values on which it is built. In a socialist state, should entrepreneurial competition be allowed to operate, it would inevitably become in some measure destructive of state property. Yet in both Vietnam and China the state is dependent for the larger part of its revenues on the profit taxes paid by SOEs. Collective enterprises and individual family businesses are also a source of revenue, but in the absence of an accounting system that allows an objective assessment of their profitability, such revenue is much harder to collect.

Therefore, in both countries the state, acting through its agents, the bureaux, feels an owner's responsibility to protect 'its' firms against the destructive effects of competition with a rapidly growing private sector. State-owned enterprises are still perceived by the old guard to be the main generators of wealth in the economy, not so much because of the revenue they generate but because of their size and their asset base; they embody more frozen labour and hence more value. The new entrepreneurs who threaten them thus often continue to be cast in the role of opportunists who appropriate for themselves value created elsewhere.

Much of the corruption that has taken place in Vietnam and China in recent years results from a failure by policy-makers to understand entrepreneurial processes and the nature of the institutions through which these function. But there is also much economic behaviour that is labelled corrupt and where labelling is the product of established beliefs concerning who creates value and how. It is perhaps worth recalling that in Ricardo's day, when Europe was still predominantly an agrarian society, the key sources of value were held to be land and labour. The entrepreneur was viewed as a middleman who created no value. The Labour theory of value has its origins in agrarian economic cultures. The Marxist Labour theory of value is an idea deeply embedded in socialist organizational practice, and in both reforming communist societies – at present Vietnam and China – as well as in post-communist societies, the state-owned sector has become its last refuge. As an implicit model, it finds expression in institutionalized attitudes and practices that keep this sector at a permanent disadvantage where it struggles to compete with an emergent bourgeois private sector.

In neither communist nor post-communist societies has there occurred any striking change in the behavior of SOEs. Where developments have taken place they have been located primarily in the private or the quasi-private sectors (i.e. in collective, township and family enterprises). Here the protective cocoon of the state has been removed and the selection environment has consequently become more rigorous, weeding out firms that cannot adapt to market governance. The reason this has been allowed to happen is instructive. Given their service orientation and their dilapidated asset base, these small firms are deemed to be of little value to the state.

The state, in other words, unleashed the most potent elements of the reform through a process of benign neglect. In those parts of the economy that it valued, the old paradigm continued to hold sway.

Where competing implicit models are incommensurate the move from one to the other cannot be performed on rational grounds; it requires a 'paradigm shift' that may be difficult if not impossible to carry out within an individual brain strongly committed to one of the models. Moreover, since such models are largely unconsciously held, modifying the articulate structures of institutions and organizational processes that give them effect may be to little avail. A new model may then only effectively replace an existing model when a new cognitively uncommitted generation gradually comes to make its own choices.

The practical implication of this point for the reform of institutions based on the Labour theory of value should be noted. It suggests effectively that neither privatization nor organizational restructuring will of themselves create viable market-oriented firms out of existing SOEs. For what needs to be changed are the implicit models held by their managers and workers and, as we have just seen, in most cases this may not be possible. Only carefully crafted socialization strategies based on new implicit models and addressed to a new generation of managers and workers can hope to do the trick.

CONCLUSION

Today China has two economies, each embodying a different socioeconomic paradigm. The first continues to regulate the state-owned sector according to the implicit precepts of the Labour theory of value. It is an economy in long-term secular decline – more than 50 percent of Chinese industrial output is today accounted for by the private sector – and kept alive by a continuous drip-feed of state subsidies. The second provides a framework for a vigorously growing private sector. It is more of a network than a market economy insofar as it is built on a tight web of interpersonal obligations based on trust rather than on atomized competitive relations (Boisot and Child forthcoming).

The two economic paradigms may be incommensurate at a conceptual level – we shall leave open the question of whether this is indeed the case – but the two economic systems that they regulate strongly interact. Indeed, each constitutes a significant part of the other's economic environment, a situation that works much to the advantage of the newly emerging private sector given the poor shape of SOEs.

In time, change may well come to SOEs. If it does, it will be because they perceive their environment to be sufficiently rich in opportunities to make change worthwhile rather than because they are threatened with privatization and restructuring. The carrot rather than the stick is likely to provide the incentive that makes a change of paradigm both possible and manageable. China in this respect has been luckier than the CIS. Its attempts at economic reforms were initiated in a growing economy, not a shrinking one.

BIBLIOGRAPHY

Alchian, A. and Demsetz, H. (1972) Production, information costs, and economic organization', *American Economic Review*, 62, December: 777–92.

Barone, E. (1935) 'Ministry of production in a collectivist state', in F. Hayek (ed.) *Collectivist Economic Planning*, London: George Routledge and Sons.

Blaug, M. (1978) *Economic Theory in Retrospect*, Cambridge: Cambridge University Press.

Boisot, M. (1986) 'Markets and hierarchies in cultural perspective', *Organization Studies* Spring.

—— (1987) 'Industrial feudalism and enterprise reform – could the Chinese use some more bureaucracy?', in M. Warner (ed.) *Mangement Reforms in China*, London: Pinter Publishers.

—— (1989) 'The long march towards bureaucratic rationality', in D. Goodman and G. Segal (eds) *China at Forty: Mid-Life Crisis?*, Oxford: Clarendon Press.

Boisot, M. and Child, J. (1988) 'The iron law of fiefs: bureaucratic failure and the problem of governance in the Chinese economic reforms', *Administrative Science Quarterly*, December.

—— (1994) 'Network capitalism: the strength of weak markets', paper presented at the Cambridge Conference on China, March.

Boisot, M. and Xing, G. (1992) 'The nature of managerial work in the Chinese enterprise reforms: a study of six directors', *Organization Studies* Spring.

Braudel, F. (1979) *Civilisation Materielle, Economie, et Capitalisme, XVe–XVIIIe Siècle*, 3 volumes, Paris: Armand Colin.

Brus, W. (1990) 'Market socialism', in J. Eatwell, M. Milgate, P. Newman (eds) *Problems of the Planned Economy*, London: Macmillan.

Burnham, J. (1960) *The Managerial Revolution*, Bloomington: Indiana University Press.

Carr, E. (1966) *The Bolshevik Revolution: 1917–1923*, Harmondsworth: Penguin Books.

Chandler, A. (1962) *Strategy and Structure: Chapters in the History of the American Industrial Enterprise*, Cambridge, Mass: MIT Press.

Cheung, S. (1983) 'The contractual nature of the firm', *Journal of Law and Economics* 3 (1), April: 1–21.

Child, J. and Markoczy, L. (1993) 'Host country managerial behaviour and learning in Chinese and Hungarian joint ventures', *Journal of Management Studies* 30.

Eatwell, J. (1990) 'Socially necessary technique', in J. Eatwell, M. Milgate, P. Newman (eds) *Marxian Economics*, London: Macmillan.

Elster, J. (1985) *Making Sense of Marx*, Cambridge: Cambridge University Press.

Fama, E. and Jensen, M. (1983) 'Agency problems and residual claims', *Journal of Law and Economics* 26, June: 327–49.

Freeman, C. and Perez, C. (1988) 'Structural crises of adjustment: business cycles and investment behaviour', in G. Dosi *et al.* (eds) *Technical Change and Economic Theory*, London: Pinter Publishers.

Granick, D. (1975) *Enterprise Guidance in Eastern Europe: A Comparison of Four Socialist Economies*, Princeton, New Jersey: Princeton University Press.

Hamel, G. and Prahalad, C.K. (1991) 'Corporate imagination and expeditionary marketing', *Harvard Business Review* July–August.

Hayek, F. (1949) *Individualism and the Economic Order*, London: Routledge and Kegan Paul.

Jensen, M. and Meckling, W. (1976) 'Theory of the firm: managerial behaviour, agency costs, and capital structure', *Journal of Financial Economics* 3 (4), October: 305–60.

Kirzner, I. (1973) *Competition and Entrepreneurship*, Chicago: University of Chicago Press.

—— (1979) *Perception, Opportunity, and Profit*, Chicago: University of Chicago Press.

Kornai, J. (1990) *Vision and Reality, Market and State: New Studies on the Socialist Economy and Society*, Hemel Hempstead: Harvester-Wheatsheaf.

Kowalik, T. (1987) 'Central Planning', in J. Eatwell, M. Milgate, P. Newman' (eds) *Problems of the Planned Economy*, London: Macmillan.

Kuhn, T. (1962) *The Structure of Scientific Revolutions*, Chicago: University of Chicago Press.

—— (1977) *The Essential Tension: Selected Studies in Scientific Tradition and Change*, Chicago: University of Chicago Press.

Lakatos, I. and Musgrave, A. (1970) (eds) *Criticism and the Growth of Knowledge*, Cambridge: Cambridge University Press.

Lange, O. (1936–7) 'On the economic theory of socialism', *Review of Economic Studies*, 4, Pt I, October 1936: 53–71; Pt II, February 1937: 123–42.

Lawrence P. and Vlachousticos, C. (eds) (1990) *Behind the Factory Walls: Decision Making in Soviet and US Enterprises*, Boston, Mass: Harvard University Press.

Lerner, A. (1936) 'A note on socialist economies', *Review of Economic Studies* 4: 72–6.

Markoczy, L. (1992) 'Managerial and organizational learning in Hungarian and Western joint ventures', research paper, Cambridge: Judge Institute of Management Studies, University of Cambridge, March.

Marris, R. (1964) *The Economic Theory of Managerial Capitalism*, Glencoe, Illinois: The Free Press.

Marshall, A. (1947) *Principles of Economics*, London: Macmillan.

Marx, K. (1970) *Capital: A Critique of Political Economy*, London: Lawrence and Wishart.

Mirowski, P. (1991) *More Heat than Light: Economics as Social Physics, Physics as Nature's Economics*, Cambridge: Cambridge University Press.

Nolan, P. (1987) 'China's economic reforms' in J. Eatwell, M. Milgate, P. Newman (eds) *Problems of the Planned Economy*, London: Macmillan.

Penrose, E. (1958) *The Theory of the Growth of the Firm*, New York: Wiley.

Pfeffer, J. (1978) *The External Control of Organizations: A Resource Dependancy View*, New York: Harper and Row.

Porter, M. (1985) *Competitive Advantage: Creating and Sustaining Superior Performance*, New York: The Free Press.

Schumpeter, J. (1934) *The Theory of Economic Development*, London: Oxford University Press.

—— (1942) *Capitalism, Socialism, and Democracy*, New York: Harper and Row.

Shackle, G. (1972) *Epistemics and Economies: A Critique of Economic Doctrines*, Cambridge: Cambridge University Press.

Talmon, J. (1952) *The Origins of Totalitarian Democracy: Political Theory and Practice during the French Revolution and Beyond*, Harmondsworth: Penguin Books.

Tidrick, G. and Chen, J. (eds) (1987) *China's Industrial Reforms*, Oxford: Oxford: Oxford University Press.

Vanek, J. (1975) 'The basic theory of financing of participatory firms', in J. Vanek (ed.) *Self-Management: Economic Liberation of Man*, Harmondsworth, Penguin Books.

Vianello, F. (1990) 'Labour theory of value', in J. Eatwell, M. Milgate, P. Newman (eds) *Marxian Economics*, London: Macmillan.

Warner, M. (ed.) (1987) *Management Reforms in China*, London: Pinter Publishers.

Weick, K. (1979) *The Social Psychology of Organizing*, Reading, Mass: Addison-Wesley.

Williamson, O. (1975) *Markets and Hierarchies: Analysis and Antitrust Implications*, Glencoe, Illinois: The Free Press.

—— (1991) 'The logic of economic organization', in O. Williamson and S. Winter (eds) *The Nature of the Firm: Origins, Evolution, and Development*, New York: Oxford University Press.

4

CREATING VALUE ON THE BALANCE SHEET

Capital structures of new businesses

Richard N. Cardozo, Paul Severn, Anne Sickels and Alexander Ardishvili

INTRODUCTION

The popular notion that new businesses are 'undercapitalized' receives support from folklore, the popular press (Barren 1989) and academic sources (Cardozo *et al.* 1991). Undercapitalization may mean

- that total assets are 'inadequate' for the level of output of the business;
- that the assets are financed with 'too much' debt and 'too little' equity.

Our purpose here is to address the second argument, which presumes that there is some level of debt that is 'excessive'; in other words, there exists some appropriate or optimum debt–equity ratio or capital structure for a fledgling firm.

Finance theory

For help in defining and identifying this optimum capital structure (if it existed), we turned to finance theory. There we encountered six theories of capital structure, including the following (in alphabetical order):

- Agency Theory (Jensen 1986);
- Asymmetric Information Theory (Brennan and Kraus 1987);
- Life Cycle Theory (Shulman *et al.* 1992);
- Pecking Order Theory (Pinegar and Wilbrecht 1989);
- Product Input Market Interaction Theory (Kim and Maksimovic 1990; Maksimovic and Zechner 1991; Sarig and Abraham 1991; Titman 1985; Titman and Wessels 1988);
- Stakeholder Theory (Cornell and Shapiro 1987).

These theories, whose propositions in some instances conflict, yield multiple criteria for managing capital structure. The three criteria that appear most prominent are:

56

1 maximizing value for present shareholders by minimizing costs, which include costs of capital (Brealey and Myers 1988), of insolvency (Carter and Van Auken 1990; Titman 1992), and of diluting current shareholders' wealth (Cornell and Shapiro 1987);
2 maintaining control (Jensen 1986; Ronen 1991);
3 maintaining financial flexibility (Cornell and Shapiro 1987).

In addition to these three criteria, which speak to firms in general, finance theory also prescribes different structures for firms in different businesses. These criteria include (but are not necessarily limited to):

- asset type (Harris and Raviv 1991; Williamson 1988);
- product type (Titman and Wessels 1988);
- profitability and cash flow (Baskin 1989; Lundstrom 1990);
- size (Gupta 1969);
- age (Shulman et al. 1992);
- growth rate (Toy et al. 1984);
- ownership (Winter 1962).

The literature also includes criteria less easily measured in objective terms; for example, strategy and investment opportunities (Kim and Maksimovic 1990; Rappaport 1986; Sarig and Abraham 1991).

We expected that this rich set of criteria reflected the existence of a theory of capital structure. But even review articles (e.g. Harris and Raviv 1991) do not present general theory, but rather they summarize and contrast different individual theories. In fact, Brealey and Myers (1988: 888) confess that, 'We still don't have an accepted, coherent theory of capital structure.' They hasten to point out, however, that the gap in knowledge comes more from lack of consensus than lack of discussion.

Although it would be presumptuous to attempt to develop a comprehensive theory of capital structure, we can pull together in a single framework many of the apparently diverse ideas and approaches from finance theory. We believe that part of the difficulty finance scholars encounter stems from their desire to have a single, simple, elegant, unifying theory from which propositions can be deduced.

Our modification and extension

We take a more modest approach; namely, to try to build a contingent theory. We argue that optimum capital structure for any firm depends principally on the objectives of that firm and the particular costs of capital it faces at a particular time.

We begin building our limited theory with wealth maximization as the objective. An optimum capital structure presumably maximizes shareholder value (Brealey and Myers 1988; Rappaport 1986). Maximization of shareholder value implies minimization of cost of funds, *ceteris paribus*.

Cost of capital

Cost of capital is minimized when the weighted average cost of capital (WACC) is minimized. WACC is the cost of any type of capital multiplied by the percentage of that type in the firm's capital structure. Debt ordinarily costs its interest rate; equity, the return requirement of the provider of equity, which in theory should be appropriate to the level of risk in the investment.

There is no economic reason for a provider of equity to accept a return lower than what he could obtain from lending to a firm with a similar risk profile. Were it not for the effects of income tax, debt might cost the same as equity. Because interest on debt is deductible from income taxes, a dollar of debt costs somewhat less than a dollar of equity (Modigliani and Miller 1958). In fact, in a firm that earns a return equal to or greater than its cost of capital, debt always costs less than equity (Mikkelson and Partch 1986). Extending this argument to its logical limit implies that a firm would minimize its cost of capital and maximize its value to shareholders, if it were financed entirely with debt (see Figure 4.1).

Insolvency cost

But every firm is not financed entirely by debt because WACC is not the sole measure of cost. There is a cost of insolvency, often defined as bankruptcy cost or financial distress (Barton *et al.* 1989; Brennan and Kraus 1987; Carter and Van Auken 1990; Davidson and Dutia 1991; Toy *et al.* 1984). This cost is negligible for firms financed entirely by equity, but rises sharply as firms become more heavily leveraged. Lundstrom (1990) argues that firms with less than 10 percent equity will experience financial crises. Past some point, higher percentages of debt lead to higher interest rates, security requirements, loan covenants – all measures that increase cost and reduce shareholder value. Anecdotal evidence suggests that the impact on shareholder value of insolvency cost is minimal until the firm takes on a substantial burden of debt. Then the cost increases – and shareholder value decreases – sharply (see Figure 4.2).

Optimizing WACC and insolvency

Conceptually, then, the total cost of capital would be lowest – and value to shareholders highest – at the debt–equity ratio which simultaneously minimized the combination of WACC and insolvency costs (see Figure 4.3).

Dilution cost

This optimum also minimizes dilution of present shareholders' wealth, because the dilution curve overlaps the WACC curve. Dilution of present

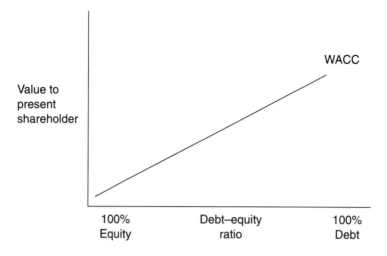

Figure 4.1 Weighted average cost of capital

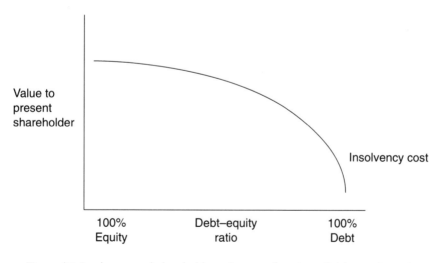

Figure 4.2 Insolvency and shareholder value as a function of debt–equity ratio

shareholders' wealth is greater when funds are added to the business through issuance of stock – present owners then own a lower percentage of the total value (even if their absolute wealth increases). Dilution does not occur if funds are added through straight debt. Thus it is in the interests of present shareholders to add funds first through retained earnings (non-dilutive), then through debt, and finally through equity. This anti-dilution (or wealth preservation) argument is consistent with pecking order theory, which holds that managers prefer to use retained earnings first as a source of funds, then to use straight debt, and finally, equity (Pinegar and Wilbrecht 1989). In graphical terms, dilution has the same impact on shareholder value as WACC (see Figure 4.4).

Control

In addition to cost, shareholders consider:

● control;
● financial flexibility.

The question of control may arise if the owners do not make all the managerial decisions, but delegate some of them to managers whom finance theory regards as agents of the shareholders. Finance theory argues that shareholders (principals) have greater control over managers (agents) under circumstances of high debt, because high debt reduces free cash flow, and thus reduces managers' freedom of action, making their decisions more consistent with those that would maximize shareholders' wealth (Harris and Raviv 1991; Kim and Maksimovic 1990). Jensen (1986) also argues that high leverage increases shareholders' claims on the residual value once debt is retired. The control of agents, then, may require carrying higher levels of debt. In graphical terms, the effect of this 'agent control premium' is to shift the optimum point to the right and downward, from M1, O1, to M2, O2 (see Figure 4.5).

Flexibility

Financial flexibility implies higher levels of equity and lower levels of debt (Cornell and Shapiro 1987). A firm with all equity can issue either equity or debt; but a firm burdened with a high level of debt may be unable to issue more debt and finds that the cost of issuing equity would dilute the wealth of present shareholders. Stakeholder theory (Cornell and Shapiro 1987) argues for higher percentages of equity so that firms can meet future cash outflows.

Flexibility is maximized at 100 percent equity and minimized at 100 percent debt; it is the inverse of WACC. As in the case of insolvency costs, anecdotal evidence suggests that flexibility may not be substantially reduced

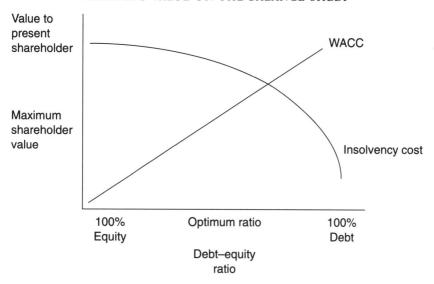

Figure 4.3 Optimizing WACC and insolvency

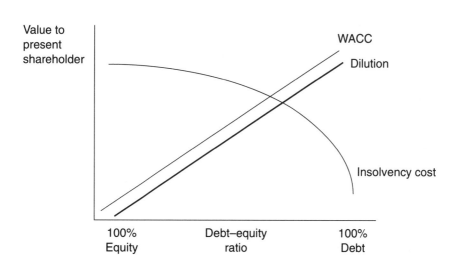

Figure 4.4 Value to present shareholder as a function of WACC, insolvency cost and dilution

until the debt exceeds 30 percent of the total capital. It appears that the curves for insolvency costs and flexibility parallel each other (see Figure 4.6).

Optimizing all criteria

In sum, the appropriate capital structure for a firm from the point of view of a composite finance theory would be that debt–equity ratio which optimized all the aforementioned considerations: WACC, insolvency costs, cost of dilution, agency (control) costs, and flexibility costs. If all these factors received equal weight in the decision, the appropriate debt–equity ratio to maximize present shareholder value could be depicted as in Figure 4.7.

If these curves could be drawn with perfect empirical accuracy, then one could compute the costs – in terms of reduced shareholder value – of flexibility and of controlling agents. If the curves could be estimated empirically, we would have a general guideline for debt–equity ratios.

Adjusting the optimum for different firms

Even if a general guideline were available, we would want to know what modifications should be made to that guideline for particular types of firms.

Finance theory and prior work in entrepreneurial studies offer some guidance here. Product Input Market Interaction Theory (Kim and Maksimovic 1990; Maksimovic and Zechner 1991; Sarig and Abraham 1991; Titman 1985; Titman and Wessels 1988) suggests that businesses providing commodity products will carry more debt than those offering specialized products, because insolvency costs to customers will be lower for highly leveraged commodity producers.

Firms whose assets are tangible and useful in a variety of situations (Harris and Raviv 1991; Williamson 1988) will carry higher levels of debt than will firms with intangible, specialized assets. Presumably insolvency costs for the former (tangible, general assets) are lower because of the salvage value of the assets. Put another way, tangible, general assets offer more persuasive collateral to most lenders than do intangible and/or specialized assets. Thus the presence of tangible general assets in a firm effectively shifts the optimum to the right, to higher levels of debt.

Firms with records of higher profitability and cash flow are likely to have lower levels of debt, because managers use earnings to pay down debt (Baskin 1989; Lundstrom 1990), and retain funds in the business rather than distribute them to shareholders (Jensen 1986). Myers and Majluf (1984) argue that firms with higher profits should carry higher levels of debt, because they have more income to shield, but this advice is evidently ignored. The converse of the relationship of higher surplus and lower debt appears also to hold; firms with lower levels of profit carry higher debt loads. Managers may

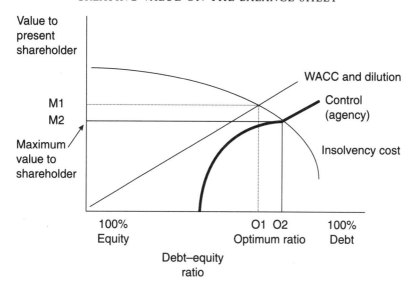

Figure 4.5 Impact of control of agents

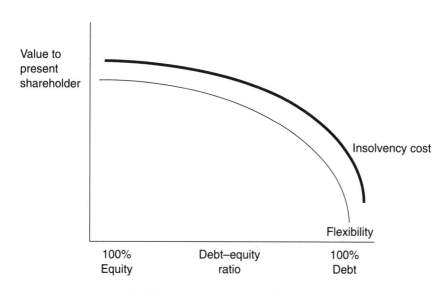

Figure 4.6 Shareholder value as a function of flexibility and insolvency

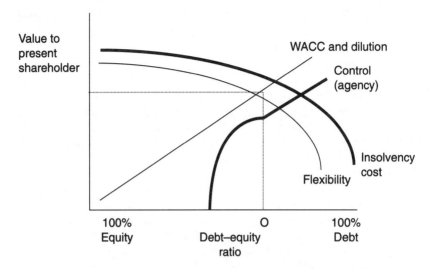

Figure 4.7 Optimum debt–equity ratio to maximize value of present shareholders as a function of WACC, insolvency costs, control (agency) costs, flexibility costs and cost of dilution

incur debt in order to preserve the business and their jobs or because the cost of equity is higher than they believe it ought to be. Brennan and Kraus (1987) argue that managers know more than investors and have more confidence in the firm. This asymmetry in information presumably raises the cost of equity more than it raises the cost of debt to the firm.

Regardless of accounting profitability, firms with high growth rates have lower levels of cash flow, and carry higher levels of debt to finance that growth (Gupta 1969; Toy *et al.* 1984).

In addition, size of firm may affect debt–equity ratios. Smaller firms may carry lower levels of long-term marketable debt than larger firms but they carry more total debt. Smaller firms have more short-term debt and more bank debt than larger ones (Gupta 1969).

A dynamic optimum

The preceding arguments are basically static in nature. But observation and literature suggest that capital structure may change during the life of a firm. Shulman *et al.* (1992) propose a life cycle theory, in which firms begin with high levels of debt, particularly short-term loans, with any longer term debt and all equity coming from the entrepreneur(s), relatives and friends. As firms mature (as measured by increases in employment), the percentage of debt decreases, debt terms become less restrictive and institutional sources replace relatives and friends as providers of funds. Shulman *et al.* (1992) reported results consistent with this description. Supporting evidence comes from Cardozo *et al.* (1991). These results are consistent with Sharpe (1990) and with pecking order theory (Baskin 1989).

Presumably the greater access to capital markets and lower cost of capital (fewer covenants and restrictions) arise from the greater confidence institutional funders have in a more experienced, larger firm – confidence that the entrepreneur(s), friends and relatives (and suppliers) had in greater measure than those institutional sources at the beginning. This explanation is consistent with asymmetric information theory.

Whether or not emerging firms experience higher interest rates at first, and then obtain lower ones, is not clear. While the preceding explanation would favor a decreasing interest rate with greater borrowing maturity, Sharpe (1990) argues that competition among lenders keeps rates for emerging firms low. It may be that, once a firm has matured to the point at which it can become a customer for regular bank credit, interest rates vary by size of borrowing and by industry more than by firm age.

If one could establish an optimum capital structure for any particular individual firm, that optimum would represent an ideal equilibrium point. If a firm were in equilibrium at the beginning of a period, and earned during that period an amount greater than its cost of capital, the firm would be out of equilibrium at the end of the period because its equity would be increased by the amount of earnings retained. The firm could regain equilibrium by paying dividends equal to the surplus, or it could take on added debt to regain equilibrium. The latter action would create shareholder value only if the new capital (retained earnings plus debt) were invested in projects with a positive net present value. Thus to maintain equilibrium in capital structure, a firm must pay out its surplus, grow, or do a combination of both.

Reconciling 'pecking order' life cycle and optimization

If decision-makers choose growth (i.e. additional investment in the business) they will probably follow a 'pecking order' (Baskin 1989; Pinegar and Wilbrecht 1989). We extend the current pecking order theory by hypothesizing that managers will indeed follow this pecking order in sequence when obtaining new funds. For each increment of funds, they will go as far down the order (from retained earnings to new equity) as needed, then begin again at the top. Our hypothesis is consistent with maintaining an equilibrium around the optimum debt–equity ratio. Retention of earnings moves a firm's actual debt–equity combination to the left on Figures 4.1 to 4.5, thereby reducing shareholders' wealth. Taking on debt shifts the actual combination to the right. If the shift to the right passes the optimum point, then additional equity or debt–equity combinations will be needed to maintain capital structure at the optimum point, or as near to it as possible. Although Bates (1990) argues that managers follow the pecking order hierarchy or general financial planning principles rather than attempting to maintain a target debt–equity ratio, the result may in fact be to maintain a target ratio, provided that the debt–equity adjustments occur around the optimum point. If that is the case, then decision-makers are behaving in a manner consistent with this extended theory.

Basic hypothesis

The argument above specifies a conceptual or theoretical optimum that may differ among firms and be maintained in a predictable manner. Observation suggests that optimum debt–equity ratios differ among industries: utilities may carry higher levels of debt than manufacturers in cyclical industries, for example. We should expect, then, to find differences in optimum points among emerging businesses across industries, with fledgling businesses mirroring their established counterparts, perhaps with less total capital and higher proportions of debt.

METHOD

To explore differences in capital structure among fledgling firms we have begun to examine data on capital structures from a panel of fledgling businesses developed by Reynolds et al. (1985). We also intend to examine data from an extensive study conducted by the Federal Reserve Board (1987).

Preliminary examinations of data indicate that we may have to redefine 'debt'. Traditionally in studies and reports of debt–equity ratios, 'debt' excludes current liabilities and includes any interest-bearing debt (typically with maturity greater than one year). Since many new businesses appear not to have long-term debt, but do 'stretch' their payables and other current liabilities, we will probably have to include all debt (current and long-term). Another definition problem comes in differentiating debt from equity within capital contributions of friends and relatives who have in some instances made loans (e.g. Stevenson et al. 1989), or supplied funds on a debt plus equity basis. From the viewpoint of senior lenders – outside institutions – the 'debt' in these transactions is seen as 'equity', subordinated to debt from institutions. When there is no clear basis for differentiation, we count friends' and relatives' contributions as 'equity'. These definitions will tend to overstate 'equity' in a new business and will understate the extent of 'undercapitalization' of a new firm relative to an established one.

PRELIMINARY RESULTS AND DISCUSSION

Our first overviews of the data are, frankly, rather surprising. We find little variation among new businesses in capital structures and no consistent pattern by industry. This lack of variation in capital structures has prompted us to formulate a 'differentiation' hypothesis: namely, that capital structures of emerging businesses resemble one another more than they match patterns of capital structures across industries in established businesses.

Emerging businesses may require time – and attainment of threshold levels of size – to take on the financial characteristics of established members of an industry; that is, firms may have to acquire a certain size and stability (reduced growth rate) to resemble established competitors. New firms may have to learn what financial ratios and capital structures are necessary to compete in a particular industry and are efficient for such competition. Firms that are new and small may not occupy well-defined competitive niches and therefore not yet need to acquire characteristics of larger competitors. Rapidly growing firms may display capital structures different from those of more stable firms that generate cash, rather than consume it.

To evaluate this 'differentiation' hypothesis, we will compare older and younger, larger and smaller firms. We should expect older, larger emerging businesses to be more similar in capital structure to their larger established counterparts in the same industry than younger, smaller businesses.

To assess the premiums that emerging firms are paying, respectively, for flexibility and lack of sufficient capital, we may have to evaluate these yet-to-be differentiated-by-industry firms against one another in addition to comparing emerging and established firms in an industry. If these comparisons that we propose can be made effectively, then we may be able to develop some relative guidelines and heuristics for capital structure for new and small businesses. Such heuristics would provide information and guidance for owner–managers, investors and lenders.

CONCLUSION

We have made an initial attempt to build a limited theory of capital structure for fledgling firms. We argue that there is indeed a conceptual or theoretical optimum capital structure for new businesses, and that we can recognize the costs to a firm of operating away from that optimum, for example, by insisting on excessive financial flexibility or by suffering excessive agency costs.

This argument prompts us to ask of new firms not only, 'Are you carrying too much debt?' but also, 'Are you using enough debt?' The latter is not an obvious question, by any means, for emerging businesses. Nevertheless, if our analysis is correct, it is a question that needs to be addressed. If there is an optimum capital structure for a firm, then entrepreneurs can increase shareholder value by thoughtful attendance to the balance sheet.

Our preliminary examination of data leads us to a 'differentiation' hypothesis. If data turn out to be consistent with this hypothesis, such a finding would open up a whole series of questions on the process by which new businesses come to resemble their counterparts.

REFERENCES

Barren, B. W. (1989) 'Avoiding undercapitalization', *Small Business Reports*, 14, August: 45.

Barton, S., Hill, N. and Gunderom, S. (1989) 'An empirical test of stakeholder predictions of capital structure', *Financial Management*, Spring.

Baskin, J. (1989) 'An empirical investigation of the pecking order hypothesis', *Financial Management* 18, Spring: 26–35.

Bates, T. (1990) 'Entrepreneur human capital inputs and small business longevity', *The Review of Economics and Statistics*, LXXII, November: 4.

Brealey, R. A., and Myers, S. C. (1988) *Principles of Corporate Finance*, 3rd edn, New York: McGraw-Hill.

Brennan, M. and Kraus, A. (1987) 'Efficient financing under asymmetric information', *Financial Management* 42, December: 1225–43.

Brophy, D. J. and Shulman, J. M. (1992) 'A financial perspective on entrepreneurship research', *Entrepreneurship Theory and Practice* Spring: 61–71.

Cardozo, R. N., Harmon B., Reynolds, P. and Miller, B. (1991) 'Initial financial partnering and new firm growth', Proceedings of the 36th ICSB Annual World Conference, Vienna.

Carter R. B. and Van Auken, H. E. (1990) 'Personal equity investment and small business financed difficulties', *Entrepreneurship Theory and Practice* 15, Winter: 2.

Chang, E. C. and Pinegar, J. M. (1987) 'Risk and inflation', *Journal of Financial and Quantitative Analysis* 22, March: 89–99.

Cornell, B. and Shapiro, A. C. (1987) 'Corporate stakeholders and corporate finance (implicit claims)', *Financial Management*, 16, Spring: 5–14.

Davidson, W. N. III and Dutia, D. (1991) 'Debt, liquidity, and profitability problems in small firms', *Entrepreneurship Theory and Practice*, 16, Fall: 2.

Federal Reserve Board (1987) *National Survey of Small Business Finances*, Washington DC: USGPO.

Gupta, M. C. (1969) 'The effect of size, growth, and industry on the financial structure of manufacturing companies', *Journal of Finance* 24: 3.

Harris, M. and Raviv, A. (1991) 'The theory of capital structure (survey of recent literature)', *Journal of Finance* 46, March: 297–355.

Jensen, M. C. (1986) 'Agency costs of free cash flow, corporate finance, and takeovers', *The American Economic Review*, 76, May: 232–9.

Kim, M. and Maksimovic, V. (1990) 'Technology, debt and the exploitation of growth options', *Journal of Banking and Finance* 14, December: 1113–31.

Lundstrom, A. (1990) 'The development of small and medium enterprises – some empirical findings (Sweden)', *Journal of Small Business Management* 28, January: 1.

Maksimovic, V. and Zechner, J. (1991) 'Debt, agency costs, and industry equilibrium (investment projects)', *Journal of Finance* 46, December: 1619–43.

Mikkelson, W. H. and Partch, M. M. (1986) 'Valuation effects of security offerings and the issuing process', *Journal of Financial Economics* 15, January–February: 31.

Modigliani, F. and Miller, M. H. (1958) 'The cost of capital, corporation finance and the theory of investment', *American Economic Review* June: 48.

Myers, S. C. and Majluf, N. S. (1984) 'Corporate financing and investment decision when firms have information that investors do not have', *Journal of Financial Economics* 13.

Norton, E. (1991) 'Factors affecting capital structure decisions', *Financial Review* 26, August: 431–46.

—— (1990) 'Capital structure and small public firms,' *Journal of Business Venturing* 6, July: 4.

Pinegar, J. M. and Wilbrecht, L. (1989) 'What managers think of capital structure theory', *Financial Management* 18, Winter: 4.

Rappaport, A. (1986) *Creating Shareholder Value*, New York: The Free Press.

Ravid, S. A. and Sarig, O. H. (1991) 'Financial signalling by committing to cash outflows (debt and dividend policies', *Journal of Financial and Quantitative Analysis* 26, June: 165–80.

Reynolds, P. D. and Miller, B. (1985) *Minnesota New Firm Study*, Minneapolis, MN: University of Minnesota Center for Urban and Regional Affairs.

Ronen, I. (1991) 'Capital structure and the markets for corporate control', *Journal of Finance* 46, September: 4.

Sharpe, S. A. (1990) 'Asymmetric information, bank lending, and implicit contracts: a stylized model customer relationships', *Journal of Finance* 45, September: 4.

Shulman, J. M., Cooper, N. K. and Brophy, D. J. (1992) 'Capital structure life cycle: static process or dynamic evolution', working paper, Ann Arbor: University of Michigan.

Stevenson, H. H. , Roberts, M. J. and Grousbeck, H. I. (1989) *New Business Ventures and the Entrepreneur*, Homewood IL: Irwin.

Thakor, A. V. (1989) 'Strategic issues in financial contracting: An overview', *Financial Management* 18, Summer: 39–58.

Titman, S. (1985) 'The effect of forward markets on the debt–equity mix of investor portfolios and the optimal capital structure of firms', *Journal of Financial and Quantitative Analysis* 20, March: 19–27.

—— (1992) 'Interest rate swaps and corporate financing choices', *Journal of Finance* 47, September: 1503–16.

Titman, S. and Wessels, R. (1988) 'The determinants of capital structure choice', *Journal of Finance* 43, March: 1–19.

Toy, N., Stonehill, A., Remmers, L., Wright, R. and Beekhuson, T. (1984) 'A comparative international study of growth, profitability, and risk as determinants of corporate debt ratios in the manufacturing sector', *Journal of Financial and Quantitative Analysis*, November.

Williamson, O. E. (1988) 'Corporate finance and corporate governance', *Journal of Finance* XLIII, July: 3.

Winter, E. L. (1962) *A Complete Guide to Making a Public Offering*, Englewood Cliffs, NJ: Prentice Hall.

5

COPING WITH INDUSTRY TRANSFORMATION

The case of the Italian tannery industry

Paola Dubini and Umberto Lago

INTRODUCTION

The Italian economic system is characterized by a few distinctive features; seven models of firm can be identified (Colombo 1992), on the basis of their structural characteristics and typical management styles:

- large state-owned companies, often monopolists in the industries in which they operate, for example, IRI;
- large private entrepreneurial companies, such as Benetton;
- large private managerial companies, such as Olivetti;
- aggregates of small companies, often located in the same geographic region and operating in the same industry; to give an example, the Italian industry of equipment for the packaging industry consists of nearly 450 companies, located in the Bologna and the Milano area. All of them are small and medium-sized enterprises (SMEs) and are spin-offs of the two main competitors. One of the key features of the firms in this cluster is their ability to develop both competitive and cooperative strategies (Lorenzoni 1990);
- independent small companies and cooperatives, particularly situated in central Italy and in the food industry;
- style-based companies, often mid-sized, are characterized by the ability to mingle creativity with the logic of industrial production or to create highly differentiated products with a good quality–price ratio.

Generally speaking, compared with international companies, the relative size of Italian firms is quite small. Moreover, four out of the seven groups identified consist of SMEs. Being so many, it is not surprising that they are widely diffused across industries. In fact, Italian SMEs have been able to gain competitive leadership in small industries characterized by a high level of internationalization for example, jewelry, industrial equipment, tiles, etc. (Corbetta 1993). Therefore, it is not necessarily true that SMEs are 'economic dwarfs' or simple entities which can be examined as having adapted management models originally developed for large corporations. On the contrary, they tend to pursue focus strategies in industries with many segmentation possibilities (Visconti 1993). This explains why they are more concentrated in fragmented industries, in niches, or tend to have marginal positions in concentrated industries.

The Italian tannery industry is representative of the aggregates of small firms. In 1992 it generated 6,900 billion lira of total turnover, 35 percent of which was exported. The industry consists of approximately 2,390 companies, employing approximately 27,400 people. Almost all the companies are located in specific geographic areas, namely in the northeastern part of Italy (Arzignano) and in central Italy (S. Croce sull'Arno). Most of them share some of the structural features characterizing Italian SMEs

- limited number of shareholders, often belonging to the same family and heavily involved in the company's management;
- simple and lean organizational structures with unsophisticated operating systems;
- rapid and centralized decision-making processes;
- limited articulation of activities performed;
- limited product range and high service orientation.

Many of them have been founded by individual entrepreneurs, with little formal education and a technical background, who left the company in which they were employed to set up an independent venture. In many cases, the new companies were spin offs of existing ones.

The Italian tannery industry has traditionally been very important for the economy as a whole and for the specific geographical areas in which companies are located. In recent years, trends occurring at the international level have stressed some of the structural weaknesses of Italian players, forcing them heavily to modify their strategies. The structural changes affecting the industry are first presented; some archetypes of entrepreneurial strategies are then identified and discussed, focusing on the major challenges from international competition facing the various archetypes, and on the emerging successful behaviors.

THE METHODOLOGY OF THE RESEARCH

The research has been based both on secondary and primary data. Secondary data have been provided by FAO analysis (*World Statistical Compendium for Raw Hides and Skins, Leather and Leather Footwear 1972–1990*) of livestock resources and world leather production by country and from industries' associations reports.

Primary data were collected from two sources:

1 Financial analysis – the balance sheets of 223 Italian tanneries have been analyzed for the period from 1988 to 1991.
2 Interview – a total of 37 in-person interviews were conducted with entrepreneurs or top managers (25 companies in the tannery industry, 6 in client industries and 3 in supplier industries), as well as with officers of industry associations.

The results of the interviews have been circulated within the work group in order to help the hypotheses generation process and to drive the research.

STRUCTURAL CHANGES IN THE ITALIAN TANNERY INDUSTRY

The major structural change affecting the Italian tannery industry is undoubtedly the emergence of major new competitors. In the last twenty years, newly industrialized countries (NICs)[1] and developing countries (DCs)[2] – located mainly in South East Asia – have emerged as significant players, heavily reducing the role of European competitors.

Price competition has traditionally characterized the industry and cost leadership explains the dominance of Italian producers over the European competitors; more than 50 percent of European production is made in Italy. Several reasons explain the loss of world leadership by Italian producers; they have experienced a systematic increase in production costs during the last decade, due to three main causes:

- the reduction of demand growth rate – occurring after a period of strong investments – determined a supply surplus which reduced production capacity utilization;
- the increase of gross national product (GNP) per capita and the high rate of inflation related to a sustained increase of labour costs:
- local environmental regulations forced companies heavily to invest in cleaners and reduced the degree of freedom of companies involved in the tanning process.

This loss of competitiveness of Italian products gave rise to the massive entrance of new competitors in the tanning industry.

Significant labour cost advantages and improvements of political, social and economic situations encouraged the rapid development of labour intensive industries in newly industrialized countries; this explains the high growth rate experienced by the Pacific area. In particular, the South East Asian shoe industry is currently the largest in the world, with a production share of nearly 60 percent. As happened in Europe, the boom of the shoe industry pushed a parallel growth of the tannery industry.

European shoe producers were forced to occupy smaller high quality–price ratio niches, characterized by high level of service – particularly to the trade – and by a significant product obsolescence, due to the fad effect. The world shoe industry, therefore, appears nowadays to be divided into two large clusters: the Asian cluster, characterized by mass production, standardized, low quality products and very low prices; and the European cluster, characterized by medium–high quality products, attention to fashion requirements as well as to service and time to market.

In order to cope with the reduction of market share deriving from the entrance of low-cost producers, many Italian shoe producers have decentralized abroad (mainly in Eastern Europe, but also in Asia) the high added value phases of the production process; in some cases, the entire manufacturing process has been transferred to low-cost countries.

This reorganization of the European shoe industry has also significantly affected the Italian tannery industry, traditionally supplying local customers. Reduced volumes and pressure to reduce cost seriously affected many companies, forcing them either to restructure or to quit. The Italian tannery industry has steadily declined since 1981: figures in 1991 showed a decline in the number of companies of about 12 percent and in the number of employees of about 23 percent.

If the main reason for the growth of the tannery industry in newly industrialized countries has been the performance of the main client industry – the shoe industry – which has stimulated the demand for tanned leather, the path in developing countries has been the opposite.

In fact, developing countries, traditionally strong exporters of raw leather, are at present reducing the export of these goods and increasing the export of semi-finished (wet-blue) or even finished products (crust). This is due to the industrial policies pursued by their governments to increase employment (the tannery industry is, at least in these countries, labour-intensive) and, at the same time, to exploit the huge livestock resources.

The rise of developing countries in the tannery industry has certainly been facilitated by the producers of Italian tanning machines. Since the Italian and the European markets were already saturated, they started to export the technology to the Far East and to South America. This contributed to an increase in the quality of the new competitors' production, thus reducing the strongest competitive advantage of the Italian companies.

The trends at the international level in the shoe, tannery and tanning machines industries have led to a dramatic change in the strategies pursued by Italian tanneries. Ten years ago the market for Italian tanneries was mostly domestic, with some export in Europe. Today the development of a strong new shoe industry in the South East Pacific area, together with the growth of new competitors, has broadened the competitive scope of Italian tanneries to a global scale.

In fact, Italian tanneries are at present serving two markets with very different characteristics: the European (mainly Italian) market; and the South

East Asian market. The first requires products of medium–high quality and a high flexibility; the second requires huge amounts of low–medium quality, standard products at low prices. However, the rapid increase of GNP per capita in the countries of the Far East seems to be opening up room for medium–high quality products.

THE STRATEGIC OPTIONS FOR ITALIAN COMPANIES

In order to face these structural changes, Italian competitors are exploring different strategic options, on the basis of the following dimensions:

- the variety of leather types produced, for example, bovine, sheep, goat;
- the degree of externalization of production;
- the client industries – shoe industry, clothing industry;
- the end-user segments served – high, medium, low quality;
- the geographic scope.

These have been determined (from interviews and analysis 'in the field') as the key dimensions upon which Italian companies formulate their competitive strategies. In fact, these dimensions capture a large percentage of the tanneries' competitive choices. This means that companies placing different values upon them are pursuing different competitive strategies. According to the choices made upon these dimensions, therefore, we can identify which competitive strategy a company is seeking and what are the conditions for the further development and the success of these strategies in the long-term.

The competitive strategies which seem to be more popular among Italian tanning companies can be classified as follows:

- focus on differentiation strategy;
- industrial strategy;
- group strategy.

FOCUS ON DIFFERENTIATION STRATEGY

Companies which pursue differentiation strategy typically produce only one or two types of leather, carry out the entire production process in-house, from raw leather to finished product, and serve mainly one client industry only in the domestic or European market, where they target the high-end segment.

This strategy is, by definition, available only to a minority of companies and those which have been traditionally pursuing a differentiation strategy over a long period of time are obviously in a better position in comparison to those which have been forced to upgrade their production by the competition of the low-cost newcomers.

In order to implement successfully the focus on differentiation strategy, it is necessary to develop specific know-how in terms of production flexibility: production of small lots, fast and frequent deliveries, and service to customers. Moreover, companies pursuing these strategic options are required to put constant emphasis on high-quality standards: selection of the best raw leathers, accurate manufacturing process, and exploitation of technology as a possible source of innovation and differentiation.

Finally, this strategy is very tightly linked to the needs of the target market segment. This means a continual stress on values such as innovation, design and fashion, in order to maintain the basis of differentiation on which the strategy relies (see Figure 5.1).

The further developments and the success of this kind of strategy for Italian companies are linked to some conditions. First, Italian tanneries should improve their ability to work with their customers in a cooperative rather than conflictual way: this means raising their production flexibility in order to be able to react quickly to demand fluctuation, designing products together with clients, widening the range of products, and so on.

At the same time, Italian tanneries should start looking for new clients in international markets, especially in the fast-growing NICs. The rapid increase in the standard of living in those countries is creating new customers who are willing to pay a premium price in order to have high quality products. This means that manufacturers (local or European with plants abroad) could be looking for the high-quality leather which Italian tanneries can supply.

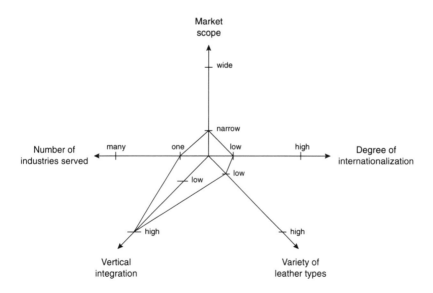

Figure 5.1 Focus on differentiation strategy

To be competitive in international markets, however, Italian companies must reduce the cost gap *vis-à-vis* the new competitors. They can, for example, externalize less critical phases of the production process which are less important for the quality of the product or which can be easily monitored.

A more radical solution could be the export of the first phases of the process to developing countries where labour costs are much lower and environmental laws less strict. This solution would not only significantly reduce production costs, but also avoid the export quota restrictions. In fact, companies which have branches in developing countries also benefit from being able to choose the raw leathers to process, thus avoiding quality problems.

INDUSTRIAL STRATEGY

Companies pursing this kind of strategy are typically focused on one or two types of leather products. In terms of the production process they aim to minimize costs, maintaining an acceptable quality *vis-à-vis* their competitors. These companies, in fact, pursue all the cost-cutting possibilities: they prefer to buy semi-finished (wet-blue) rather than raw leather and to use outside suppliers for production processes which require particular skills. At the same time, they give emphasis to those characteristics, such as design or finishing, which can significantly raise the quality of the product without adding relevant costs.

These companies are significantly present in the international markets where they serve mainly the shoe industry, targeting a wide range of segments, from low to medium-high (see Figure 5.2).

This strategy is available to those companies which are able to mix a continuous pressure to reduce costs – through the rationalization of the production process and the control of production costs – and the ability to maintain a flexible process in order to meet the requirements of Western clients and to differentiate from emerging competitors. Conditions for further development and success of this strategy seem to be:

- growth in international markets with the aim of playing a significant role in the South East Pacific, targeting Italian shoe manufacturers going abroad as well as local manufacturers.
- the location of the first phases of the tanning process in developing countries, in order not only to lower production costs and directly to supply with raw leather, but also to create a bridgehead in emerging markets.

GROUP STRATEGY

Almost all Italian tanneries are SMEs located in specific areas (economic districts). The changes in the industry structure have highlighted some intrinsic weaknesses of this mode of organization, namely related to the small

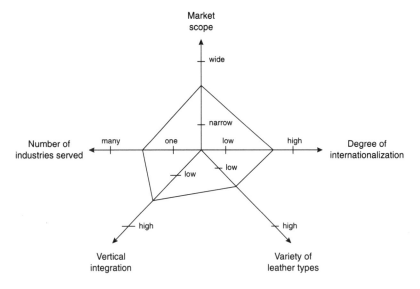

Figure 5.2 Industrial strategy

size of companies. Weakness in the supply as well as in the sale markets, difficulties in investing in research or marketing and a general waste of resources have pushed many companies to find new ways of organizing production. The group strategy emerged as a viable solution for Italian tanning companies to overcome the weaknesses associated with small size.

In the Italian tanning industry two kinds of group can be identified: the 'trust' and the groups dominated by one company. Groups of the first type generate a significant turnover and allow small companies to gain access to international markets but, being created mainly for opportunistic reasons, they are fairly unstable and weak.

Groups of the second kind, which are widespread in the area of Arzignano and S. Croce, are typically created by a company aiming to implement a strategy of external growth. Groups of this kind have a very large competitive scope: they produce a wide range of leathers directed to a broad range of segments in different industries, in domestic as well as in international markets (see Figure 5.3).

Groups dominated by one company in the tanning industry were founded for different historical reasons, which can be summarized as the willingness (or the need) of the founder company:

- to buy companies in crisis, taking advantage from industry reorganization;
- to grow rapidly to a size which can give a relevant bargaining power without creating new production capacity;
- to stop the growth of a competitor;

- to acquire rapidly specific know-how;
- to make the most of valuable employees.

Moreover, the group is also able to exploit significant synergy and to take advantage of the larger size without losing the typical flexibility of SMEs. In fact companies which are part of a group can offer a wide range of products and share the same marketing people and technicians, thus improving market penetration and research. The larger size of the group also allows it to increase its bargaining power, to invest in communication and brand promotion and to optimize financial management.

Further development of the group strategy seems to lead to a rationalization – concentration of the market segments served and the type of leather produced, improvements in coordination activities in order to exploit synergy and to reduce risk of cannibalization or overlapping areas. The strengthening of the position in international markets, namely with direct investments, also appears as a condition of success for the group strategy.

TYPICAL PROBLEMS OF ITALIAN TANNERIES

In the previous paragraphs, the most significant strategic archetypes in the Italian tannery industry are identified and their strategic patterns in reaction to the dramatic industry changes are discussed.

Although the devaluation of Italian lira contributed to an increase in revenues and export in 1993, Italian tanning companies are facing a significant crisis. In addition to international competitive pressures, increased

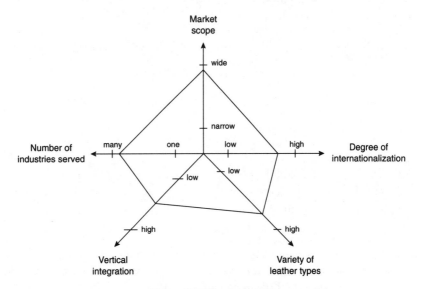

Figure 5.3 Group strategy

78

awareness of environmental problems is reducing the social acceptance of this highly polluting industry in the domestic market. Firms are forced to bear heavy investments that can hardly be made individually; at the same time, the institutional problems of the Italian public administration make it difficult to generate the necessary consensus to implement environmental strategies at local level.

Some of the difficulties of Italian tanneries are shared by Italian SMEs and derive from their structural features. A small group of shareholders sharing a cohesive culture, limited size, the convergence of a multitude of roles around the entrepreneur, growth through self-financing, the limited possibility of gathering financial resources, the simplicity and lack of formalization of organizational assets all define a consistent picture of a successful SME, but can be interpreted as the determinants of pathological situations hindering future growth. This is particularly evident in the case of major structural changes, requiring consistently different strategic as well as organizational solutions. Part of the failure in the Italian tanneries can be analyzed according to this perspective.

As far as the institutional framework is concerned, top management often consists of family members. The existence of family ties may make it very difficult to set the borderline between firm and family. The ambiguity of the relationship may be problematic in different respects: the need to fund growth via self-financing may generate discontent among family members who are not directly involved in the firm management and who are expecting increased dividends. As a partial balance, the firm is sometimes considered as the natural job destination for all family members, regardless of their expectations, skills and commitment and the company's actual needs. The presence of incompetent family members in the company may quite easily generate tensions among the management; at the same time, the need to maintain long-lasting relationships within the family makes it hard to discriminate among family members, particularly where the entrepreneur's successor is concerned. Compromises are often inevitable; some SMEs diversify mainly to create organizational conditions for the entry of family members, rather than to exploit perceived competitive opportunities.

The presence of a charismatic leader – the founder – undoubtedly has several advantages. However, the delicate moment of the entrepreneurial succession (Corbetta and Demattè 1994) makes Italian SMEs particularly vulnerable. Given the fact that many companies were started immediately after World War II, a lot of them are facing entrepreneurial succession during this decade. Because the entrepreneur directly controls people and activities and operating mechanisms have not been activated, the company lacks consolidated procedures. Substituting the entrepreneur is a very real problem. When succession takes place, the company not only has to adjust to a new personality, but also has very little to capitalize on, since all the information is stored in the entrepreneur's mind. For this reason, financial institutions often view the presence of a sole entrepreneur as a risk when they are considering financing opportunities.

From a different viewpoint, the presence of a cohesive culture may lead to a form of insulation from external stimuli; the company will tend to replicate past successful behaviors without challenging them. Moreover, the entrepreneur's viewpoint will be systematically regarded above the others, thus contributing to an increase in frustration for the management. Finally, the firm's development will tend to be consistent with the entrepreneur's own inclination and skills; the result is an inconsistent structure.

As far as the organizational assets are concerned, the entrepreneur's personality and activism may lead him to surround himself with yesmen. Brilliant managers and direct collaborators may find it frustrating to work in a company in which little room is left for their creativity. As a consequence, managerial positions within SMEs are still viewed as second-best career opportunities by smart graduates. Over time the human resources base of SMEs may become rather weak. In the case of the tannery industry, this is particularly relevant due to the fact that an increase in size is often a requisite for successful strategies.

Simplicity of organizational structure and focus on operational activities can be major hindrances when a company is exploring strategic alternatives or is facing significant growth. Some companies, for example, are unable to internationalize, in spite of a good product system. This can be due to the lack of resources and knowledge of how to approach a foreign market or to the lack of basic skills, such as knowledge of a foreign language, to be able to develop relationships with international counterparts. Moreover, changes in structure tend to follow changes in strategy, thus contributing to great stress on the organization during radical transformation processes (see Depperu 1993, for pressures on an organization as a consequence of internationalization strategies).

From the economic and financial viewpoint, willingness to maintain status quo as far as institutional relationships are concerned and fears of losing institutional control are key determinants of the structural undercapitalization of Italian SMEs. As a consequence, even companies with high potential do not grow due to lack of investments. The delicate relationships between shareholders in family businesses determine over-conservative behavior. Given the fact that many Italian tanneries have focused investments in environmental protection due to regulatory pressures, they tend to lack capital for further investments.

Implications on strategy are quite evident. First, SMEs tend to react to competitive pressure, rather than anticipate it, putting competitors in the position of leveraging on their own strengths or – as in the case of the tannery industry – of developing alternative strategies without fear of retaliation. If the company is unable to face the high level of competition, it is generally confined in progressively smaller and overcrowded niches. The result is that it finds itself engaged in dangerous price wars or pushed to increase the level of service and accelerate product obsolescence. Leadership strategies in international niches appear to be those which enable SMEs better to defend their competitive advantage. However – as the tannery industry shows – focus strategies present the problem of sustainability of the competitive territory and significantly challenge the innovative potential of Italian SMEs.

ACKNOWLEDGEMENTS

Data for this paper derive from a research project carried by SDA Bocconi and sponsored by the Nino Lodi foundation. The authors wish to acknowledge the contribution of the members of the research team: Guido Corbetta, Gianluca Colombo, Mario Marelli, Federico Visconti. Data for the research are published and extensively discussed in Corbetta *et al.* (1993).

NOTES

1 For newly industrialized countries (NICs) we mean here and further in this chapter countries such as China, Taiwan and Korea.
2 For developing countries (DCs) we mean here and further in this chapter countries such as India and Pakistan in Asia and Argentina and Brazil in South America.

REFERENCES

Colombo G. (1992) *Modello italiano di management*, Milan: SDA Bocconi research report.
Corbetta, G. (1993) 'I ruoli delle imprese di piccole e medie dimensioni', *Sistema impresa* 11 (5).
Corbetta, G. and Demattè, C. (1994) *I processi di transizone delle imprese familiari*, Milan: SDA Bocconi research report.
Corbetta, G., Lago, U., Marelli, M. And Visconti, F. (1993) *Strategie per la competitività dell'industria conciaria italiana*, Milan: EGEA.
Depperu, D. (1993) *L'internazionalizzazione delle piccole e medie imprese*, Milan: EGEA.
Lorenzoni, G. (1990) *L'architettura di sviluppo delle imprese minori* Bologna: Il Mulino.
Visconti, F. (1993) 'Le strategie competitive delle piccole e medie imprese', *Sistema impresa* 11 (5).

6

EXTRAORDINARY FEATS OF ENTREPRENEURIAL ENTERPRISE

Strategies for rapid, sustained growth

Thomas D. Kraemer and S. Venkataraman

INTRODUCTION

This chapter constitutes a first and exploratory attempt to understand the rapid, sustained growth of what we call extraordinary entrepreneurial enterprises. These firms have been founded after 1945 and, in this short time, have succeeded in entering the *Fortune 500*, becoming some of the largest industrial firms in the USA. Growth of this magnitude and scale represents some of the most extraordinary feats of entrepreneurial enterprise in the post World War II American economy. Measured in any terms, share of new job creation, new wealth creation, or technical innovation, these firms contribute massively to societal welfare and, therefore, deserve further attention. This exploratory and descriptive exercise seeks to develop a deeper understanding of the key elements of their growth processes.

RESEARCH QUESTIONS

Through this chapter, we investigate five substantive questions about the rapid, sustained growth of these enterprises.

1　To what degree did these firms possess proprietary assets or inventions near the time of their founding that conferred a substantial competitive advantage to them?
2　Since founding, to what extent do these firms rely on alternative modes of growth, internal venturing, acquisitions, and joint ventures, to generate sales?
3　Do a proprietary asset or skill at founding and the product market mix of the firm imply more common modes of growth or patterns of new business entrance?

4 Do a proprietary asset or skill at founding and the mode of growth yield preferred methods of expansion?

5 To what extent are differences in return based on differences in growth processes?

THEORETICAL DEVELOPMENT

In examining each of these five questions, we rely principally on the resource-based view of the firm and on theories which attest to the crucial nature of founding conditions and imprinting on future development. The fundamental point of the resource-based view of the firm is that certain key attributes of the resources and resource configurations of a firm provide it with the necessary competitive insulation required for sustained abnormal profits, which in turn are a crucial fuel for sustained growth over time (Rumelt 1987; Penrose 1959). The fundamental point of the imprinting argument is that the circumstances of an organization's founding contribute significantly to imprinting those founding conditions and channeling the organization's attention and resources along certain feasible and often unique opportunity sets (Kimberly 1975; Stinchcombe 1965). We combine these ideas to suggest linkages between possessing a proprietary asset or invention at founding, the firm's product market mix, its mode of growth, and relative performance differentials between firms.

Proprietary asset of invention at founding

We expect to see a majority of the extraordinary entrepreneurial enterprises to possess a unique proprietary asset or invention at their founding. As Schumpeter (1976) compellingly argued several decades ago, a proprietary invention or knowledge affords an enterprising firm the ability to build the necessary monopoly power, such as entry barriers, which may be crucial for sustained growth. Further, such assets also confer the ability to these firms to create inimitable configurations of co-specialized assets and routines around the proprietary assets, thus creating new paths for future growth (Dierickx and Cool 1989; Nelson and Winter 1982; Penrose 1959; Rumelt 1984). The existence of such proprietary assets, inventions, tacit routines, and inimitable resource configurations allow firms to appropriate, even in the face of competition, the crucial fuel for sustained growth, namely abnormal profits and slack.

Certain types of innovation can also destroy or make irrelevant the competencies or skill set currently used within an industry. Such a competence destroying innovation simultaneously devastates one class of producers in a market while replacing them with a new industry and a new dominant player in that industry (Abernathy and Clark 1985). If properly tended, possessing such an asset at founding would allow a firm to create new markets and appropriate new and old markets in order to generate the profits needed to finance the tremendous rates of growth over many years. Perhaps more importantly, possessing such an asset would significantly impact opportunities available to the firm in the future: 'Managers of organizations must recognize that they operate within constraints [and opportunities], many of which come from the initial establishment of structures, routines, and repertoires that become institutionalized over time' (Boeker 1989). Stiglitz's (1989) view of learning as a competitive weapon, in turn, means that experience with this initial asset would confer a competitive advantage to the originating firm for not only this particular asset but also for any extensions of it. Hence, as long as the skill sets which spawned the initial asset or invention at founding could contribute to developing new assets or products, the firm possessing it should have an advantage over all others.

Hypothesis 1: A majority of the extraordinary entrepreneurial enterprises will possess a proprietary asset or invention at the time of the firm's founding.

Proprietary asset or invention and the product market mix

We argue, that of the firms which own a proprietary asset or invention at founding, a greater proportion of the extraordinary entrepreneurial enterprises will be more likely to select a focused product-market as they grow. Dierickx and Cool (1989) argue that firm assets and endowments exhibit the quality of 'stickiness' – they are not easily changed, refocused, or shifted. The capability development process and the character of assets and capabilities cause firm endowments to be 'sticky'. Capability development is complex in the extreme and most firms lack the ability to develop new ones quickly. 'From the capabilities perspective, strategy involves choosing among and committing to long term paths or trajectories of organizational competence' (Teece *et al.* 1991). Consequently, as a firm successfully moves along a path or trajectory, the new assets and capabilities which it builds will be closely related to the old ones. Klein, Crawford, and Alchian call these new assets or capabilities co-specialized assets. Path dependency makes them specialized and the 'co' element permits their redeployment but only in a limited range of tightly related areas (Teece 1987). Hence, the development and evolution of capabilities suggest that a firm with a proprietary asset or invention would pursue a specific trajectory and develop co-specialized assets over time. If it deviated from its original business trajectory at all, the entrance would be into a closely related sector since the firm's co-specialized assets would favor that.

The character or nature of such assets or capabilities should also motivate fast-growing enterprises to focus their product market mix. Many assets and capabilities are inarticulable, non-tradable, not observable, and tacit. This severely limits the ability of a firm to recognize the importance or value of external opportunities and to assimilate and utilize successfully those opportunities which it does recognize (Cohen and Levinthal 1990). The extent to which a firm is able to recognize and seize opportunities rests on its prior experience and knowledge (Cohen and Levinthal 1990) and its ability to learn (Stiglitz 1989). Together, these two criteria create a learning range (Dosi *et al.* 1990) which severely delimits the ability of a firm to recognize and seize external opportunities. The presence of inarticulable or tacit capabilities at founding limits the firm to recognizing and executing successfully only those initiatives which are closely related to its original capabilities.

Hypothesis 2: Firms which possess a proprietary asset or invention at their founding will be more likely to pursue a focused product market mix.

Proprietary asset or invention and the mode of growth

Here, we believe that an enterprise with a proprietary asset or invention will emphasize a mode of growth which favors venturing over acquisitions or strategic alliances. Barney (1986) and Dierickx and Cool (1989) argue that critical assets are accumulated not acquired in strategic factor markets – capabilities cannot be easily bought, they must be built. Building requires venturing. Asset stocks contain a strategic value, capacity to generate rents, only to the extent that they are non-tradable, not imitable, and not substitutable. This causal ambiguity (Wernerfelt and Montgomery 1986) allows a firm both to insulate and sustain its competitive advantages. It also erodes the ability of a firm to acquire a strategic advantage in two ways. First, a firm seeking to acquire competitive capabilities cannot ascertain if a potential acquisition target owns the sought after capabilities. Second, even if a firm could determine that a potential target firm possessed the capabilities it required, the acquirer could still not be sure of its ability to transplant successfully those strategic capabilities. For a firm which owned a proprietary asset or invention at founding, this difficulty would motivate it to build strategic assets with a strategy that emphasizes venturing.

These arguments, however, do not simply preordain that all firms will venture. Those firms lacking a proprietary asset or invention could not select a trajectory and, through time, develop a host of co-specialized assets. Instead, they would be forced to attempt to acquire, at least during their infancy, some asset stocks. In addition to the dilemmas of purchasing a strategic capability, some capabilities are simply not for sale. Possessing a proprietary asset or invention at founding may often mean that the enterprise has a monopoly on it and, thus, would derive little benefit from any acquisition. Creating a stream of co-specialized assets and successfully leveraging the new asset or invention would then require a firm to venture. That ventures may, from time to time, receive transfusions in the form of acquisitions does not alter the basic thrust of our argument.

A different perspective on growth offered by Penrose (1959) also supports our view. Since no firm can utilize its assets at 100 percent efficiency, slack or fallow resources exist within the firm. These spur growth. As a firm brings more resources on line, it simultaneously increases its stock of assets and, therefore, slack. This requires the firm to utilize still more slack – growth begets growth. Given inarticulable and tacit assets which are often embedded within a firm's routines, internal venturing would have a greater likelihood of isolating and utilizing successfully the slack imbedded within a firm's proprietary asset or inventions.

Hypothesis 3: Firms which possess a proprietary asset or invention at their founding will be more likely to choose venturing over acquisitions or joint ventures as their mode of growth.

Raw return and risk weighted return

We measure profitability with two performance measures, one unadjusted for risk and one incorporating risk, to ensure that the analysis of profitability includes the fluctuations in profits over time. To do otherwise would be myopic in the extreme, as the variation in profitability, the risk of an investment, constitutes a crucial component of an investor's return. A risk return paradox has been identified which showed that the most well-managed firms have both higher performance and lower risk, an important contradiction of a lot of finance literature. It is this ability to generate higher returns at lower levels of risk that we expect to observe.

Combining the three different constructs here, we arrive at a total of eight different possible growth processes.

		Focused product market mix		Unfocused product market mix	
		Venture	Acquisition/ other	Venture	Acquisition/ other
Proprietary asset or invention at founding	YES	1	2	3	4
	NO	5	6	7	8

We expect to observe performance differentials in rates of return between cells. Much of the literature from strategy argues that owning a proprietary asset or invention allows a firm to generate superior rates of return when compared to competition which lacks such an endowment. This asset or invention often enlivens a first mover advantage and the ability quickly to build market share. Market share, in turn, allows the firm to insulate itself from competition. In addition to allowing the firm to extract monopoly rents, such assets and inventions typically afford it the opportunity to capture Pareto and Ricardian rents once competition does enter an industry. The firm continues to insulate its stream of profits because such assets typically exhibit the quality of causal ambiguity – copying or even understanding them well vexes most competition (Dierickx and Cool 1989).

Different product market focuses should also enliven differing rates of return. Much of the strategy literature on mergers and acquisitions and diversification demonstrates that a related or more tightly focused strategy outperforms a less related or more unfocused one (Rumelt 1984). Focus is argued to be superior, because it confirms the strength of a firm's endowment or capabilities. If a firm possesses assets it can continually modify and utilize to generate rents, it will not have to attempt to enter new markets. Similarly, focus also implies that the enterprise's competition does not have competitive capabilities which force the firm to enter into unfamiliar markets and industries. Christiensen and Montgomery found that:

> the performance problems of unrelated-portfolio firms [unfocused] may go deeper than this [entering fragmented, low profit, and unrelated markets]: They may lack the critical skills or resources needed to participate successfully in faster growing, more concentrated markets
> (Christiensen and Montgomery 1981: 340)

Competitive weakness in the face of competition and the inability to redeploy the capabilities and assets of the firm would result in a relatively poorer performance.

Finally, the degree to which a firm emphasizes venturing or acquisitions in its growth process should yield different rates of return. Barney (1986) and Dierickx and Cool (1989) argue that valuable strategic assets are accumulated not acquired. Capabilities must be built; they cannot be bought. Even if one relaxes the perfect market assumptions used to make these conclusions, the general thrust of their argument remains valid. Two central dilemmas hamper the ability to acquire a useful strategic asset. First, given the tacit and causally ambiguous character of most of such assets, determining if such an asset is capable of producing the synergies required to make such an acquisition lucrative is quite difficult. Second, transplanting capabilities from one setting to another is uncertain at best. Hence, firms which emphasize venturing should achieve higher rates of return than those which do not drive growth through internal methods.

Hypothesis 4: The different growth processes of the extraordinary entrepreneurial enterprises will have different rates of raw return and risk weighted return.

Hypothesis 5: Those extraordinary entrepreneurial enterprises having a growth process consisting of a proprietary asset or invention at founding, an emphasis on venturing, and a focused product market mix, will have a higher risk weighted return than any other growth process.

METHOD

Sample selection

We drew the sample of extraordinary entrepreneurial enterprises from the 1992 *Fortune 500* list and the earliest three *Fortune 500* lists which appeared in 1956, 1957, and 1958. The firms present in 1992 but not present in any of the earlier *Fortune 500* lists were isolated. Of these 360 firms, we excluded those known to be founded before 1 January 1946. The Coca-Cola Company is an example of a deleted firm. For the remainder, research assistants contacted public relations departments within each firm to determine the year of founding. Since many firms experienced difficulty with supplying a date, research assistants augmented the self-reported information with *Moody's* business histories and the *International Catalogue of Business Histories* to find founding dates. The initial round of coding for age yielded 136 firms in the *Fortune 500* which were founded after 1946.

As a precaution against different types of firm origin which might contaminate founding date data, we classified the firms into the following categories using the self-reported information, *Moody's* business histories, and the *International Catalogue of Business Histories* (hereafter *ICBH*). They totaled 131 and are:

- spin-offs: 12;
- mergers: 19;
- independent start-ups: 69;
- holding companies: 26;
- foreign subsidiaries: 2;
- went public: 3.

Spin-offs were included if the original starting date for the division or subsidiary was after 1946. In the absence of a founding date, we excluded the spin-off firms. Mergers between two firms or divisions qualified if each division or firm was known to be founded after 1946. Firms qualified as independent start-ups if archival sources confirmed this and if no other information implied that they might fit into any of the other categories. Holding companies would have been included if the founding dates for all member firms and groups comprising the holding entity were known to be before 1946. None met this criterion. Foreign subsidiaries were excluded as they received huge financial infusions and managerial support from their mother corporation. We included firms which 'went public' if we confirmed that they were founded after 1946 and if archival data at the time of founding was available. This resulted in 105 possible extraordinary entre-preneurial enterprises.

This initial list of firm founding dates and classifications then underwent several iterative checks to ensure accuracy, reducing the available N. First, in cases of disagreement between self-reported dates and founding dates found in *Moody's* or the *ICBH*, we discarded the self-reported data, as we could not be positive of a respondent's accuracy. Second, while attempting to locate annual report and 10K information at the Library of Congress, we found reports from firms which preceded the then current founding dates. We adjusted these backward. Third, using the archives at Harvard Business School, the dates for other firms needed to be shifted backward. Fourth, the annual reports and/or 10K reports within a span of eight years from the founding date were read to verify founding dates and classifications. If, at any of these four checks, a founding date or classification was found to be incorrect, we consulted additional annual reports and/or 10Ks to find the correct informa-tion. In the many cases where an annual report or 10K was unavailable to lock down a founding date or classification, we excluded the firm from the sample.

After completing this process, we eliminated 23 firms as possible extraor-dinary entrepreneurial enterprises, reducing their potential number to 82. Of these 82 firms, the ability to collect data reduced our sample size. We encoun-tered the greatest difficulty with mode of growth, as we had to rely on the firms themselves to report it. Some were unwilling to divulge the informa-tion; some did not have it; and some simply failed to respond in time. The unavailability of archival information for many firms precluded us from including many others. Our sample size for this chapter consists of 55 enter-prises or 76.1 percent of the population of firms of interest.

Industry membership

The extraordinary enterprises in our sample operated in 28 different two-digit SIC code product markets. Four SIC categories appeared more than five times. If we roughly construe computers, measuring devices, and electronics as one industry (codes 35, 36, 38, and 50), we encountered them 87 times which constitutes 44.8 percent of the total number of SIC codes. While this source of potential bias is unavoidable, it is understandable. Heavy technology, inten-sive defense spending, the space race, and the birth and boom of information technology drove this trend. Furthermore, it is unclear whether 44.8 percent represents an overestimate or underestimate of computer and electronics firms. The inclusion of interim firms, those founded after 1 January 1946 who became *Fortune 500* members and then dropped off the list at some point prior to 1992, could either raise or lower the percentage. We will be revisit-ing this point in our discussion of the study's limitations.

MEASURES

To address our research questions, we used the following variables which we explain below.

A   Proprietary asset or invention
B   Product market mix
C   Mode of growth
D   Raw return and risk weighted return

Proprietary asset or invention

To determine the presence or absence of a proprietary asset or invention, annual reports, 10Ks, and company histories supplied by the firms themselves were coded by the authors and research assistants. Before elaborating on the coding procedure, further explanation of the operationalization of this variable is necessary. Instead of noting the presence of a competency or comparative advantage, we imposed a more difficult standard. A firm had to possess not only a competitive advantage, but also a clearly insulatable and sustainable competitive advantage. In the case of technology, it had to be not only advanced, but also a competence destroying technology. We chose this higher benchmark to preclude trivial advantages which most if not all firms would have possessed. A proprietary asset or invention should augment significantly the prospects for growth and the ability to grow. In short, such an asset or invention should be of tremendous import.

While we attempted to use annual reports and 10Ks at the year of founding, availability precluded us from doing so. Consequently, we used information that was up to eight years old and, in one case, an eleven-year-old annual report. Even with these older materials, assets and inventions which were present but clearly acquired or built after founding were still excluded. The coding rules required that the report information used to make a positive determination was explicit or a 'no' was entered. Each firm was coded independently by three research assistants. In cases of disagreement, they were asked first to discuss the differences of opinion and, if necessary, to resolve the dispute by vote. Of the 55 firms, the group of three failed to reach immediate agreement five times. In only two cases, were they forced to resolve these disagreements by vote.

Product market mix

To determine the product market mix, we selected the change in SIC codes from the year of founding to the present. Using annual reports and/or 10Ks within eight years of the founding date, research assistants coded for product lines. For those annual reports and 10Ks not from the year of founding, coders excluded any product line not underway during the founding year and any line initiated after the founding year. Using 'SIC Info-Base' software obtained from the US Department of Commerce, we derived the SIC codes for each product line. By combining these two figures, we computed the proliferation and change in SIC codes. Note that this was not a simple subtraction. In some cases, firms had abandoned their original business lines and entered new ones. We regarded this as an important distinguishing factor and, therefore, included SIC codes present at founding which the firm had later discarded. Two illustrations best clarify the procedure. Firm 1, at founding was in SIC code A and, in 1992, was found to be in A, B, C, and D. We therefore eliminated the double counted A and assigned Firm 1 a product market mix score of four. Conversely, Company 2 began in SIC code A at founding and, in 1992, offered products in SIC codes B, C, and D. Company 2 received a score of five, reflecting the four SIC codes and the additional movement out of the original product line. Finally, we split the scores along the mean and defined the half with smaller values as a focused product market mix and the upper half as an unfocused product market mix.

Mode of growth

To determine the mode of growth, research assistants contacted the investor relations or the treasury departments in each firm. Where possible, Wharton alumni were contacted to provide the information. In each reported case, they interviewed a senior manager or managers. The following questions and clarification were used either in direct telephone interviews or in a fax survey following a brief conversation. On the phone, the ordering of A, B, and C was altered at random to avoid any priming effects.

A What proportion of your total sales are generated by products or services developed in house?

B What proportion of your total sales are generated by products or services which you acquired or purchased?

C What proportion of your total sales are generated by products or services created through cooperative alliances or joint ventures?

Clarification: For those acquisitions which you have substantially altered, please estimate the value of the original acquisition in the 'Acquisition' category and any improvements made thereafter in the 'In House' category.

The respondents were asked to provide precise ratios but were also told that checking 20 percent blocks (0–20, 20–40, 40–60, 60–80, and 80–100) would be acceptable. In three cases, response overlap occurred where interviewees checked the 80 to 100 percentile box for in house venturing and the 0 to 20 boxes for both acquisitions and joint ventures. These were classified as 80 percent venturing, 10 percent acquisitions, and 10 percent joint ventures. In cases where no overlap occurred, respondents checked 80 to 100 for venturing and 0 to 20 for acquisitions, for example, we recorded the average value of each cell, 90 percent for venturing and 10 percent for acquisitions. We were also heartened to find that 32 firms or 58.2 percent recorded and disclosed exact percentages. Using these percentages, we categorized the mode of growth as either venture or acquisition/other based, because the mean reliance on joint ventures for all those who used them was only 13.04 percent. Furthermore, only 23 firms in the sample reported that joint ventures contributed to sales at all.

Those firms who estimated to generate over 50 percent of their sales with venturing were classified as emphasizing ventures as a mode of growth. Similarly, those firms who estimated acquisitions to generate over 50 percent of their sales were classified as emphasizing acquisition/other as the mode of growth. Four firms, however, did not fit into this heuristic.

	Venturing %	Acquisition %	Joint venture %
Firm 1	40	0	60
Firm 2	40	40	20
Firm 3	44	14	42
Firm 4	24	8	68

For these cases, we based the mode classification on the higher of the venturing and acquisitions percentages. Firm 2, being a tie, was coded as acquisition/other.

Raw return and risk weighted return

The CRISP database served as the data source for both the raw return and the risk weighted return. We utilized daily return figures for each firm and used all of the data points which the database contained. The raw return consists of the mean for all of these data points. The risk weighted return is this mean divided by the standard deviation of the returns over the time period for which data was available. As the database did not contain at least five years of returns for one firm (1,825 data points), we excluded it. The procedure substantially altered the ranking of only one cell and this, in turn, was due to an extremely high return and standard deviation figures for one firm about which we only had four years' worth of data. Note of this is made in the results section.

Statistical tests

The sample size, non-normally distributed data, and four observed counts less than five precluded the use of ANOVA or a chi-square test. Instead, we chose to test our hypotheses using log linear modeling on a three-dimensional contingency table. This allows us to ensure that the relationships present in our hypotheses and in the table actually exist. It also allows us to test for direct and moderating interactions after having derived the model with the best fit.

RESULTS

The following tables answer the first two questions. Table 6.1 contains the distribution of firms for each factor and Table 6.2 presents the distribution of the firms between mode of growth, product market mix and proprietary asset or invention at founding.

These two tables confirm Hypothesis 1: a majority of the extraordinary entrepreneurial enterprises did possess a proprietary asset or invention at the time of their founding. A high share of these enterprises, 56.4 percent, were determined to possess a proprietary asset or invention which enlivens an insulatable, sustainable, and substantial competitive advantage. The tables also lend support to Hypotheses 2 and 3. Enterprises which owned a proprietary asset or invention at founding were more likely to offer a focused product market mix. Of the 31 enterprises, 23 had such an asset

Table 6.1 Distribution of firms for each factor

Proprietary asset or invention	Yes	No	Total sample
	31	24	55
Mode of growth	Venture	Acquisition	Total sample
	44	11	55
Product market mix	Focused	Unfocused	Total sample
	36	19	55

Table 6.2 Distribution of firms between mode of growth, product market mix and proprietary asset or invention at founding

		Focused product market mix		Unfocused product market mix	
		Venture	Acquisition/other	Venture	Acquisition/other
Proprietary asset	YES	22	1	5	3
or invention					
at founding	NO	9	4	8	3

and were focused and only 8 did not. The support for Hypothesis 3 was even stronger: 27 extraordinary entrepreneurial enterprises began life with a proprietary asset or invention at founding and leveraged this endowment with venturing and only 4 did not. While the raw distribution of the data confirms Hypothesis 1 and lends support to Hypotheses 2 and 3, interactions still need to be demonstrated and other features of the data warrant further discussion.

Venturing figured prominently in the growth strategies employed by the extraordinary entrepreneurial enterprises. Over three-quarters of the firms, 80 percent, reported to emphasize a venturing strategy as a mode of growth. To further underscore its central role, the mean amount of sales generated by venturing for all 55 firms, including those who favored acquisition/other, reached 73.1 percent. Acquisition/other accounted for 20.1 percent and joint ventures for 6.2 percent. While not as pronounced, 65.5 percent of these firms emphasized a focused product market mix. The odds ratios between the left and right two-by-two's comprising Table 6.2, however, are of considerably more interest as they address the interaction between measures. Typically, the ratios for each two-by-two matrix move in the same direction. This is not the case here. For the matrices above, the odds ratios are:

$$\frac{22 \times 4}{9 \times 1} = \frac{88}{9} \qquad \frac{5 \times 3}{8 \times 3} = \frac{5}{8}$$

The odds ratios show that, given a focused product market mix, an enterprise with a proprietary asset is over nine times more likely to use a venturing strategy. Given an unfocused product market mix, however, an enterprise with a proprietary asset or invention is likely to use a venturing strategy in only five out of every eight cases. The interaction between a proprietary asset or invention at founding and the mode of growth is governed by the focus of the product market mix.

For each permutation of the matrix, the different odds ratios or different movements between the left and right halves of each two-by-two hold. One may locate any variable in any of the three possible positions and obtain the same pattern. When firms emphasize venturing as their mode, firms with a proprietary asset or invention are 3.9 times more likely to adopt a focused product market mix than those without such an asset or invention. Conversely, given an acquisition/joint venture based strategy, firms adopt a focused product market mix in only one out of four cases. A final odds ratio is also of interest. If a firm possesses a proprietary asset or invention, the firm is 13.2 times more likely to utilize venturing as its mode of growth and to offer a focused product market mix. In the absence of such an asset or invention, a firm is only likely both to venture and to use a focused product market mix in one out of four cases. Pooling these results obtained from the odds ratios lends support to our hypotheses:

94

1   A majority of the extraordinary entrepreneurial enterprises owned a proprietary asset or invention at the time of their founding.
2   Firms with a proprietary asset or invention emphasize a focused product market mix.
3   Firms possessing a proprietary asset or invention also favor venturing as the mode of growth.
4   The preferred or most likely observed strategic growth agenda consists of firms which owned a proprietary asset or invention at founding, relied on venturing to generate their sales, and focused their product market mixes.

While our data seem to move in the posited directions, the relationships observed in the odds ratios have not yet been confirmed. Log linear models will define which odds ratios may be believed or, more broadly, which observed relationships exist and which do not.

The log linear model

Log linear modeling allows us to ask a much more robust set of questions regarding the nature of potential interactions between our factors. The log linear procedure generates predicted values by forcing the odds ratios of the observed and predicted values to be as similar as possible. Then, conceptually resembling an OLS regression, it reports the degree to which the model fits the observed data. Listed below are the possible combinations of interactions between the three different variables. The first model [Asset] [FPMM][Mode] is the independence model.

Log linear output			
	DF	Likelihood chi-square	Probability
[Asset] [FPMM] [Mode]	4	9.69	0.0460
[Asset Mode] [FPMM]	3	7.46	0.0585
[FPMM Mode] [Asset]	3	7.36	0.0614
[Asset FPMM] [Mode]	3	7.29	0.0631
[Asset FPMM] [Asset Mode]	2	5.07	0.0795
[Asset Mode] [FPMM Mode]	2	5.13	0.0770
[Asset FPMM] [FPMM Mode]	2	4.96	0.0838
[Asset FPMM] [Asset Mode]	1	3.48	0.0620
[FPMM Mode] [Asset FPMM Mode]	0	0.00	0.0000

Key
Asset = Proprietary asset or invention
FPMM = Focus of product market mix
Mode = Mode of growth (venturing or acquisition/other)

The independence model holds that the product market mix, mode of growth, and possession of a proprietary asset or invention are unrelated to or do not depend on one another. Each subsequent model posits one or more interactions between the variables – interacting variables are enclosed within the same parenthesis. For example, [Asset Mode][FPMM] means that possessing a proprietary asset at founding and the mode of growth interact with each other while the focus of the product market mix exerts no impact on this relationship. In addition, each interaction is, by convention, hierarchical; [Asset Mode] includes not only the interaction, but also the main or independent effects of [Asset] and [Mode]. The main effects are nested in the interaction effects.

The heuristic for selecting the model with best fit relies on the Likelihood Chi-Square figure and uses three tests. The Likelihood Chi-Square is the difference between the expected and observed values – the smaller the Chi-Square, the better the fit. First, using the chosen level of significance, one should reject every model with a significant Chi-Square at the degrees of freedom of the model. We use 10 percent as this study is exploratory in nature. Then one should select the least significant, best fitting, model. If all of the models must be rejected, the saturated model best fits the data. Second, one should ensure that the fit cannot be improved by adding another interaction term to the model. Third, one should find that deleting an interaction term significantly harms the fit.

As each of the first models has a likelihood chi-square probability below 0.100, none of these models fits the data well. As a result, the saturated model [Asset FPMM Mode] bests fits the data. Recall that the chi-square reflects the difference between the expected and observed values. The saturated model means that every possible two-way interaction exists, but that this interaction is controlled by the third variable. More concretely, firms possessing a proprietary asset or invention at founding will offer a focused product market mix if they also favored venturing as their mode of growth. Enterprises leveraging their proprietary assets or inventions through venturing will do so with a focused product market mix. Companies pursuing a growth strategy consisting of focused or related products and reliance on in house development will own proprietary assets or inventions. This supports Hypotheses 1, 2, 3, and 4.

The saturated model merits further clarification. The interpretation of this model means that, while owning a proprietary asset, venturing and a focused product market mix constitutes the preferred strategic growth agenda, each of the additional seven possible permutations represents a viable strategic growth agenda in its own right. In short, each of the eight possibilities exhibit unique characteristics and dynamics, and deserve consideration alone.

Industry concentration

The widely varying presence of the computer, electronics, and measurement industries strengthens the argument that each of the eight strategic growth agendas possesses its own distinct logic. We found 52.7 percent of our sample to be concentrated in this group when they were founded. We would have expected to see roughly half of each cell to be filled by this group, if strategic growth agendas resembled one another. The number of firms within each cell is enclosed in parentheses. (See Table 6.3.)

Computers, electronics, and measuring devices dominated strategic growth agendas involving a proprietary asset or invention and venturing while being sparsely represented in those agendas which emphasized acquisitions to generate sales. This provides a link, albeit weak, between industry features and strategic growth agendas.

Rates of growth

Interestingly, the more frequently occurring growth process did not correspond to the growth agendas that yielded the fastest *Fortune 500* entry. This result means two things. First, like the preceding discussion, it underscores the finding that the eight strategic growth agendas are unique and viable. Second, it implies differential rewards and risks associated with the eight possible strategic growth agendas. In Table 6.4, the mean number of years required for firms to become *Fortune 500* members is presented by cell.

Were the different strategic growth agendas to represent merely irrelevant features of growth companies, we would again expect firms in each cell to require roughly the same entry time. This does not happen. The differences in time required to enter suggest a set of unique dynamics at work within each strategic growth agenda.

A proprietary asset or invention at founding generates the different times to entry. Even if one excludes the cells with less than five firms, eliminating the mode distinction, firms lacking a proprietary asset or invention at founding became *Fortune 500* members faster than those with such an asset. The result holds for both focused and unfocused product market mixes, with the faster strategic growth agenda consisting of firms which lack a proprietary asset or invention at founding while offering a focused product market mix. The fastest were the firms which ventured without a proprietary asset or invention at founding along focused trajectories. The second fastest, if one ignores cells with few firms, were companies which owned a proprietary asset or invention at founding, who ventured, and who offered a focused product market mix.

Comparing the four cells with five or more firms shows a potential trade off between speed and risk. In both focused and unfocused cases, firms lacking a proprietary asset became *Fortune 500* members faster than those owning

Table 6.3 Computer, electronics, and measurement industries concentration

		Focused product market mix		Unfocused product market mix	
		Venture	Acquisition/ other	Venture	Acquisition/ other
Proprietary asset or invention at founding	YES	72.0% (22)	0.0% (1)	100.0% (5)	33.3% (3)
	NO	44.4% (9)	0.0% (4)	25.0% (8)	33.3% (3)

Table 6.4 Mean years to *Fortune 500* entry

		Focused product market mix		Unfocused product market mix	
		Venture	Acquisition/ other	Venture	Acquisition/ other
Proprietary asset or invention at founding	YES	17.5 (22)	31.0 (1)	20.6 (5)	16.3 (3)
	NO	16.5 (9)	8.0 (4)	18.3 (8)	24.7 (3)

such an asset (16.5 years versus 17.5 and 18.3 years versus 20.6). While marginally faster, 17 firms managed to become *Fortune 500* members while lacking such an asset and 27 did so while owning one. In short, lacking a proprietary asset or invention at founding could shorten the time required to attain *Fortune 500* membership, but wanting this resource early on may increase the difficulty associated with achieving this type of growth. If, for example, the 8.0- and 16.3-year figures are to be believed, speed to *Fortune 500* membership would depend on generating sales through acquisitions and joint ventures with product focus either being irrelevant or unfocused being best. This trajectory, then, may be fraught with both the greatest danger and opportunity.

Raw return and risk weighted return

The raw return and risk weighted return closely approximated each other. Cells 5, 3, 8, and 1 had the four highest raw return figures. These are presented in Table 6.5. For the risk weighted return, cells 5, 3, 1, and 2 displayed the highest risk weighted return. These results can be found in Table 6.6

Table 6.5 Mean daily raw return by growth process

		Focused product market mix		Unfocused product market mix	
		Venture	Acquisition/ other	Venture	Acquisition/ other
Proprietary asset	YES	0.000795 (22)	0.00074 (1)	0.001035 (5)	0.000246 (3)
or invention at founding	NO	0.001176 (8)*	0.000218 (2)**	0.000619 (8)	0.000886 (3)

Note: * and ** One firm is missing from each of these cells as its performance data were unavailable at the time of this writing. In addition, an additional firm from cell** was deleted as its performance was over 400 percent higher than average and we only had three years of performance data for it.

Table 6.6 Mean daily risk weighted return by growth process

		Focused product market mix		Unfocused product market mix	
		Venture	Acquisition/ other	Venture	Acquisition/ other
Proprietary asset	YES	0.031698 (22)	0.031693 (1)	0.035429 (5)	0.022817 (3)
or invention at founding	NO	0.03811 (8)*	0.007933 (2)**	0.018811 (8)	0.024179 (3)

Note: * and ** One firm is missing from each of these cells as its performance data were unavailable at the time of this writing. In addition, an additional firm from cell** was deleted as its performance was over 400 percent higher than average and we only had three years of performance data for it.

The variation in returns between cells confirms Hypothesis 4 while the third place of cell 1 for both raw and risk weighted return disproves Hypothesis 5. We had expected this growth process to outperform all of the others.

Since the risk weighted return of strategic growth agenda 8 is the only exception to an otherwise stable trend, we will discuss it first. The high return of this strategic growth agenda suggests the potential for successful conglomertization. These firms grew by emphasizing acquisitions which were spread across a relatively wide band of SIC codes and they accomplished this without the luxury of a proprietary asset or invention at founding. Only three of the fifty-five firms attained *Fortune 500* member status and the relatively long time period (24.7 years from Table 6.4) required to do so by these enterprises suggests a much higher degree of difficulty associated with this growth process.

Excepting cell 8 of the raw return, a stable pattern for both raw returns and risk weighted returns emerges.

Best return profile	*Second best profile*	*Third best profile*
Growth process 5	Growth process 3	Growth process 1
No proprietary asset/ invention	Proprietary asset/ invention	Proprietary asset/ invention
Focused	Unfocused	Focused
Venturing	Venturing	Venturing

The long periods of return data, well over ten years of daily returns in most cases, and the overall increasing trend of returns probably eliminates the differences in standard deviations or risk of returns. The deviation from our hypothesized growth process of cell 5 may reflect several things or a combination of them. It may be that these firms came to own a proprietary asset or invention near the point of founding but after the eight-year cut off point we utilized for coding. In addition, the development of assets may exhibit a different character for this growth process. It may be that product development capabilities are crucial during this time period and that growth explodes after the first innovation. Firms investing heavily in research and development for revolutionary technologies may require more lead time than our coding allowed to bring on stream their particular innovation or product. In any case, additional specification and intermediate time points will be required.

In the case of growth process 3, we believe specification error may account for performance here exceeding that which was posited. This chapter has consistently cast the construct of focus in the spirit in which relatedness is used in much of the strategy literature. While SIC codes are used in much of this literature, the classification developed by Rumelt (1984) may be more appropriate. Although our measure does incorporate the cognitive and organizational difficulties associated with operating across many strategic business units, SIC-based relatedness measures can be problematic. Relatedness, to be theoretically consistent, must be measured *ex post*. The MRI scanner provides an excellent case in point. This combined medical X-ray technology, spectrometry, and computer driven image enhancing skills. An SIC-based measure would surely classify these as unfocused when they are clearly related. This potential problem is understandable because, to our knowledge, this is the first effort to separate the outcome of relatedness, a focused product market mix, from the vehicle of achieving a related set of SBUs, the mode of growth.

Finally, that the posited growth process performed in the top three in both return classifications does encourage us somewhat. In addition to occurring most frequently and permitting the third fastest *Fortune 500* entry, its healthy performance profile is still noteworthy. Combining a proprietary asset or invention at founding with a relatively focused product market mix, and leveraging this with in-house venturing yielded a healthy performance profile, albeit 20 percent less than the best possible.

Limitations and efforts to address them

It is important to note that the nature of our data and our results do not imply causality. They constitute descriptions of a unique and important population; at best, we could argue that the patterns observed are associated with sustaining rapid growth. Without the presence of a control group, we cannot address causal links.

The most glaring weakness of this study is its failure to include firms founded after 1 January 1946 which succeeded in becoming *Fortune 500* members but which dropped out before 1992. We call these 'the in-between firms' and they number roughly 80. While we are attempting to collect data on them, we elected to proceed without them for several reasons. Most important, many of these companies simply no longer exist. Some suffered bankruptcy while others were sucked into the vortex of merger and acquisition activity. Tracking firms which have been acquired, reorganized, partially divested, and merged is quite difficult. Obtaining information on these firms, especially the mode of growth data, is nearly impossible. Finally, we cannot locate an address for many of them and simply have no idea where they are or if they exist. Our sampling procedure, therefore, generates two types of bias. One, relatively older *Fortune 500* entrepreneurial enterprises survived when many others failed to do so. This creates a clear survivor bias among the older part of the sample. Conversely, the sample may contain proportionately more new firms than would be the case if information on a significant portion of the in-between firms were available.

On a related note, computer, electronics, and measurement industries represent a large percentage of the firms in the sample. The addition of the in-between firms may either increase or decrease the weight of these industries within a complete sample. The importance of this related set of industries in our sample, however, should not eliminate the generalizability of our results. The computer and electronics firms present in the sample achieved and sustained tremendous rates of growth in the face of intense competition from other firms within the same industries. They still constitute some of the most successful firms in the post-World War II American economy.

Measuring the presence or absence of a proprietary asset or invention only at founding will also enliven criticism. We are currently collecting data points between the present and founding to ensure that the connections observed here remain independent of time. It will also be useful in explaining and clarifying some of the performance differentials observed. We hope that this will produce a much richer mosaic of firm resource bundles and their metamorphosis over time.

Finally, the reliance on firm reported data to determine the mode of growth constitutes the largest potential source of error for the data which we have. While we made every effort to contact executives and Wharton alumni, we cannot establish the reliability of the responses which we received. Although we searched for an alternative measure which would illuminate the importance of venturing, acquisitions, and joint ventures and not just their frequency, we were unable to develop one.

CONCLUSION

This examination of the rapid, sustained growth of the USA's most extraordinary entrepreneurial enterprises revealed distinct patterns.

- A majority of the extraordinary entrepreneurial enterprises possessed a proprietary asset or invention at the time of their founding.
- Enterprises possessing a proprietary asset or invention are more likely to favor venturing as the mode of growth if they have a focused product market mix.
- The preferred or most likely growth process contained firms which owned an insulatable, sustainable, and substantial competitive advantage, relied on venturing to generate sales, and focused their product market mix.
- Each of the eight identified growth processes represents a viable and distinct way for firms to achieve and sustain rapid growth. Each will exhibit unique characteristics and dynamics.
- Industry characteristics interact differently with different strategic growth agendas.
- Different growth processes contain distinct potentials for rates of growth.
- Enterprises which lack a proprietary asset at founding, that offer a relatively focused product market mix, and that emphasize venturing exhibit both the best raw return and risk weighted return profiles.

These results imply the need to refocus or shift a portion of the research on the resource-based view of the firm. Usually, research in this tradition has concentrated on a few constructs – capability development, learning, the importance of relatedness, and others. The results of our research, however, imply that the interaction between these constructs is of greatest import. Alone or even in groups of two, the ability of our constructs to describe the phenomena of firm growth depends on the impact of a third construct. Significantly, this third variable relates not only to the interaction between the first two, but also moderates or controls the interaction relationship. If we really intend to deepen our understanding of sustained, rapid growth, focusing on the co-development or co-evolution of constructs will be necessary.

The potential value of focusing on the interactions between varying constructs can be demonstrated by fusing the central results of our research. Together, we have distilled the preferred and most likely growth processes for extraordinary entrepreneurial enterprises. Companies capable of achieving and sustaining rapid rates of growth will probably possess or be close to developing an insulatable competitive advantage which has a competence destroying element. They will most fruitfully exploit the value of this asset or invention through a strategy of focused venturing. The ventures should seek to generate new proprietary assets or inventions which are closely related to those already possessed; the firm should intend to offer a tightly focused set of products and services. While this does not preclude a strategic growth agenda which emphasizes other choices, our research does suggest that this combination of strategic choices and characteristics occurs most frequently.

Although the perspective offered here described well the location of the extraordinary entrepreneurial enterprises across the three dimensions discussed, it did not do well in predicting the relative performance between the different groups. Additional specification of focus and the introduction of intermediate data may substantiate our last hypothesis. Yet, two growth processes performed better than expected. Perhaps, the importance of assets is not as crucial in one growth process. Similarly, another process may be less sensitive to relatedness or focus of its products.

Future research efforts

Extending this research will require progress on four interrelated fronts. Up to this point, we have been unable to claim that the elements of the observed growth processes generate or account for the tremendous success of these extraordinary entrepreneurial enterprises. Research designed to demonstrate causality holds much promise and we plan to use a matched sample with the hope of drawing this causal link.

Measurement of constructs and illuminating the character of the interactions which we argue are critical will also require much creative effort. We made some headway in our measurement of a proprietary asset or invention, but mode of growth and the focus of the product market mix require further work. Specifically, measuring mode of growth requires a reliable and falsifiable alternative. The specification of focus needs to be changed to reflect the classification used by Rumelt as well as the notion that cognitive and organizational features limit the number of SBUs in which a firm can profitably operate. More generally, developing inferences and theories which describe in detail the interaction of, for example, the ability to learn and an insulatable, competitive advantage would, based on our results, seem to offer much promise.

Similarly, the addition of intermediate data for the firms used here and the inclusion of the in-between firms with intermediate data would allow much progress in describing the co-evolution of the dimensions identified. Capturing longitudinal development is the only way to develop greater descriptive and prescriptive power for theory. It is also the best vehicle to facilitate building additional dimensions through more elaborate and well-informed theory.

Finally, this research fails to supply any inferences for the enterprises whose growth process deviated from that posited above. That 60 percent of our sample achieved tremendous feats of growth by utilizing other strategic growth agendas must not be forgotten. We seem to understand the behavior of the firms which fall into the left two-by-two matrices, but theory does not explain the alternative strategic growth agendas utilized by the other firms. While progress on the above four fronts holds much promise for description of a prescriptive theory for achieving and sustaining rapid rates of growth, the daunting nature of these tasks should also serve to underscore the paucity of understanding surrounding the phenomena of rapid, sustained growth.

ACKNOWLEDGEMENTS

This research was supported by grants from the Entrepreneur Program at the University of Southern California and the Sol C. Snider Entrepreneurial Center at the Wharton School. We would like to thank Jon Goodman for several discussions on the nature and scope of this project. We would like to thank Paul Rosenbaum, Ian MacMillan, James Mohr of KPMG Peat Marwick, and Ming Hone Tsai for their helpful comments. We would also like to express our gratitude to our research assistants, David Choi, Philip Kim, Edward LaPuma, Aidan Riordan, Angel Rowley and Carlos Schonfeld for the development of this ongoing research.

REFERENCES

Abernathy, W. and Clark, K. (1985) 'Innovation: mapping the winds of creative destruction', *Research Policy.*

Barney, J. (1986) 'Strategic factor markets: expectations, luck, and business strategy', *Management Science*, 32: 1231–41.

Boeker. W. (1989) Strategic change: the effects of founding and history, *Academy of Management Journal.*

Cohen, W. and Levinthal D. (1990) 'Absorptive capacity: a new perspective on learning and innovation', *Administrative Science Quarterly.*

Dierickx, I. and Cool, K. (1989) 'Asset stock accumulation and sustainability of competitive advantage', *Management Science*, 35: 1504–13.

Dosi, G. Teece, D. and Winter, S. (1990) *Toward a Theory of Corporate Coherence: Preliminary Remarks*, working paper.

Reference Publishers International (1988) *International Directory of Company Histories*, Toronto: Reference Publishers International.

Kimberly, J. (1975) 'Environmental constraints and organizational structure. A comparative analysis of rehabilitation organizations', *Administrative Science Quarterly.*

Moody's (1992) *Moody's Industrial Manual*, New York: Moody's Investor Services.

Nelson, R. and Winter, S. (1982) *An Evolutionary Theory of Economic Change*, Boston: Belknap Press of Harvard University.

Penrose, E. (1959) *The Theory of the Growth of the Firm*, White Plains, NY: M.E. Sharpe.

Rumelt, R. (1984) 'Toward a strategic theory of the firm', in R. Lamb (ed.) *Competitive Strategic Management*, Englewood Cliffs, NJ: Prentice Hall.

—— (1987) 'Theory, strategy, and entrepreneurship', in D. Teece (ed.) *The Competitive Challenge*, New York: Harper & Row.

—— (1991) 'How much does industry matter?', *Strategic Management Journal.*

Schumpeter, J. (1976) *Capitalism, Socialism, and Democracy*, New York: Harper & Row.

Stiglitz, J. E. (1989) 'Learning to learn, localized learning, and localized progress', in P. Dasgupta and P. Stoneman (eds) *Economic Policy and Technological Performance*, Oxford: Basil Blackwell.

Stinchcombe, A. (1965) 'Social structure and organizations', in J. March (ed.) *Handbook of Organizations*, Chicago: Rand McNally.

Teece, D. J. (1987) 'Profiting from technological innovation: implications for integration, collaboration, licensing and public policy' in D. J. Teece (ed.) *The Public Challenge: Strategies for Industrial Innovation and Renewal*, New York: Harper and Row.

Teece, D. J., Pisano, G. and Shuen, A. (1991) 'Dynamic capabilities and strategic management', unpublished manuscript.

Wernerfelt, B. and Montgomery, C. (1986) 'What is an attractive industry?', *Management Science.*

APPENDIX I CRITERIA FOR PROPRIETARY ASSET OR INVENTION

Creates an insulatable, sustainable, and substantial advantage
Is a competence destroying technological innovation

Characteristics

- unique to the firms in question;
- ground breaker or first mover;
- unique manufacturing process;
- possesses high entry or exit barriers;
- creates a significant, sustainable competitive advantage;
- firm creates substantially more value with its products or services than competitors;
- firm's products or services command a premium.
- insulatable for the competition;
- geographical location;
- unique access to resources;
- monopoly over a technology;
- provides unique efficiency to the firm compared to its competition;
- meets customer or consumer needs that were never met before;
- firm offers a revolutionary improvement in quality or value.

These characteristics were examined in the following four contexts:

A Products and services

- Competing firms do not presently offer it and a substitute does not exist for it.
- Copying or developing a substitute for the product or service would require many years and major expenditures to do so.
- Examples: the 486 chip; 747 Jumbo Jet.

B Physical asset, natural resource, or an exclusive legal claim to a resource or technology

- Competing firms do not possess comparable assets, resources, or claims.
- Competing firms cannot acquire comparable assets, resources, or claims without making a prohibitively expensive investment.
- Examples: first continuous cast steel mill; patent on a jet engine assembly; monopoly on oil supply in a given region.

C A set of defined standard operating procedures, manufacturing practices, or routinized operations

- Allows the firm to offer a product or service which competing firms do not presently offer and for which a substitute does not exist.
- Comparable practices do not exist among the competition.
- Copying these practices or developing substitutes would require a significant time period and high expenditures.
- Examples: a Wharton education; Mercedes Benz engineering; an innovation which uses superconductivity to manufacture chips.

D A set of standard operating procedures, manufacturing practices, or routinized operations

- Confers an efficiency advantage which allows the firm to be the lowest cost producer.
- Comparable practices do not exist among the competition.
- Copying these practices or developing substitutes would require a significant time period and expenditure.
- Examples: just-in-time; GE credit.

APPENDIX II CONCENTRATION OF STANDARD INDUSTRIAL CLASSIFICATION CODES

Frequency	SIC	Description
2	10	Metal mining
1	12	Coal mining
3	13	Oil and gas extraction
3	14	Mining and quarrying of non-metallic materials
2	20	Food and kindred products
4	22	Textile mill products
4	23	Apparel and other finished products
1	26	Paper and allied products
6	28	Chemicals and allied products
2	29	Petroleum refining
1	30	Rubber and miscellaneous plastics
1	32	Stone, clay, glass and concrete
2	33	Primary metal structures
1	34	Fabricated metal
15	35	Industrial and commercial equipment/machinery (includes computers)

Frequency	SIC	Description
8	36	Electronic and other electrical equipment (excludes computers)
1	37	Transport equipment
9	38	Measuring, analyzing and controlling devices
1	39	Miscellaneous manufacturing
1	45	Transportation by air
1	49	Electric, gas and sanitary services
7	50	Wholesale trade – durable goods – computer
3	51	Wholesale trade – non-durable goods
1	57	Home furnishings, furniture and equipment
1	61	Non-depository credit industries
1	65	Real estate
3	73	Business services
2	87	Engineering, accounting, research, management, and related services
87		TOTAL

7

TEAM PROCESSES AND PROGRESS IN INNOVATION

The role of job satisfaction at project level

Atul A. Nerkar, Rita Gunther McGrath and Ian C. MacMillan

INTRODUCTION

Prahalad and Hamel (1990) made the observation that 'the survivors of the first wave of global competition . . . are all converging on similar and formidable standards for product cost and quality – minimum hurdles for continued competition, but less and less important as sources of differential advantage.' This implies that few competitive advantages are really sustainable today – eventually every current advantage will be matched, imitated or superseded, and with increasing rapidity. In contemplating the rate at which global competitors are reducing the time to match any firm's offerings in the market, a number of authors conclude that continuous innovation is the primary mechanism through which firms will secure and maintain a place in the competitive world of the future (Itami 1987; Senge 1990) and that continuous innovation is the principal mechanism by which firms will survive.

In this hypercompetitive world, the easily exploited 'low hanging fruit' type of innovations are soon picked, and the cost of innovation then rapidly begins to increase at the same time that the probability of success at innovation comes down (D'Aveni 1994). It therefore becomes imperative for scholars and managers alike to assemble all the tools possible to better understand and to manage the increasingly expensive and risky but crucial challenge of generating successful innovations.

Innovation requires more than the creative capacity to invent new ideas; it requires managerial skills and talents to transform the new ideas into practice (Van de Ven and Angle 1989). While the management of innovation has been the focus of many scholars over the years (Damanpour 1991; Ettlie *et al.* 1992; Robertson *et al.* 1972; Van de Ven 1986; Zajac *et al.* 1991), this research has focused primarily on the antecedent conditions to successful innovation. Scholars have examined determinants of individual innovative behavior in organizations (Scott and Bruce 1994), political processes of innovation (Frost and Egri 1991), motivational predictors of development of innovative ideas (Monge *et al.* 1992), tensions in the management of innovation (Venkataraman *et al.* 1993), psychology of innovation (Angle 1989) and organizational culture and innovation (Morris *et al.* 1993).

This work is useful and essential, but it is important to deploy these insights to focus more attention to the managerial part of the equation of innovation progress in organizations (Tornatzky *et al.* 1983). We concur with Lewin and Minton (1986) who called for a managerial perspective on innovation that focuses on the key problems and challenges confronting managers initiating and directing the development of an innovation. If we are to help managers improve their ability to innovate, it is necessary to deepen our understanding of the managerially actionable factors that shape the process of innovation. By managerially actionable factors we mean those factors which managers can use and act upon to direct the progress of innovation in their organization.

Three years of field work observing managers wrestling with over twenty major innovation projects leads us to suggest one such managerially actionable factor. We will argue that job satisfaction plays a major role in helping or hindering the progress of an innovation, and suggest that this factor is very much under-explored in the literature. Thus, the purpose of this chapter is to examine one part of the innovation performance puzzle by investigating the linkages among innovation activities, innovation performance and job satisfaction.

WHY DO PEOPLE INNOVATE IN EXISTING FIRMS?

In his classic work Schumpeter suggests three motives for innovation by the entrepreneur:

> First of all, there is the dream and the will to found a private kingdom, usually, though not necessarily, also a dynasty. Then there is the will to conquer: the impulse to fight, to prove oneself superior to others, to succeed for the sake, not of the fruits of success, but of success itself. Finally there is the joy of creating, of getting things done or simply of exercising one's energy and ingenuity.
>
> (Schumpeter 1942)

Unfortunately, these motives for innovation have been posited in the context of the 'hero entrepreneur' perspective of innovation, where the entrepreneurs reap all (if any) of the benefits of their innovative efforts. Schumpeter does not discuss the role of motives in the context of innovation within the bounds of the organization. It is this context which we explore in this chapter. While there have been studies on the impact of organizational characteristics like size, decentralization, autonomy, structure on innovation there have been very few studies of the effects of motives of the organization members on the progress of innovation in organizations (Scott and Bruce 1994).

Within an established business, innovative processes manifest themselves in two ways. The first is through internal new business creation, in which a firm extends its activities into products or markets which are new to it. This process is the focus of a growing body of research on corporate venturing (see Block and MacMillan 1993). A second outcome of innovative activity within the firm is thought to be revitalization; meaning that existing patterns of resource deployment are altered without this activity necessarily resulting in an identifiably new business (Guth and Ginsberg 1990: 5–6; Henderson and Clark 1990; Miller 1983). In either case, the objectives are to discover and create unique combinations of resources with the potential to generate new revenue and rent streams as the old streams are eroded by competitive attack (Burgelman 1983; Venkataraman et al. 1993). Despite the importance attached to continuous innovation within organizations as a source of future competitiveness, empirical evidence suggests that there are daunting barriers. Internally developed ventures take a long time (Biggadike 1979), are uncertain (Miller et al. 1988), are expensive (Block 1989) and often go awry (Fast 1981). The practices which are associated with sound management of a going concern can be anathema to innovation (Kanter 1985). Failure is often encountered along the way and may in fact be an integral component of the process (Maidique and Zirger 1985). Innovations can threaten to disrupt established routines, relationships and power flows (Frost and Egri 1991; More, 1985; Schon, 1963; Van de Ven 1986). In short, innovation within an established organization is apt to be highly problematic.

This brings us to the research question of this chapter: Given the strong barriers to innovation, what various motives propel people to innovate in an existing organization and how do the motives of these people influence the processes and the progress of an innovation?

Along with other scholars (Monge et al. 1992; Tushman and Nadler 1986; Utterback and Abernathy 1975; Van de Ven 1986) we use a process perspective to study innovation within the firm. The process perspective is a convenient way of abstracting and comprehending this highly complex phenomenon. Thus Van de Ven and Poole (1989) define innovation as the introduction of a new idea and the process of innovation as a temporal sequence of events that occurs as people interact with others to develop their innovation ideas within an institutional context. The different stages to the innovation process can be classified as the initiation, development and implementation periods (Utterback and Abernathy 1975; Van de Ven 1986).

However, as an innovation progresses from initiation to implementation it is not 'the process,' but people who push, change and kill it (Van de Ven 1986). We are interested in what motives propel these people to push, change, kill or otherwise engage in the innovation process. They do not experience the innovation as a process, but as a set of activities in which they are engaged.

110

We submit that their satisfaction with the activities associated with the innovation significantly shapes their decisions to engage. In the past some researchers have looked at the effect of job satisfaction of individuals as a global concept on the performance of project group in R&D organizations (Keller 1986). Others have examined the impact of work climate on organizational innovation (Abbey and Dickson 1983), but little or no work has been done to examine the independent multidimensional influence of the job satisfaction of those engaged in the innovative effort. Most of the research on job satisfaction has been done in the area of organizational behavior and psychology (Brockhaus and Horwitz 1986; Landy and Becker 1987) and does not find a significant place in innovation literature. Job satisfaction simply does not feature in the extant literature in the area of innovation. We now briefly review some important insights from the organizational behavior (OB) and organizational psychology literature on job satisfaction.

Aspects of job satisfaction

Job satisfaction has been hugely studied – in 1976 Locke reported that a survey using the key words 'job satisfaction' yielded approximately 3,350 articles or dissertations. By 1995 a similar computer search conducted on PSYCINFO yielded more than 7,000 articles or dissertations. Despite the extensive literature done in the area of job satisfaction there is wide disagreement on definitions and on measurement of job satisfaction (Jayaratne 1993). Another problem is that the literature has examined the relationship of job satisfaction and individual performance in great detail but has not found any significant results. We are interested in exploring the different dimensions of job satisfaction in the context of innovation within organizations and researching its impact on innovation performance.

Our concern with the linkage between innovation processes, job satisfaction and innovation performance suggests three major issues that need attention before we can begin to link it to the progress of an innovation project: How job satisfaction is to be defined, how it is to be measured and then how it is to be linked to performance. We now address these three issues.

Definition of job satisfaction

Two major theories have dominated the job satisfaction literature, namely, the expectancy theory (Hollenbeck 1989; Katzell 1964; Locke 1969; Vroom 1964) and the two-factor theory (Herzberg et al. 1959).

While the two-factor, motivator-hygiene theory argues that job satisfaction is a result of the presence of motivator factors (elements of work itself) and job dissatisfaction is the result of the lack of hygiene factors (elements of the context of work), the expectancy theory argues that an individual's assessment of job satisfaction is a function of the discrepancy between what an individual expects from the job and what the individual receives. The debate over the more appropriate theory remains unresolved but has caused job satisfaction to be defined in very different ways by researchers. For instance, job satisfaction is defined by Porter (1961) as the extent to which rewards actually meet or exceed the perceived equitable level of rewards, whereas it is defined by Locke (1976) as a 'pleasurable or positive emotional state resulting from the appraisal of one's job or job experiences.'

Jayaratne (1993) states that two major approaches hold sway with regard to the conceptualization and definition of job satisfaction. The first approach takes a macro perspective, in which the concern is with general feelings about a job (Brayfield and Rothe 1951; Dunham and Herman 1975; Kunin 1955). Although job satisfaction is viewed as a multifaceted or composite phenomenon, the emphasis is on global assessment or overall evaluation.

In contrast the second approach emphasizes facets of the job. The extent to which the individual is satisfied with different aspects, or facets, of the job determines the overall degree of job satisfaction (Herzberg et al. 1959; Quinn et al. 1974; Smith et al. 1969).

Jayaratne (1993) concludes that job satisfaction is a purely subjective assessment of one's work, that there exists no single satisfactory definition of job satisfaction, and that there is general acceptance that job satisfaction is multifaceted, although the specific facets remain arguable (Dunnette et al. 1967: 143; Ferratt 1981).

Because of its multifaceted nature, the measurement of job satisfaction has posed a formidable if not insoluble problem to researchers in the past. Extant literature in the area of job satisfaction has measured it along many different dimensions such as work environment; pay, promotion and benefits; co-workers and supervisors (Brayfield and Rothe 1951; Dunham and Herman 1975; Hackman and Oldham 1980; Hartman et al. 1986; Hoppock 1935; Kornhauser 1965; Kunin 1955; Quinn and Staines 1977; Quinn and Shepard 1974; Smith et al. 1969; Weiss et al. 1967).

Locke (1976) identified several facets which typically appear in research on job satisfaction, such as quality and quantity of work, satisfaction with pay, promotional opportunity and fairness, recognition and credit for one's work, nature and style of supervision, feelings about self supervisors and co-workers, working conditions, satisfaction with company and management. Locke proposed that each facet be examined and measured within the context of needs, expectancies and values.

In his meta-analytic study on the relationship between perceived control and variety of outcome variables, Spector (1986) included job satisfaction and noted that many different measures were used – the most popular being the Job Descriptive Index (Smith et al. 1969), Minnesota Job Satisfaction Questionnaire (Weiss et al. 1967) and Job Diagnostic Survey (Hackman and Oldham 1980). These all employ a 'facet-sum' approach to derive an overall measure of satisfaction. Thus many researchers accepting the above have adopted a 'facet-sum' approach to measure job satisfaction by assuming that these facets can be summed across to arrive at a measure for job satisfaction.

However, there are problems with this measurement approach. In his review Jayaratne (1993) states that it is not unusual to find facets of job satisfaction being employed as independent variables and overall job satisfaction as the dependent variable, resulting in a confusing circular logic in the discussion of cause and effect or in selection of independent and dependent variables. A job facet cannot be a predictor of job satisfaction if it is also a dimension of the summative index of job satisfaction.

Thus, while we agree with the multiple facets of job satisfaction, we disagree with the summing up of these facets to arrive at a single global measure (Ferratt 1981). We argue instead for an intermediate approach which uses and measures distinctly different facets of satisfaction. The reason we suggest this is that we suspect that the different facets of job satisfaction will have different antecedents (Dunnette *et al.* 1967: 143) and impact the outcomes of an innovation project differently, as we argue below.

What are these facets? In this chapter we are interested in the linkages among activity, satisfaction and performance in major innovations. In the case of people involved in major innovations, since there is a certain element of risk and uncertainty involved in participating at all, job satisfaction of the team members would certainly have a dimension related to their satisfaction with the way in which the project is progressing – what we call here the 'instrumental' job satisfaction they derive from knowing they are accomplishing their purposes.

Next, in any organization, but particularly in a major innovation project, the team's satisfaction with their relations and interactions with superiors, subordinates and coworkers would be an important factor, which we will call 'social' job satisfaction.

Finally the members of the project team would expect specific, individual rewards for participating in the project, which suggests that satisfaction with personal benefits would be another facet, which we call 'egocentric' satisfaction (Cook *et al.* 1981; Locke, 1976; Smith *et al.* 1969; Weiss *et al.* 1967).

While researchers have looked at facets or components of job satisfaction in the past, no research has been conducted to investigate whether these facets are independent of each other and represent an important aspect of job satisfaction in the context of innovation performance. Hence the following hypothesis:

Hypothesis 1: There are at least three independent facets of job satisfaction: social, instrumental, and egocentric in the context of innovation projects.

We now turn to the expected relations among these facets and innovation performance.

ANTECEDENT CORRELATES AND OUTCOME CORRELATES OF JOB SATISFACTION

Studies of the relation between job satisfaction and performance have tended to focus on the effect of dissatisfaction. For instance, considerable research has been done on the negative consequences of job dissatisfaction on personal well-being (French and Caplan 1972; Mangione and Quinn 1973; O'Brien and Feather 1990; O'Toole 1975; Quinn et al. 1974).

Similarly, at the organizational level, job dissatisfaction has been associated with work-related fatigue and injury (Quinn and Sheppard 1974); theft and sabotage (Mangione and Quinn 1973); turnover (Lawler 1973). In contrast, studies of the relationship between job satisfaction and productivity have shown no consistent negative or positive associations.

Most of the above research uses an overall measure of job satisfaction to relate with the outcome variables. In addition to our objections concerning the use of an overall measure of satisfaction, there are two further weaknesses to using overall measures. The first is that while people may be satisfied with one facet of the job, they may be unhappy with other facets, to the detriment of the project. The second follows from the first: by looking only at overall satisfaction, these studies do not get to the origins of dissatisfaction, and thus the linkages between satisfaction, the processes taking place which lead to this satisfaction, and the performance of the project cannot be fleshed out.

This chapter suggests that it will be more fruitful to examine separately the three different facets of job satisfaction, together with the antecedent processes that lead to such satisfaction, in studying performance of innovation projects.

Project performance as an outcome of organization processes

People involved in the early stages of any major innovation are facing conditions of simultaneous high uncertainty (absence of information) and ambiguity (lack of clarity about the meaning of data). Such a situation is 'characterized by rapid change, unanalyzable technology, unpredictable shocks (Daft and Lengel 1986: 558). Under such conditions the success of any organization attempting to innovate depends to a large extent upon the performance of various work groups within it (Herold 1982). In the case of innovations, these work groups are generally project teams. The question which arises is what are the particular team processes that affect the outcome of a major innovation. Drawing off recent empirical work by McGrath et al. (1996) and McGrath et al. (1995) we start with two important team processes: development of comprehension and development of team deftness.

Antecedents to performance in innovation projects: Comprehension

To be able to attain project goals presupposes that those responsible understand which combinations of resources, assembled in which sequences, and applied to which situations, will lead to this desirable result. For major innovations this implies an understanding of interrelationships of enormous complexity. Those pursuing a new initiative are initially faced with unknown and intricate causal relationships which exceed the ability of any individual to grasp.

Often what little is known about the causal relationships is embedded in the minds of individuals, where it is retained in the form of inarticulatable know-how or skill. Weick and Roberts (1993) suggest that 'comprehension' is the outcome of a process by which elements of individual know-how and skill become linked. This linkage allows a group of people working together to respond as if the complexity of the system in question were understood by the group, even though such understanding would be beyond the cognitive capabilities of any single member. In their words, 'when we say that a collective mind "comprehends" . . . we mean that heedful interrelating connects sufficient individual know-how to meet situational demands' (1993: 366).

At the start of a new initiative, such comprehension is generally limited. There is apt to be considerable uncertainty about what factors will drive performance (see Block 1989; Block and MacMillan 1993; Kanter 1983, 1989; Vasconcellos and Hambrick 1989; Vesper 1990).

For an innovation to progress, the set of objectives of the project and the understanding of what must be done to meet them must become sharper, more precise and better understood among members of the project team. Unless this occurs, such lack of comprehension retards the progress of the innovation project. This has been demonstrated in McGrath *et al.* (1995) and provides a backdrop hypothesis for our discussion of the role that job satisfaction plays in shaping innovation progress. Hence:

Hypothesis 2a: In an innovation project the development of the comprehension of the project team will be positively associated with performance.

If development of comprehension in a group represents a critical antecedent of its ability reliably to achieve objectives, a second important antecedent reflects the nature of the group's interrelationships. We next turn to a discussion of this issue.

Antecedents to performance in innovation projects: Deftness

The literature which speaks most directly to the relationship between interpersonal processes and organizational outcomes is that which examines teams. Indeed, a veritable avalanche of publications urge organizations to use teams to pursue a broad variety of objectives. Thus, Miller (1992) identified ninety-one 'teamwork' articles in a database search of publications which appeared between 1986 and 1990.

In a new team people are brought together who lack knowledge about one another's aptitudes, motivation and level of commitment. Such a team lacks the history of repetitive interactions which render people predictable to one another, and aids the development of trust (Larson 1992: 91) which is a powerful form of social control. In the absence of trust, resources must be invested to create other forms of control – investments must be made in checking and evaluating performance, as well as in establishing sanctions and rewards.

McGrath *et al.* (1995) use the term 'deftness' to reflect those qualities of team relationships in which there is mutual confidence, trust and fluency of execution of tasks among team members. They demonstrate empirically that team deftness represents a second necessary antecedent for the attainment of project goals. This provides the second backdrop hypothesis for our discussion of the role that job satisfaction plays in shaping innovation progress.

Hypothesis 2b: Development of the team deftness of a project team is positively associated with performance

Job satisfaction as mediator

With these two major process variables, deftness and team comprehension, as backdrops we turn now to the effects of job satisfaction.

Research by Gladstein (1984), among others, suggests that there is a relation between team satisfaction and self-reported effectiveness, suggesting that progress on an innovation project will be severely inhibited if those involved are dissatisfied. We now argue that the role of job satisfaction is to mediate the effects of team processes on performance.

Furthermore, as we have posited, there are three facets to job satisfaction and we suggest that these forms of job satisfaction separately mediate the effects of comprehension and deftness on the team's performance.

First, high dissatisfaction with the people and relations in the project, in other words poor social satisfaction, will obstruct deftness. In a team dissatisfied with other players, agency and transaction cost issues will distract the team from accomplishing their objectives (Guth and MacMillan 1986; Mintzberg *et al.* 1976). Also lower deftness among members of an innovation project team will result in lower social satisfaction. Hence:

Hypothesis 3a: Social satisfaction will mediate the effect of deftness on innovation performance.

Next consider people who are dissatisfied with the progress of their project. This instrumental job satisfaction could be a result of incomplete development of comprehension of the innovation project and will have a negative impact on project performance. Webb (1992), describing the case of a company where innovation projects were in progress, states that the management response to the disaffection expressed by the engineers was not to seek some improvement through collaborative project management, but to adopt a highly directive stance which resulted in the innovation projects getting slowed down. Similarly, in our field studies an information services project in a large financial house stalled because team members became dissatisfied with the progress of systems development. Instead of identifying and working on the causes of systems delays among team members, the team started to mistrust one another's motives and commitment. Hence:

Hypothesis 3b: Instrumental satisfaction will mediate the effect of comprehension on innovation performance.

Finally, since people will generally tend to act in their own self-interest, those projects where individuals perceive themselves as being unable to accomplish their egocentric purposes will not receive their commitment. This low egocentric satisfaction can result out of lack of comprehension as well as low deftness of project members, thus inhibiting innovation project progress. Hence:

Hypothesis 3c: Egocentric satisfaction will mediate the effects of both comprehension and deftness on innovation performance.

We turn now to empirical testing of the hypotheses proposed.

Research method

Level of analysis

As described in the technology, innovation and corporate venturing literature (for example, Ancona and Caldwell 1988; Burgelman 1983; Gersick 1988; Kogut and Zander 1992; Leonard-Barton 1991), the locus for such activities is within organizational task groups. Members of these groups or teams are simultaneously the principal actors in the drama of an unfolding innovation project and are also the most expert observers of what is going on. Their expectations and interactions are likely to have the most direct impact upon substantive outcomes for the innovation project. Therefore the expectations of those on the team were measured for this study; in other words, the level of analysis for the present study is the group level, specifically the management group for an innovation project.

Sample

The data for the study were collected from 168 major innovations in 40 different firms. One or more major innovation attempts were identified by senior executives of the participating firms. An innovation project was defined as the development of a new offering, entry into a new market, or a significant attempt to restructure or improve an internal process (such as the adoption of a new processing technology or design and implementation of a new computer system). The sample includes substantial variety in both firms and innovation projects, with wide variation on size, age, performance, industry, objectives and other potentially important contingent variables, to increase confidence in the generalizability of the results. The industries represented are presented in Appendix II. Most of the innovation projects are in US-based firms, although 24 percent are from firms based in other countries.

The senior executive in charge (usually in conjunction with key project team members) determined the composition of the team. All individuals who were classified as part of the project team were included in the respondent set for that project, since their expectations for future outcomes are the central focus of this study. Questionnaires were developed which operationalize and provide measures for each independent and dependent variable. These were administered to each of the individuals in the respondent set. The response rate for each innovation project was 100 percent.

Constructs and measures

For each of the central constructs tested in this study, a search of the innovation literature revealed a number of variables related to or thought to measure the construct. Questionnaire items were then created which reflected each of these variables. The questionnaires used are presented in Appendix I.

Team respondents' scores were averaged for each item. The resulting value was summed for all the items to yield the innovation project's score for the construct. Appendix I lists the items with which each construct is measured. Means, standard deviations, Cronbach alphas and correlations among variables created by the constructs are listed in Table 7.1

1 Performance is a composite of ten items which represents the extent to which *ex post* results met or exceeded *ex ante* expectations. All measures are reported in Appendix I with an extensive list of literature citations used to tap each measure.
2 Comprehension is measured using sixteen items derived from the literature.
3 Deftness was measured using fifteen items.
4 Satisfaction is measured using eleven items tapping the three different facets of satisfaction: social, instrumental and egocentric. These eleven items were then factor analyzed.

The Cronbach alphas for all variables were above 0.7 Most other common forms of reliability check are not appropriate for this study. One might expect to find change over time in the variables of interest, so intertemporal stability is not meaningful. One would expect to find some differences in assessment among members of the project team, hence inter-rater reliability is not meaningful.

Results

Factor analysis was used to explore Hypothesis 1 and ordinary least-squares regression analyses were used to test the remaining hypotheses in this study. Table 7.2 reports the results of the factor analysis conducted on the items measuring satisfaction. Table 7.3 reports OLS regression results for performance, the different facets of satisfaction, comprehension and deftness.

Factor analysis

The results for the factor analysis support Hypothesis 1. The loadings from the rotated factor pattern clearly show the satisfaction items fall into three facets related to social, instrumental and egocentric aspects as hypothesized. Each factor has an Eigen value of greater than one.

Regression analyses

We turn now to the regression results. Standardized beta coefficients and significance levels are reported in Table 7.3 and Table 7.4. Models 1 and 2 test the influence of each of the main-effect variables: deftness and comprehension on the dependent variable performance (Hypotheses 2a and 2b).

Model 3 tests Hypothesis 3a by checking for the mediating effect of social satisfaction on the relation between deftness and performance. Model 5 repeats this test, but controls also for instrumental satisfaction and egocentric satisfaction.

Model 4 tests Hypothesis 3b by checking for the mediating effect of instrumental satisfaction on the relation between comprehension and performance. Model 5 repeats this test, but controls also for social satisfaction and egocentric satisfaction.

Model 7 tests Hypothesis 3c by checking for the mediating effect of egocentric satisfaction on the relations between comprehension and deftness on performance.

The results support Hypotheses 2a, 2b, 3a and 3b as we discuss below. Hypotheses 2a and 2b predicted that deftness and comprehension would be positively associated with performance. Model 1 suggests a direct association of deftness with performance ($\beta = 0.32$ and $p < 0.0001$) while Model 2 suggests a direct association of comprehension with performance ($\beta = 0.30$ and $p < 0.0001$).

Hypothesis 3a predicted that social satisfaction would mediate the relation between deftness and performance. Model 3 supports this – the Beta coefficient for deftness becomes insignificant ($\beta = 0.09$ and $p < 0.7$) while the coefficient for social satisfaction is significant ($\beta = 0.41$ and $p < 0.0001$). This mediating effect is repeated in Model 5 which controls for the other

Table 7.1 Means, standard deviations and Pearson correlation coefficients

Variable	Mean	Std dev.	Cronbach alphas	Social satisfaction	Instrumental satisfaction	Egocentric satisfaction	Performance	Deftness	Causal understand
Social satisfaction	18.69	2.40	0.83	1.00					
Instrumental satisfaction	11.33	1.50	0.72	0.65[a]	1.00				
Egocentric satisfaction	10.31	1.32	0.76	0.30[a]	0.27[c]	1.00			
Degree of performance	32.01	5.38	0.87	0.42[a]	0.43[a]	0.06	1.00		
Deftness	54.56	5.82	0.90	0.70[a]	0.47[a]	0.27[b]	0.32[b]	1.00	
Comprehension	57.02	6.71	0.89	0.41[b]	0.44[a]	0.22[c]	0.30[b]	0.43[a]	1.00

Notes: [a] - p < .0001   [b] - p < .001   [c] - p < .05

Table 7.2 Results of varimax rotated factor analysis

Items	Factor 1 Instrumental	Factor 2 Egocentric	Factor 3 Social
Working relationships in the project team	0.85	.	.
Skill set of the project team	0.72	.	.
Morale of the project team	0.72	.	.
Project leadership	0.63	.	.
Team's understanding of how to meet project goals	0.62	.	.
Your opportunities for promotion	.	0.86	.
Your pay and compensation	.	0.79	.
Your job as currently defined	.	0.77	.
Benefit to the company	.	.	0.82
Current direction of the project	.	.	0.77
Overall performance to date	.	.	0.63
Eigen values	4.32	1.71	1.01

Note: Values less than 0.5 have been printed as .

Table 7.3 Results of regression analyses on performance

Variables	Model 1	Model 2	Model 3	Model 4	Model 5	Model 6	Model 7
Hypotheses tested	H2a	H2b	H3a	H3b	H3a	H3b	H3c
Deftness	0.32[a]		-0.09	0.13	0.03	0.11	0.24[b]
Comprehension		.30[a]					0.20[b]
Social satisfaction			0.41[a]		0.22[b]	0.23[c]	
Instrumental satisfaction				0.37[a]	0.29[b]	0.26[b]	
Egocentric satisfaction					-0.09	-0.10	-0.04
Adjusted R^2	0.09	0.09	0.17	0.20	0.21	0.22	0.12
F	18.59[a]	16.53[a]	13.01[b]	20.96[a]	11.96[a]	12.64[a]	8.58[a]

Notes: one-tailed tests were used for hypothesized relationships. Entries represent standardized regression coefficients, N = 168
[a] - $p < .0001$ [b] - $p < .001$ [c] - $p < .05$

Table 7.4 Results of regression analyses on performance with controls

Variables	Model 1	Model 2	Model 3	Model 4	Model 5	Model 6	Model 7
Hypotheses tested	H2a	H2b	H3a	H3b	H3a	H3b	H3c
Deftness	0.36[a]		0.11	-0.01	0.16	0.11	0.33[b]
Comprehension		.20[c]					0.04
Social satisfaction			0.35[b]		0.02	0.15	
Instrumental satisfaction				0.53[a]	0.44	0.43[b]	
Egocentric satisfaction					-0.03	-0.02	0.02
Project age	0.02	0.01	0.02	0.05	0.05	0.05	0.02
Project size	0.10	0.05	0.11	0.06	0.05	0.07	0.09
Firm size	0.02	0.00	0.00	-0.09	0.06	0.07	0.01
Industrial sector	-0.04	-0.05	-0.02	0.00	-0.07	-0.08	-0.03
Adjusted R^2	0.10	0.01	0.16	0.23	0.24	0.22	0.09
F	3.32[b]	1.13	4.19[b]	5.96[a]	4.86[a]	4.59[a]	2.36[c]

Notes: one-tailed tests were used for hypothesized relationships Entries represent standardized regression coefficients, N = 103.
[a] - $p < .0001$ [b] - $p < .001$ [c] - $p < .05$

facets of job satisfaction(β = 0.03 and p < 0.77 for deftness while β = 0.22 and p < 0.05 for social satisfaction).

Hypothesis 3b predicted that instrumental satisfaction would mediate the relation between comprehension on performance. Model 4 supports this hypothesis. The coefficient for comprehension is insignificant (β = 0.13 and p < 0.15) while the coefficient for instrumental satisfaction is significant (β = 0.37 and p < 0.0001). This mediating effect is repeated in Model 6 which controls for other facets of satisfaction (β = 0.11 and p < 0.15 for comprehension while β = 0.26 and p < 0.05 for instrumental satisfaction).

Hypothesis 3c predicted that egocentric satisfaction would mediate the association of deftness and comprehension with performance. However, this is not supported by the results of Model 7 (β = 0.24 and p < 0.05 for deftness, β = 0.20 and p < 0.05 for comprehension while β = 0.04 and p < 0.30 for egocentric satisfaction). Table 7.4 reports the results of regression with control variables like project age, project size, firm size and industrial sector included. None of the controls were significant, offering strong support for the relationships suggested.

All of the F-statistics are significant at the p < 0.0001 level, thus showing good fit of the models to the data. The constructs used also account for a sizable proportion of the variance in performance.

DISCUSSION AND IMPLICATIONS

Tests of hypotheses

The original framework depicted in Figure 7.1 appears, for the most part, to be supported by our results. Hypothesis 1 was supported by the factor loadings in the rotated factor pattern. Hypotheses 2a, 2b, 3a and 3b received support in both the correlation and regression analyses. There is a positive association between performance and deftness through social satisfaction. Similarly there is a positive association between performance and comprehension through instrumental satisfaction.

However, egocentric satisfaction does not seem to mediate the effects of deftness and comprehension on performance. The result from Model 7 would extend the findings of researchers in the past that satisfaction is not related to performance for the specific case of major innovations.

Our results advance our understanding of the management of the venturing phenomenon in several ways. First, they suggest that there are at least three facets to the satisfaction of employees. Second, deftness is related to performance but mediated by social satisfaction. This is an important conclusion for those who would like to understand the management of innovation projects. Third, comprehension and its relation to performance is mediated through instrumental satisfaction, which has important implications for those managing major innovations on a 'need to know basis'.

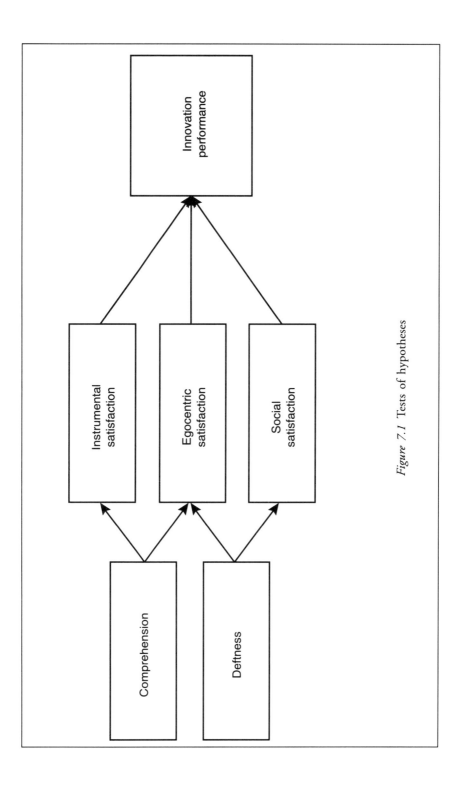

Figure 7.1 Tests of hypotheses

Future research

The research presented here suggests several substantive and interesting future opportunities to learn about the circumstances under which team processes and satisfaction of team members relates to outcomes of major innovations within a firm, a few of which we will now discuss.

Consider first the question of whether performance is causally related to all the other constructs in our study. Our approach was to view the different facets of satisfaction as an outcome of team processes. In fact it may be the case that it is the different facets of satisfaction that drive the team processes.

Similarly another question which arises is about other facets of job satisfaction than the three we identified here, and their association with innovation project outcomes. This needs to be explored in the future.

A third issue is whether there is a hierarchy of 'satisfactions' or if one has an effect on another. Finally, it would be important to include other antecedents to innovation like organization structure in future research to explore their impact on the hypotheses developed by us in this chapter.

Limitations and efforts to address them

Before turning to the implications of our results, the reader should bear in mind a number of limitations, and the steps we have taken to address them.

Possible multicollinearity

There is a possible multicollinearity problem caused by the high correlation between social satisfaction and deftness. We suggest that this expected strong relationship between social satisfaction and effectiveness does not pose major problems of collinearity for the following reasons:

1   The item scales for both the constructs are based on different theoretical concepts. Also, as can be seen from Appendix I the wording of the items in the two measures are very dissimilar.
2   We systematically dropped items in each of the measures, and then reran the correlations. This did not substantially change the correlations.

Cross-sectionality of study

The study is not longitudinal, and thus it is improper to assume causality among the variables. To some extent we have addressed this limitation by including innovation projects at various stages of evolution. Project leaders were asked to categorize their innovation project in terms of their stage of development. For those cases where the project leaders provided information, their stage of development is reported in Appendix II.

A third potential limitation is that our results are partially a result of common response bias. To address this limitation, responses of the innovation project group without the team leader's response were compared with the responses of the innovation project leader (the individual with arguably the greatest amount of external access, but with substantial expertise on the status of the innovation project). Correlations among leader's responses and team responses were positive and significant, reducing this concern. Another way in which we reduced this concern was by running Harman's one-factor test as suggested by Podsakoff and Organ (1986). Responses to items from all constructs were pooled and subjected to a factor analysis. The factor analysis yielded seven factors with Eigen values greater than one with items from each construct loading cleanly and separately on different factors, which reduces our concerns about common method bias.

CONCLUSION

This study was undertaken with the idea of gaining theoretical insight into influences of team processes upon outcomes of major innovations.

Our empirical results lend considerable support to the central thesis of the chapter. The first major conclusion of the study is that there are different facets to the satisfaction of the project team. The second major finding of the study is that team processes affect performance of outcomes through the satisfaction of the members of the team along different facets.

In conclusion, we have made a beginning, albeit an exploratory one, on the fascinating problem of understanding team processes and their correlates in a highly complex, uncertain situation such as a major innovation. The results of the study are encouraging and suggest that this is a fruitful area for further inquiry.

ACKNOWLEDGEMENTS

We appreciate the insightful comments of S. Venkataraman. Financial support from the Sol C. Snider Entrepreneurial Center at the Wharton School and the Crosby Foggitt Fellowship was crucial. This paper was presented at the 4th Global Entrepreneurship Conference at INSEAD in March 1994.

REFERENCES

Abbey, A. and Dickson J.W. (1983) 'R&D work climate and innovation in semiconductors', *Academy of Management Journal* 26 (2): 362–8.

Alutto, J.A. and Acito, F. (1974) 'Decisional participation and sources of job satisfaction: a study of manufacturing personnel', *Academy of Management Journal* 17 (10): 160–7.

Ancona, D.G. and Caldwell, D.F. (1988) 'Beyond task and maintenance: defining external functions in groups', *Group and Organizational Studies* 13 (4): 468–93.

—— (1992) 'Demography and design: predictors of new product team performance', *Organization Science* 3 (3): 321–41.

Angle, H.L. (1989) 'Psychology and organizational innovation', in A. Van de Ven, H. Angle and M. Scott Poole (eds) *Research on the Management of Innovation: The Minnesota Studies*, New York: Harper & Row.

Ansoff, H.I. (1979) *Strategic Management*, New York: Wiley.

Biggadike, R. (1979) 'The risky business of diversification', *Harvard Business Review* May–June: 103–11.

Block, Z (1989) 'Damage control for new corporate ventures', *Journal of Business Strategy* March–April: 22–8.

Block, Z. and MacMillan, I.C. (1985) 'Milestones for successful venture planning', *Harvard Business Review* September–October: 4–8.

—— (1993) *Corporate Venturing*, Cambridge, MA: Harvard Business School Press.

Brayfield, A.H. and Rothe, H.F. (1951) 'An index of job satisfaction', *Journal of Applied Psychology* 35: 307–11.

Brockhaus, R.H. and Horwitz, P.S. (1986) The psychology of the entrepreneur, in D. L. Sexton and W.R. Smilor (eds) *The Art and Science of Entrepreneurship*, Cambridge: Ballinger.

Buchanan, B. (1975) 'To walk an extra mile: the whats, whens and whys of organizational commitment', *Organizational Dynamics* Spring: 67–8.

Burgelman, R.A. (1983) 'A process model of internal corporate venturing in the major diversified firm', *Administrative Science Quarterly* 2.

Burns, T. and Stalker, G. (1961) *The Management Of Innovation*, London: Tavistock.

Castaneda, M. and Nahavandi, A. (1991) 'Link of manager behavior to supervisor performance rating and subordinate satisfaction', *Group & Organization Studies* 16 (4), December: 357–66.

Cook, J.D., Hepworth, S.J., Wall, T.D. and Warr, P.B. (1981) *The Experience of Work*, London: Academic Press.

Cook, J. and Wall, T. (1980) 'New attitude measurements of trust, organizational commitment and personal need non-fulfillment', *Journal of Occupational Psychology* 53: 39–52.

Daft, R.L. and Lengel, R.H. (1986) 'Organizational information requirements, media richness and structural design', *Management Science* 32 (5): 554–71.

Damanpour, F. (1991) 'Organizational innovation: a meta-analysis of effects of determinants and moderators, *Academy of Management Journal* 34 (3), September: 555–90.

D'Aveni, R. (1994) *Hypercompetition: Managing the Dynamics of Strategic Maneuvering*, New York: The Free Press.

Dougherty, D. (1992) 'Understanding new markets for new products', *Strategic Management Journal* 13, Summer special issue: 77–92.

Dunham, R. and Herman, J. (1975) 'Development of a female faces scale for measuring job satisfaction', *Journal of Applied Psychology* 60: 629–31.

Dunnette, M.D., Campbell, J.P. and Hakel, M.D. (1967) 'Factors contributing to job satisfaction and job dissatisfaction in six occupational groups', *Organizational Behavior and Human Performance* 2: 143–74.

Ettlie, J.E. and Reza, E.M. (1992) 'Organizational integration and process innovation', *Academy of Management Journal* 35 (4): 795–827.

Fast, N. (1981) 'Pitfalls of corporate venturing', *Research Management* 24 (2).

Feldman, S. (1988) 'How organizational culture can affect innovation', *Organizational Dynamics* 16: 57–68.

Ferratt, T.W. (1981) 'Overall job satisfaction: is it a linear function of facet satisfaction?', *Human Relations* 34: 463–73.

French, J.R.P. and Caplan, R.D. (1972) 'Organizational stress and individual strain', in A.J. Marrow, (ed.) *The Failure of Success*, New York: AMACOM.

Frost, P.J. and Egri, C.P. (1991) 'The political process of innovation', *Research in Organizational Behavior* 13: 229–95.

Gersick, C.J.G. (1988) 'Time and transition in work teams: toward a new model of group development', *Academy of Management Journal* 31 (1), March: 9–41.

Gladstein, D.L. (1984) 'Groups in context: a model of task group effectiveness', *Administrative Science Quarterly* 29: 499–517.

Gorman, M. and Sahlman, W.A. (1989) 'What do venture capitalists do?' *Journal of Business Venturing* 4 (4): 231–48.

Gresov, C., Drazin, R. and Van de Ven, A.H. (1989) 'Work-unit task uncertainty, design and morale', *Organization Studies* 10 (1): 45–62.

Guth, W.D. and Ginsberg, A. (1990) 'Guest editors' introduction: corporate entrepreneurship', *Strategic Management Journal* 11: 5–15.

Guth, W.D. and MacMillan I.C. (1986) 'Strategy implementation versus middle management self-interest', *Strategic Management Journal* 7 (4): 313–27.

Hackman, J.R. (1987) 'The design of work teams', in J. Lorsch (ed.) *Handbook of Organizational Behavior*, Englewood Cliffs, NJ: Prentice-Hall.

Hackman, J.R. (1990) *Groups that Work (and those that don't)*, San Francisco, CA: Jossey-Bass.

Hackman, J.R. and Oldham, G.R. (1980) *Work Redesign*, Massachusetts: Addison-Wesley, Reading.

Hartman, S., Grigsby, D.W., Crino, M.D. and Chhokar, J.S. (1986) 'The measurement of job satisfaction by action tendencies', *Educational and Psychological Measurement* 46: 317–29.

Hauser, J.R. and Clausing, D. (1988) 'The house of quality', *Harvard Business Review* 66 (3): 63–73.

Henderson, R.M. and Clark K.B. (1990) 'Architectural innovation: the reconfiguration of existing product technologies and the failure of established firms', *Administrative Science Quarterly* 35 (1), March.

Herold, D.M. (1979) 'The effectiveness of work groups', in S. Kerr (ed.) *Organizational Behavior*, Columbus, Ohio: Grid Publishers.

Herzberg, F., Mausner, B. and Snyderman, B. (1959) *The Motivation at Work*, New York: Wiley.

Hollenback, J.R. (1989) 'Control theory and the perception of work environments: the effect of focus of attention on affective and behavioral reactions to work', *Organizational Behavior and Human Decision Processes*, 43: 406–30.

Itami, H. (1987) *Mobilizing Invisible Assets*, London: Harvard University Press.

Jayaratne, S. (1993) 'The antecedents, consequences, and correlates of job satisfaction', in R. Golembiewski (ed.) *Handbook of Organizational Behavior*, New York: Martin Dekker.

Kanter, R.M. (1983) *The Change Masters: Innovation and Entrepreneurship in the American Corporation*, New York: Simon and Schuster.

—— (1985) 'Supporting innovation and venture development in established companies', *Journal of Business Venturing* 1: 47–60.

—— (1987) 'When to persist and when to give up', *Management Review*, January.

—— (1989) 'The new managerial work', *Harvard Business Review* 67 (6), November–December: 85–92.

Katzell, R.A. (1964) 'Personal values, job satisfaction and job behavior', in H. Borow (ed.) *Man in a World of Work*, Boston: Houghton-Mifflin.

Keller, R.T. (1986) 'Predictors of the performance of project groups in R&D organizations', *Academy of Management Journal* 29 (4), December: 715–26.

Kerzner, H. (1987) 'In search of excellence in project management', *Journal of Systems Management* 38 (2), February: 30–39.

Kiernan, M.J. (1993) 'The new strategic architecture: learning to compete in the twenty first century', *Academy of Management Executive* 7 (1): 7–21.

Kogut, B. and Zander, U. (1992) 'Knowledge of the firm and the speed of transfer and imitation of technologies', working paper, The Wharton School, University of Pennsylvania.

Kornhauser, A. (1965) *Mental Health of the Industrial Worker: A Detroit Study*, New York: John Wiley.

Kunin, T. (1955) 'The construction of a new type of attitude measure', *Personnel Psychology* 8.

Larson, C.E. and Lafasto, F.M. (1989) *Teamwork: What Must Go Right/What Can Go Wrong*, Newbury Park: Sage Publications.

Lawler, E. L. (1973) *Motivation in Work Organizations*, Monterey, CA: Brooks/Cole Publishers.

Leonard-Barton, D. (1991) 'Corporate culture and the dual nature of core capabilities in new product development', paper prepared for the conference on the Evolution of Firm Capabilities, Reginald Jones Center for Corporate Strategy, Management, and Organization, The Wharton School, University of Pennsylvania.

Lewin, A.Y. and Minton, J.W. (1986) 'Organizational effectiveness: another look and an agenda for research', *Management Science* 32: 514–38.

Locke, E.A. (1969) 'What is job satisfaction?', *Organizational Behavior and Human Performance* 4: 336–409.

—— (1976) 'The nature and causes of job satisfaction', in M.D. Dunnette (ed.) *Handbook of Industrial and Organizational Psychology*, Chicago: Rand McNally.

Long, W.A. and Ohtani, N. (1986) 'Facilitating new venture development through market and design feasibility study', in Ronstadt (ed.) *Frontiers of Entrepreneurial Research*, Boston, MA: Babson College.

McGrath, R. Gunther (1993) *The Development of New Competence in Established Organizations: An Empirical Investigation*, doctoral dissertation, University of Pennsylvania.

McGrath, R. Gunther, MacMillan, I.C. and Venkataraman, S. (1995) 'Defining and developing competence: a strategic process paradigm', *Strategic Management Journal* 16 (4) May: 251–75.

McGrath, R.G., Tsai, M.H., Venkataraman, S. and MacMillan, I.C. (1996) 'Innovation, competitive advantage and rent: a model and test', *Management Science*.

Maidique, M.A. and Zirger, B.J. (1985) 'The new product learning cycle', *Research Policy* 14: 299–313.

Mangione, T.W. and Quinn, R.P. (1973) *Job Satisfaction, Counterproductive Behavior and Self-Narcotizing Withdrawal from Work*, Michigan, Ann Arbor: Institute for Social Research.

March, J.G. and Simon, H.A. (1958) *Organizations*, New York: Wiley.

Miller, D. (1983) 'The correlates of entrepreneurship in three types of firms', *Management Science* 29: 770–91

Miller, J.A. (1992) 'Book reviews: whose team are you on?' *Human Resource Planning* 15 (2): 83–95.

Miller, A., Wilson, B. and Adams, M. (1988) 'Financial performance patterns of new corporate ventures: an alternative to traditional measures, *Journal of Business Venturing* 3: 287–300.

Mintzberg, H., Raisinghani, D. and Theoret, A. (1976) 'The structure of "unstructured" decision processes', *Administrative Science Quarterly* 21: 246–75.

Mohrman, S.A. (1979) 'A new look at participation in decision making: the concept of political access', *Academy of Management Proceedings*: 200–205.

Monge, P.R., Cozzens, M.D. and Contractor, N.S. (1992) 'Communication and motivational predictors of the dynamics of organizational innovation', *Organization Science* 3, May: 250–74.

More, R.A. (1985) 'Barriers to innovation: intraorganizational dislocations', *Journal of Product Innovation Management* 3: 205–8.

Morris, M.H., Avila, R.A. and Allen, J. (1993) 'Individualism and the modern corporation: implications for innovation and entrepreneurship', *Journal of Management* 19 (3): 595–612.

Nelson, R.N. and Winter, S.G. (1977) 'In search of a useful theory of innovation', *Research Policy* 6: 36–76.

Nelson, R.R. and Winter, S.G. (1982) *An Evolutionary Theory of Economic Change*, Harvard: Belknap.

Nunnally, J. (1978) *Psychometric Theory*, 2nd edn, New York: McGraw-Hill.

O'Brien, J.E. and Feather, N.T. (1990) 'The relative effects of unemployment and quality of employment on the affect, work values and personal control of adolescents', *Journal of Occupational Psychology* 63: 151–65.

O'Toole, J. (1975) *Work in America*, Cambridge, MA: MIT Press.

Pascale, R. (1990) *Managing on the Edge*, New York: Simon and Schuster.

Pettigrew, A.M. (1973) *The Politics of Organizational Decision Making*, London: Tavistock.

Pinto, J.K. and Prescott, J.E. (1990) 'Planning and tactical factors in the project implementation process', *Journal of Management Studies* 27 (3): 305–27.

Porter, L.W. (1961) 'A study of perceived need satisfaction in bottom and middle management jobs', *Journal of Applied Psychology* 45: 1–10.

Porter, M. (1980) *Competitive Strategy*, New York: Free Press.

Portigal, A.H. (1976) *Towards the Measurement of Work Satisfaction*, Paris: OECD.

Prahalad, C.K. and Hamel, G. (1990) 'The core competence of the corporation', *Harvard Business Review* May–June: 79–91.

Quinn, R.P. and Sheppard, L.J. (1974) *The 1972–73 Quality of Employment Survey*, Ann Arbor, Michigan: Institute for Social Research.

Quinn, R.P., Staines, G.L. and McCollough, M.R. (1974) 'A longitudinal study of a valence model approach for the prediction of job satisfaction of new employees', *Journal of Applied Psychology*, 68: 307–12.

Robertson, A.B., Achilladelis, B.G. and Jervis, P. (1972) 'Success and failure in industrial innovation', *Report on Project Sappho*, London: Centre for the Study of Industrial Innovation, Science Policy Research Unit.

Schon, D.A. (1963) 'Champions for radical new intentions', *Harvard Business Review* March–April: 77–86.

Scott, S.G. and Bruce, R.A. (1994) 'Determinants of innovative behavior: a path model of individual innovation in the workplace', *Academy of Management Journal* 37 (3): 580–607.

Schumpeter, J.A. (1942) *Capitalism, Socialism and Democracy*, New York: McGraw-Hill.

Senge, P.M. (1990) *The Fifth Discipline: The Art and Practice of the Learning Organization*, New York: Doubleday.

Smith, P.C., Kendall, L.M. and Hulin, C.L. (1969) *The Measurement of Satisfaction in Work and Retirement: A Strategy for the Study of Attitudes*, Chicago: Rand McNally.

Spector, P.E. (1986) 'Perceived control by employees: a meta-analysis of studies concerning autonomy and participation at work', *Human Relations* 39 (11): 1005–16.

Stata, R. (1989) 'Organizational learning: the key to management innovation', *Sloan Management Review* Spring: 63–74.

Stokes, S.L. Jr (1990) 'Building effective project teams', *Journal of Information Systems Management* 7 (3), Summer: 38–45.

Sykes, H.B. and Block, Z. (1989) 'Corporate venturing obstacles: sources and solutions', *Journal of Business Venturing* 4: 159–67.

Tornatzky, L.G. *et al.* (1983) *The Process of Technological Innovation: Reviewing the Literature*, Washington DC: National Science Foundation.

Tushman, M.L. (1977) 'A political approach to organizations: a review and rationale', *Academy of Management Review* 2: 206–16.

Tushman, M.L. and Nadler, D. (1986) 'Organizing for innovation', *California Management Review* XXVII (3), Spring: 74.

Utterback, J.M. and Abernathy, W.J. (1975) 'A dynamic model of process and product innovation', *Omega* 3 (6): 639–56.

Van de Ven, A. (1986) 'Central problems in the management of innovation', *Management Science* 32 (5): 590–607.

Van de Ven, A. and Angle, H.L. (1989) 'An introduction to the Minnesota Innovation Research program', in A. Van de Ven, H. Angle and M. Scott Poole (eds) *Research on the Management of Innovation: The Minnesota Studies*, New York: Harper & Row.

Van de Ven, A., Hudson, R. and Schroeder, D.M. (1984) 'Designing new business startups: entrepreneurial, organizational and ecological considerations', *Journal of Management* 10 (1): 87–107.

Vasconcellos, J.A. and Hambrick, D.C. (1989) 'Key success factors: test of a general framework in the mature industrial-product sector', *Strategic Management Journal* 10 (4): 367–82.

Venkataraman, S., Shane, S., McGrath, R.G. and MacMillan, I.C. (1993) 'Some central tensions in the management of corporate venturing, in S. Birley and I.C. MacMillan (eds) *Entrepreneurship Research: Global Perspectives*, Amsterdam: Elsevier Science Publishers.

Vesper, K.H. (1990) *New Venture Strategies*, Englewood Cliffs, NJ: Prentice-Hall.

Vroom, V.H. (1964) *Work and Motivation*, New York: Wiley.

Webb, J. (1992) 'The mismanagement of innovation', *Sociology: The Journal of the British Sociological Association* 26 (3), August: 471–92.

Weick, K.E. and Roberts, K.H. (1993) 'Collective mind in organizations: heedful interrelating on flight decks', *Administrative Science Quarterly* 38 (3), September: 357–81.

Weiss, D.J., Dawis, R.V. and England, G.W. (1967) 'Manual for the Minnesota satisfaction questionnaire', *Minnesota Studies in Vocational Rehabilitation* 22.

Wernerfelt, B. (1989) 'From critical resources to corporate strategy', *Journal of General Management* 14 (3): 4–12.

Zajac, E.J., Golden, B.R. and Shortell, S.M. (1991) 'New organizational forms for enhancing innovation: the case of internal corporate joint ventures', *Management Science* 37 (2), February: 170–84.

APPENDIX I MEASURES USED IN THE STUDY
Performance

To measure the extent to which the team has attained its goals respondents are asked to 'assess the performance of your project over the last two months' where a score of 1 indicates that results were far worse than expected and a score of 5 indicates that results were far better than expected. These scores are applied to ten generic kinds of business objectives, described in the innovation/corporate venturing literature as more or less universal to new products.

The use of 'subjective' ratings follows the logic articulated by a number of authors. Ancona and Caldwell (1992) note that: 'We use subjective ratings of performance because these ratings are most often used to make budget and promotion decisions. They are related to final performance evaluations, and more "objective" results are often a product of "subjective" ratings'.

Items comprising the construct 'performance'

Respondents are requested to: 'Please assess the performance of your project over the last two months, on each of the following dimensions.'	*Reference Source*
Construct overall	Related to notions of 'effectiveness' (Gresov *et al.* 1989: 45).
2.01 Meeting budget objectives	Block (1989: 24,26,32); Ancona and Caldwell (1988: 324); Sykes and Block (1989: 162); Van de Ven *et al.* (1984: 91).
2.02 Meeting staffing objectives	Block (1989: 29); Block and MacMillan (1985: 5); Van de Ven (1986: 602); Van de Ven *et al.* (1984: 91).
2.03 Meeting major deadlines	Block and MacMillan (1985: 7); Sykes and Block (1982: 163); Van de Ven (1986: 590–607): 'Among the most powerful temporal features we observed were time limits and deadlines' (Hackman 1990: 480).
2.04 Meeting quality objectives	Hauser and Clausing (1988); Block and MacMillan (1985: 7); Van de Ven *et al.* (1984: 91).
2.05 Meeting reliability objectives	Block and MacMillan (1985: 7); Van de Ven *et al.* (1984: 91).
2. 06 Meeting cost objectives	Block (1989: 24,26,32); Block (1989: 26); Block and MacMillan (1985: 5); Sykes and Block (1989: 162); Van de Ven *et al.* (1984: 91).

Items comprising the construct 'performance'

Respondents are requested to: 'Please assess the performance of your project over the last two months, on each of the following dimensions.'	Reference Source
2.07 Meeting efficiency objectives	Block (1989: 26); Sykes and Block (1989: 162); Van de Ven *et al.* (1984: 91).
2.08 Meeting user/client satisfaction objectives	Block and MacMillan (1985: 7); Van de Ven *et al.* (1984: 91).
2.09 Meeting service objectives	Block and MacMillan (1985: 7); Van de Ven *et al.* (1984: 91).
2.10 Meeting objectives overall	Block (1989: 26); Block (1989: 23); Sykes and Block (1989: 162).

Comprehension

The operationalization of comprehension is derived from several literatures. First is the corporate venturing/innovation literature, in which the acquisition of knowledge and subsequent reduction in uncertainty is seen as a key process (see Block and MacMillan 1985; Dougherty 1992). Second is learning theory, as discussed by March (1991) in which he proposes that the amount of knowledge possessed by an organization about 'm-dimensional' space is strongly related to performance. To measure the extent to which members of a project team feel they understand cause/effect relations on the most significant drivers for their projects, respondents are asked to score 16 items on a scale in which a 1 is equivalent to 'we have no idea at this stage' and 5 is equivalent to 'we know exactly'. Two sets of items are used, one which is tailored toward projects intended to generate revenues directly, and one which is tailored toward projects not intended to generate revenues directly. The items used to measure 'comprehension' are:

Items comprising the construct 'causal understanding' variable GRN

Projects intended to generate revenues directly	Reference source	Projects not intended to create direct revenue
Overall concept of a shared paradigm or code	March (1991); McCaskey (1972: 22); Stata (1989: 67).	
Concept of causal understanding as a link to superior performance	Barney (1986); Alchian and Demsetz (1972); Hackman (ed.) (1991: 9); Stata (1989); Bryson and Bromily (1993: 320).	

Items comprising the construct 'causal understanding' variable GRN

Projects intended to generate revenues directly	*Reference source*	*Projects not intended to create direct revenue*
4.01 Key sources of revenue	Vesper (1990: 99); Block (1989: 22–8); Block and MacMillan (1985: 4–8); Vesper (1990: 486).	Key sources of funds
4.02 Who key customers are	Block (1989: 23–26); Vesper (1990: 99,122,160); Gorman and Sahlman (1989: 429); Zirger and Maidique (1990: 871)	Who key clients or users are
4.03 The customer need being satisfied	Day (1991): Dougherty (1990: 60,66); Vesper (1990: 55); Kanter (1987: 15); Block and MacMillan (1985: 4–8); 'the product was a good match with customer's needs' (Zirger and Maidique, 1990: 877).	The client/user need being satisfied
4.04 The competition you face in filling this need	Porter, 1980 (one of the five forces); Gorman and Sahlman (1986: 439); Vesper (1990: 55); Block (1989: 23–8); Ancona and Caldwell (1992: 329).	The competition you face in filling this need
4.05 Where, when and how customers will use your offering	Gorman and Sahlman (1989: 231–48); Vesper (1990: 122); Block and MacMillan (1985: 4–8); Block (1989: 22-8).	Where, when and how clients will use your offering
4.06 Risks to the customer of buying your offering	MacMillan (1983: 6,8); Vesper (1990: 199).	The risks to the client of using your offering
4.07 How to price your offering	Vesper (1990: 160,121); Block and MacMillan (1985: 7,8); Block (1989: 22–8).	How to assess the value of your contribution
4.08 Legal or regulatory matters affecting your business	Vesper (1990: 99–100, 133); Block 1982: 28).	Legal or regulatory matters affecting your business

Items comprising the construct 'causal understanding' variable GRN

Projects intended to generate revenues directly	*Reference source*	*Projects not intended to create direct revenue*
4.09 The main sources of risk to your firm	Vesper (1990: 121,101); Block (1989: 26, 27, 28); Sykes and Block (1989: 169); Block and MacMillan (1985: 5).	The main sources of risk to your firm
4.10 Support services which must be provided	Block (1989: 20; Day and Wensley (1988); Zahra (1991: 264).	Support services which must be provided
4.11 The cost of resources	Long and Ohtani (1986: 463); Kanter (1987: 15); Block and MacMillan (1985: 6), Block (1989: 26).	The cost of resources
4.12 How key operations need to be carried out	Vesper (1990: 57); Long and Ohtani (1986: 463); Block and MacMillan (1985: 6); Block (1989: 20).	How key operations need to be carried out
4.13 Factors which interfere with operations reliability	Vesper (1990: 99); Block (1989: 26); Block and MacMillan (1985: 6).	Factors which interfere with operations reliability
4.14 Factors which interfere with output quality	Block and MacMillan (1985: 6); Block (1989: 26); Barney (1986: 1232).	Factors which interfere with output quality
4.15 Costs of your operations	Sykes and Block (1989: 162); Kanter (1987: 15); Block and MacMillan (1985:6).	Costs of your operations
4.16 Major bottlenecks preventing improved operations	Block (1989: 22); Block and MacMillan (1985:7); Block (1989: 31).	Major bottlenecks preventing improved operations

Deftness

Deftness represents the extent to which the processes by which a team solves problems are effortless, effective and well-honed. A higher score is always associated with greater process 'deftness' for a team. To tap the deftness of a group, project group members are asked to position their projects on a five-point scale between two semantic differentials. A score of 1 implies processes which are clumsy or unresponsive, requiring substantial expenditures of resources to coordinate tasks and solve problems. A score of 5 indicates maximum effortlessness of task coordination and problem-solving.

The wording of these items is drawn primarily from writers examining intra-organizational and team political processes. Exact items, together with reference sources for each are presented below (item numbers refer to item numbers in the survey instrument):

Items comprising the construct 'deftness'		
Less deft pole	Reference source	More deft pole
Few of the others in the team always know what to do	Ansoff (1979: 77); Mohrman (1979: 201); Pettigrew (1973: 233); Wernerfelt (1989: 7)	All the others on the project team always know what to do
Few of the others in the team are competent to do what is needed	Ansoff (1979: 77); Cook and Wall (1980: 40); Guth and MacMillan (1986: 315); Larson and Lafasto (1989).	All the others in the team are competent to do what is needed
Few people on the team can depend on one another to do what is needed	Guth and MacMillan (1980: 315); Cook and Wall (1980: 45); Mohrman (1979: 200, 201); Tushman (1977: 212); Wernerfelt (1989: 7); 'a common interest in nonshirking' Alchian and Demsetz (1972: 790).	All people on the team can depend on one another to do what is needed
Few people on the team know what information is important to the others	Ansoff (1979: 100); Mohrman (1979: 200); Pettigrew (1973: 169).	All people on the team know what information is important to the others
On this project, there are many hidden agendas	Alutto and Acito (1974: 160–67); Guth and MacMillan (1986: 314); Mohrman (1979: 200, 201); Pettigrew (1973: 234); Stata (1987: 70).	On this project there are very few hidden agendas
Important information often gets held up	Ansoff (1979: 100); Guth and MacMillan (1986: 314); Pettigrew (1973: 169,234);Tushman (1977: 210).	Information flows quickly

135

Items comprising the construct 'deftness'

Less deft pole	Reference source	More deft pole
Important information often gets withheld	Ansoff (1979: 100); Guth and MacMillan (1986: 314); Pettigrew (1973: 169, 234); Tushman (1977: 210).	Information never gets withheld
Important information is often distorted	Ansoff (1979: 100); Guth and MacMillan (1986: 314); Pettigrew (1973: 169, 234); Tushman (1977: 210).	Information is always accurate
New people joining the project find it very difficult to be accepted	Ansoff (1979: 84); Buchanan (1975: 67,68); Guth and MacMillan (1986: 315).	New people joining the project are very easily assimilated
Few people on the team understand one another	Ansoff (1979: 98,108); Guth and MacMillan (1986: 314,321); Tushman (1977: 210); Larson and Lafasto (1989); Wernerfelt (1989: 7); Stata (1989: 70).	All people on the team understand one another – we all 'speak the same language'
Few people on the team can depend on one another to implement decisions	Ansoff (1979: 108); Pettigrew (1973: 26); Wernerfelt (1989: 7).	All people in the team can depend on one another to implement decisions
Information needed to move the project forward is simply not available	Hackman (1990: 11).	We have all the information that we need to move the project forward
The project is very short of key skills	Hackman (1990: 9); Kerzner (1984: 168,451); Morton (1983: 537); Pinto and Prescott (1990: 323).	All key skills are in place
Team members are uncomfortable challenging one another	Kiernan (1993: 12–13), Pascale (1990: 256) Stata (1989: 70).	Team members are very comfortable challenging one another
There is little agreement that correct decisions are being made	Wernerfelt (1989: 7); Stata (1989: 70).	There is general agreement that correct decisions are being made

Job satisfaction

Job satisfaction was measured by the following items derived from extant literature.

How satisfied are you with the progress of the project in each of the following areas right now: Please check the box which most closely matches your views.	*Variable SAT Reference source*
Current direction of the project	Kerzner (1987); Pinto and Prescott (1990: 320,323).
Overall performance to date	Kerzner (1987); Pinto and Prescott (1990: 323); Vesper (1990: 329).
Benefit to your company	Kerzner (1987); Pinto and Prescott (1990; 323); Vesper (1990: 329).
Skill set of the project team	Kerzner (1987); Pinto and Prescott (1990: 323)
Working relationships in the project team	Kerzner (1987); Stokes (1990: 38–45).
Morale in the project team	Kerzner (1987); Stokes (1990: 44).
Project leadership	Castaneda and Nahavandi (1991: 363); Kerzner (1987); Pinto and Prescott (1990: 323); Vesper (1990: 327).
Your team's understanding of how to meet project goals	Kerzner (1987).
Your pay and compensation	Smith *et al.* (1969); Cook *et al.* (1981); Weiss *et al.* (1967); Locke (1976).
Your opportunities for promotion	Smith *et al.* (1969); Cook *et al.* (1981); Weiss *et al.* (1967); Locke (1976).
Your job as it is currently defined	Smith *et al.* (1969); Cook *et al.* (1981); Weiss *et al.* (1967); Locke (1976).

APPENDIX II INDUSTRIAL BASE OF FIRMS WHICH PROVIDED DATA ON INNOVATION PROJECTS

Industry	%
Airlines	2.5
Automobiles	2.5
Banking	7.5
Chemicals	7.5
Distribution services	5.0
Environmental services	5.0
Farming/agriculture	2.5
Financial services	7.5
Glass and ceramics	2.5
Insurance	2.5
Medical/hospital	2.5
Mining	2.5
Oil	2.5
Pharmaceuticals/consumer	7.5
Retailing	2.5
Shipping	2.5
Small manufacturing	7.5
Software	2.5
Steel	2.5
Telecommunications	17.5
Transportation	2.5
Travel	2.5

APPENDIX III DISTRIBUTION OF PROJECTS IN TERMS OF STAGE OF EVOLUTION

Project's primary challenge	%
Developing or defining initial concept	17
Entering the market for the first time	15
Growth	24
Stabilization/maturation	8
Not categorized	36

8

REGIONAL BUSINESS CREATION AND 'PUSH' FACTORS

The case of Quebec

Gilles Roy, Jean-Marie Toulouse and Luc Vallée

INTRODUCTION

The question of regional variation in the rate of firm creation has long been the focus of a wide range of studies and analyses by specialists in the field of entrepreneurship, particularly in the USA and UK. Clearly, interest in this issue must be placed in the context of the broader research trend concerning the economic and social contributions of entrepreneurs in terms of job creation, technological innovation and economic development.

Entrepreneurship is a multidimensional process that can be analyzed from different points of view, depending on the goals and orientations of the researchers. Many of the studies that have been conducted on the subject of inter-regional variations in new firm formation have focused on the factors that could 'explain' these differences. However, not all of them have used the same conceptual framework or variables because research objectives have been different.

From a regional development perspective, four sets of factors have been identified to account for the growth in new business formation (Keeble 1990; Mason 1992; Mason and Harrison 1990). These are the recession-related factors (redundancy, rising unemployment and job insecurity, shedding of peripheral activities by large firms, reduction of start-up costs resulting from the availability of cheap second-hand plant, equipments and premises), corporate restructuring factors (fragmentation strategies, spin-outs of existing activities, externalization process), income growth factors (increase in spendings on discretionary items, new market niches) and technological factors (new opportunities created by new technologies).

In the industrial economics perspective, there has been a traditional emphasis on the pull factors which underlie new business formation (Geroski 1990; Storey 1991; Vivarelli 1991). With few exceptions, studies have generally focused on the microeconomic aspects of market entry rather than on macro-economic considerations. According to this school of thought, entry takes place in response to some combination of pre-entry and expected post-entry prices in the chosen market and in associated markets, and in response to the level of perceived barriers in both markets (Storey 1991; Vivarelli 1991).

We have decided to explore the phenomena of new business formation from a more macroeconomic point of view. Using the general framework developed by Johannisson (1991) for his study of Swedish regional entre-preneurship, we have grouped a series of macroeconomic and socio-demographic statistics into five broad models that highlight alternative categories of explanatory factors: the push, pull, resource, contextual and network models. The models used are not exclusive: they just put emphasis on different aspects of the entrepreneurial process.

We must stress here that our immediate objective is not to define a unidi-mensional 'true' explanatory model for regional variations in the province of Quebec. It appears obvious that a multidimensional phenomenon requires a multidimensional explanation, including cultural and sociological observa-tions that cannot be represented in statistical data. Our short-term goal is solely to analyse relations between groups of variables, as they emerge from the available statistical series, in order to underline which macroeco-nomic and socio-demographic factors seem to be more related to the entrepreneurial process. In other words, we are not looking to established causality between certain variables and entrepreneurial activities but rather, in a first stage, we are trying to identify good predictors of such activities. Once the individual models have been tested, we will combine them to test a more global and multidimensional model eventually to infer some causal relations. We think that this methodology offers an efficient framework to achieve our ultimate objective.

The push model represents an essentially reactive conception of the entre-preneurial process. It is based on the hypothesis that individuals are driven to create their firm in reaction to difficulties encountered in the labour market. These difficulties may be the result of harsh macroeconomic condi-tions (recession, high unemployment rate, company closings), personal problems experienced as a wage earner (job dissatisfaction, threat of lay-off or closure, impossibility of career advancement), or integration problems resulting from an individual's immigrant status. This model is also called the 'push-recession' model because of its close links to macroeconomic cycles.[1] According to this theoretical framework, the most entrepreneurial regions should be those where these negative motivational factors are the strongest: that is, in regions with high unemployment, difficult economic conditions and a large proportion of new arrivals.

Contrary to the push model, the pull model considers entrepreneurship to be the end result of a positive force; the voluntary and carefully thought out action of a person who was able to detect and exploit a promising business opportunity in a particular market. According to this model, then, the most entrepreneurial regions should be those where business opportunities are the most numerous and where demand is the strongest or on the increase. The agglomeration/rurality factor is generally the most important factor in this model, with variables such as the income level, demographic growth and the progression of regional demand.[2]

We have undertaken to examine regional variations in business formation rates in Canada by concentrating first of all on the province of Quebec. This chapter provides a summary of the main results obtained in the context of our preliminary work on the push model. It should be underlined here that the other models will also be tested in subsequent work. Our objective is to compare the explanatory power of these different points of view and then to combine the most correlated variables in a global and cumulative model. Moreover, the study will eventually be extended to all Canadian provinces. Our ultimate goal is to arrive at a better understanding of the dynamic of inter-regional variations in firm formation in Canada. We believe that this is an important step toward improving interventions in this area.

VARIATION IN THE REGIONAL RATE OF FIRM CREATION IN QUEBEC

Choice of a database

We have used two alternative sources of data to represent the rate of firm creation in Quebec: the Dun and Bradstreet (D&B) data bank and the data bank of the Commission des Normes du Travail du Québec (CNT). Both banks present certain advantages and disadvantages in terms of methodology.

The D&B group compiles data on companies for which it receives information requests as part of its credit information service. The main advantage of this bank is its extensive range: indeed, D&B operates in all Canadian provinces as well as in several other countries, including the USA. This assures a uniform database for the different regions we wish to study. It should also be mentioned that D&B exercises strict control over the quality of the information it gathers.

The D&B nonetheless also comprises a number of weaknesses (Birch 1979). Its major disadvantage is its fragmentary nature. Indeed, the company is only interested in companies for which it receives formal information requests. This does not necessarily mean that small firms are under-represented, since such firms usually pose a greater risk financially, but rather that certain types of firms are under-represented, notably those in the service sector. As several authors have noted, the D&B indexes are designed more for the conducting of market research than for economic research. Certain conventions used are methodologically unsound. Last, it should be mentioned that not all companies agree to reveal their figures to D&B.

The CNT data bank does not present the same problems. Indeed, this bank is produced on the basis of information transmitted to it by the Bureau du fichier central des entreprises du Québec (BFCE) and based on information it gathers itself. This means that all incorporated companies are automatically entered into this database. Partnerships and self-employed individuals are also recorded when they register directly with the organization. This data bank is consequently much more comprehensive that that of the D&B. It is also important to note that the CNT data are available for a significant number of previous years, while those of the D&B are only available for 1991.

All of these factors contribute to make the CNT database appear much more interesting at first glance. However, there is a major disadvantage which must be taken into account: the bank is only available for the Quebec census divisions. As a result, similar data for the rest of Canada will have to be found when the time comes to extend our study, and chances are that this will not be an easy task. Thus, the advantages of the Quebec model may be lost at the level of Canada as a whole. It is for this reason that we decided to test both databases concurrently. As we shall see below, only the data obtained from the CNT provided significant results, both in terms of the 'push' model and in terms of the correlation coefficient matrix.

For the explanatory variables, we used the data from Statistics Canada's 1986 census. With the exception of a few minor areas, the results of the 1991 census had not yet been rendered public at the time our study was conducted.

Firm creation rate: methodological definition

The literature proposes various methods for measuring regional variations in the business creation rate. For example, a number of authors have used net annual variations in the number of companies as an estimator of the phenomenon under study. Others have used the ratio of new companies to the existing stock of companies or to sectorial employment (Schell 1983). More recent studies, however, tend to reject these approaches due to the biases introduced in the calculation of estimators (impact of the regional industrial structure, for example). Currently, the most common approach is to consider only the gross number of new companies, weighted by the number of inhabitants or households (Garofoli 1992; Johannisson 1991; Westhead and Moyes 1992). This is the method we have adopted in this study.

In this study, we will test the push model using, in turn, four dependant variables obtained from the D&B and CNT bases. The first of these variables, DB0191, reflects the number of firms created in 1991. Two others, DB1291 and DB3591, take into account lags of one to two years, and three to five years. The last of these variables, CNT8692, is a weighted annual mean of new firms' formation for the period between 1986 and 1991. This approach has been chosen to reflect the dynamic aspect of the phenomena (see Table 8.1)

Entrepreneurial profile of Quebec

Statistics Canada uses a certain number of geographical units to group the numerous statistics it publishes. The smallest standardized unit is called an enumeration area (EA). These areas (150 to 300 households) are then grouped into census subdivisions (CSD), which are in turn grouped into census division (CD) and into subprovincial regions (SR). There also exists a grouping of census agglomerations (CA) for urban centres with at least 10,000 inhabitants, and of metropolitan census areas (CMA) for urban centres with at least 100,000 inhabitants.

For methodological reasons, the breakdown into census divisions seems to be the best alternative for testing the various models we have defined. Indeed, the number of units (99) is sufficient to render the tests statistically significant. We have also combined the census metropolitan areas (5) and the census agglomerations (25) in order to underscore the impact of the urban factor.

For the purposes of this study, we have used the new territorial boundaries defined by Statistics Canada in the 1991 Standard Geographical Classification (SGC). It should be noted that this classification has been substantially modified since the 1986 census, when the federal government decided to adjust its classification to make it conform with the Quebec government's Municipalité régionale de comté (MRC). The census divisions (CD) were thus changed to imitate the boundaries of the various MRCs. This reform presented a number of significant constraints at the methodological level: it was necessary to establish a table of equivalencies between the old and the new census divisions in order to process the chronological series. This was done by means of the census subdivisions (CSD) which, in spite of a change in numeration, kept the same boundaries.

Table 8.1 Anticipated dependent variables

DB0191	Number of firms registered with D&B in 1991, in existence for less than one year, per 1,000 inhabitants.
DB1291	Number of firms registered with D&B in 1991, in existence for between one and two years, per 1,000 inhabitants.
DB3591	Number of firms registered with D&B in 1991, in existence for between three and five years, per 1,000 inhabitants.
CNT8692	Average annual number of firms registered with the CNT over the period 1986–92, in existence for less than one year, per 1,000 inhabitants.

We have grouped all of the CDs (census divisions) into their respective subprovincial region (SR) in order to determine the different regional mean rates of firm creation. The figures in brackets indicate the rank of the regions in each category. The population of the 1991 census was used to weight the indicators (see Table 8.2).

The rank of the CMAs (Table 8.3) confirms the importance of Montreal, which dominates in all categories except for DB0191. It should be pointed out that, for the purposes of our analysis, we have divided this CMA into its regional constituents (Montreal Urban Community, Laval, Montérégie, Lanaudière). The Ottawa-Hull CMA (the Quebec portion of the national capital) is that which shows the weakest entrepreneurial propensity, followed closely by the Quebec City-Chaudière-Appalaches area. This suggests that the strong presence of the public service in these two cities does not encourage entrepreneurial activity.

The results presented in Tables 8.2 and 8.3 underscore the following principal characteristics:

1 Regardless of the database used to define the rate of firm creation, the region where entrepreneurial activity is most frequent is Montreal,

Table 8.2 Rank of the subprovincial regions (SR) in Quebec

SR	Designation	POP91	DB0191	DB1291	DB3591	CNT8692
10	Gaspésie-Iles-de-la-Madeleine	105,080	0.67 (15)	0.84 (16)	0.99 (15)	7.80 (15)
15	Bas-Saint-Laurent	202,140	1.10 (09)	1.34 (11)	1.30 (08)	8.53 (13)
20	Quebec City	607,087	1.19 (07)	1.30 (12)	1.33 (05)	12.66 (07)
25	Chaudière-Appalaches	362,820	0.99 (14)	1.29 (13)	1.25 (10)	10.21 (11)
30	Estrie	263,710	1.05 (12)	1.34 (10)	1.17 (14)	13.01 (06)
35	Montérégie	1,187,342	1.09 (10)	1.36 (09)	1.28 (09)	13.54 (05)
40	Montreal	1,749,303	1.35 (02)	1.77 (01)	1.86 (01)	18.81 (01)
45	Laval	311,170	1.21 (06)	1.52 (05)	1.48 (02)	16.54 (02)
50	Lanaudière	331,208	1.14 (08)	1.29 (14)	1.21 (13)	13.78 (04)
55	Laurentians	377,342	1.27 (04)	1.55 (04)	1.33 (06)	15.69 (03)
60	Outaouais	281,765	0.59 (16)	0.97 (15)	0.84 (16)	10.39 (10)
65	Abitibi-Témiscamingue	150,625	1.25 (05)	1.59 (02)	1.34 (04)	10.55 (08)
70	Mauricie-Bois-Francs	459,038	1.07 (11)	1.37 (08)	1.23 (12)	10.46 (09)
75	Saguenay-Lac-Saint-Jean	283,596	1.38 (01)	1.55 (03)	1.47 (03)	9.43 (12)
80	Côte-Nord du Québec	102,557	1.28 (03)	1.43 (06)	1.24 (11)	8.27 (14)
90	Nord-du-Québec	36,041	1.03 (13)	1.39 (07)	1.30 (07)	6.22 (16)
	Province of Quebec	6,807,362	1.17	1.46	1.42	13.96

followed closely by Laval and the Laurentians. This result seems to confirm Montreal's importance as a centre of economic activity.

2 Regardless of the database, the two areas with the weakest entrepreneurial activity are Gaspésie-Iles de la Madeleine and the Outaouais regions.

3 Certain regions appear more entrepreneurial when only the D&B data are taken into account, and less entrepreneurial when the CNT data are used. The three regions for which there is a difference in ranking according to the database used are Abitibi-Témiscamingue, the Bas-Saint-Laurent and the Saguenay region.

4 The rates of firm creation obtained using the D&B data show little variation – which leads us to believe that the bank's entry criteria has a uniformization effect or that regions with service companies are penalized.

Although it is not presented here for the sake of brevity, we extended our analysis to examine small urban regions (those with a population of at least 10,000). We observe that the intensity of entrepreneurial activity varies according to the time period considered. For example, the city of Cowansville appears very entrepreneurial if the number of surviving firms less than one year old (DB0191) is considered. On the contrary, if we use the number of surviving firms between one and two years old (DB1291), the city no longer seems entrepreneurial. Yet, if we consider the number of surviving firms which are three to five years old (DB3591) or the number of firms created

Table 8.3 Rank of the census metropolitan areas (CMA) of Quebec

CMA	Designation	POP91	DB0191	DB1291	DB3591	CNT8692
408	Chicoutimi-Jonquière (Sanguenay)	159,610	1.43 (01)	1.60 (02)	1.42 (03)	9.63 (10)
421	Quebec City (Québec)	524,000	1.16 (04)	1.28 (07)	1.36 (04)	13.23 (06)
421	Quebec City (Chaudière-Appalaches)	113,750	1.10 (05)	0.99 (09)	0.98 (09)	10.70 (07)
433	Sherbrooke	136,700	1.02 (07)	1.36 (05)	1.24 (07)	14.37 (04)
442	Trois-Rivières	134,884	0.99 (09)	1.22 (08)	1.09 (08)	10.66 (08)
462	Montreal (Montérégie)	676,135	1.10 (06)	1.35 (06)	1.25 (06)	14.30 (05)
462	Montreal (MUC)	1,749,303	1.35 (02)	1.77 (01)	1.86 (01)	18.81 (1)
462	Montreal (Laval)	311,170	1.21 (03)	1.52 (03)	1.48 (02)	16.54 (02)
462	Montreal (part Lanaudière)	71,230	1.01 (08)	1.43 (04)	1.31 (05)	14.51 (03)
505	Ottawa-Hull (Outaouais)	225,305	0.53 (10)	0.92 (10)	0.78 (10)	10.53 (09)
	Metropolitan census areas	4,102,087	1.20	1.51	1.51	15.66

between 1986 and 1992 (CNT8692), Cowansville appears fairly entrepreneurial. At the other extreme, Granby appears very entrepreneurial if CNT8692 is used and not very entrepreneurial if DB0191 is used.

There are three possible explanations for this phenomenon: the databases differ significantly, or rankings based on short periods are very unstable, or there is no regularity in the phenomenon of firm creation. Our knowledge of this particular milieu leads us to believe that it is preferable to work with a period of between three and five years: the results obtained based on DB3591 and CNT8692 coincide more closely with our perception of this phenomenon than DB0191 and DB1291.

In order to identify the best variable and, especially, to gain an understanding of the elements associated with firm creation, we focused our attention on one model: the push model.

THE 'PUSH' MODEL

The unemployment rate constitutes the basic theoretical variable of the push model (Johannisson 1991), since it is the statistic which best reflects the problem of integration in the labour force. Other variables may also be associated with this model provided that they represent the same phenomenon; that is, negative forces which push individuals toward entrepreneurship. Researchers who gather their data by means of questionnaires obviously do not face the same constraints as those who rely on official statistical indexes. For example, Storey (1982) uncovered the following push factors based on an interview of 156 new entrepreneurs in the region of Cleveland, UK: lay-off, termination of employment, company closure, early retirement, threat of lay-off, and job dissatisfaction. For their part, Binks and Jennings (1986a) obtained the following factors: lay-off, job insecurity, disagreement with employer, and company closure. While all of these variables provide a more refined understanding of the push phenomenon, it appears very difficult to measure these variables statistically.

Review of the literature

The impact of unemployment: a conceptual background

For years, authors have been defending the theory that difficult economic conditions, particularly at the level of employment, encourage the process of firm creation.[3] The key historical precedent on this approach is Knight's (1921) insistence that an individual would switch from employee to employer depending on the relative expected return in these two types of activities.

This argument, that the formation of the new business is adopted in some sense in preference to employment in other capacities, has been well summarized by Oxenfeldt:

A majority of new businesses are established by individuals who have, or could obtain, other employment. Three important reasons for entry may be distinguished. First, many businesses are established by persons who, by accumulation, gift, inheritance or loan become financially able to realise a long-cherished ambition to be entrepreneurs. These people are probably influenced to set up businesses by the desire for higher social status and relative freedom from domination as by a hope of securing higher income. Second, a sudden worsening of working conditions, or outlook for the future, drive some people into business for themselves. Finally, some new businesses are established by persons who are induced to leave their jobs, or abandon their present enterprises, by the discovery of tempting opportunities.

(Oxenfeldt 1943: 118–19)

Starting from the premise that new firm formation implies the movement from paid employment (or unemployment) to self-employment, it has been argued that the formation/transfer decision will be made when the perceived net benefits (monetary and non-monetary) of self-employment (P_s) exceed those of remaining in paid employment (P_e). A fall in P_e with P_s constant, will push a latent entrepreneur into self-employment. On the other hand, a rise in P_s, with P_e constant, will have the effect of pulling an individual into self-employment, as the perceived net benefits of self-employment exceed those of paid employment (Johnson and Darnell 1976). According to this theory, a rise in the unemployment rate constitutes a push factor because the perceived threat to job stability and security in paid employment increases and the desire to assert independence and be responsible for one's own future becomes more significant.

Unemployment can be construed as a core element of either the push or the pull models. There is therefore an analytical imperative to ensure that model specifications cover both possibilities if the explanatory framework is to be adequate. According to Storey:

The pull hypothesis is closely related to the SCP tradition. It argues that new firm formation takes place when an individual perceives an opportunity to enter a market to make at least a satisfactory level of profit. Ceteris paribus, this is more likely to happen when demand is high and when the individual is credit-worthy or has access to personal savings. In such a situation, individuals are 'pulled' or attracted into forming their own businesses and are more likely to have access to the assets necessary to start the business.

The converse 'push' hypothesis suggests that depressed market conditions mean individuals experiencing or facing the prospect of unemployment are more likely to establish new firms. In the Knight frameworks, even though the expected income from self-employment is low, it is higher than the expected income from unemployment or from searching for employment as an employee. Furthermore, as Binks and Jennings (1986) point out, unemployment in an economy is likely to coincide with the closure of businesses and hence lead to the increased availability of low cost of second-hand equipment. In this sense, a key barrier to new firm formation may, somewhat paradoxically, be lower in times of depressed than in time of buoyant demand.

(Storey 1991: 171)

Recently, it has been argued that the relationship between unemployment and new firm formation is a non-linear one. At low levels of unemployment, increases in unemployment lead to increases in new firm formation; however, beyond a 'critical' level, increases of unemployment lead to redirections in new firm formation (Hamilton 1989).

The impact of unemployment: some empirical evidence

Empirical studies which have been conducted to test the positive influence of unemployment on firm formation are far from conclusive in this regard. It seems that the general relationships observed differ along with the methodology used.

The micro-level questionnaire surveys of new business founders generally indicate a positive relationship between unemployment and new business formation. For example, Storey (1982) conducted a survey of 156 new entrepreneurs in the region of Cleveland, UK: at the time 26 percent of respondents claimed to have been unemployed immediately prior to going into business. The results obtained by Binks and Jennings (1986a) from a survey of 100 entrepreneurs in the Nottingham region are even more revealing: in this case, 47 respondents claimed that they were motivated by 'push' factors to create their firm. More recently, Barkham (1992) administered a questionnaire to about 120 new entrepreneurs in three regions of the UK. A high proportion of the respondents declared that they were 'pushed' toward entrepreneurship (32 percent in the West Midlands) and that they were unemployed immediately prior to creating their firm (27 percent in the North-East).

The large majority of the cross-sectional studies, using more or less sophisticated econometric techniques, do not support the findings of the surveys by questionnaire. For example, Pennings (1982) found no positive correlation between the unemployment rate and the rate of new firm creation for certain selected industrial sectors (plastics, telecommunications, electronics) in a study conducted in 70 urban American centres for the period of 1966 to 1970. Foreman-Peck (1984) arrived at the same conclusion for the rate of firm creation in the English and Welsh manufacturing sector as a whole between 1918 and 1939.

Rather, several studies have observed a negative relation between the unemployment rate and the rate of firm creation. This is true of the studies realized

148

by Binks and Jennings (1986b) and Westhead (1989), which covered the years 1971–81 and 1979–83 in the UK. Recently, Johannisson (1991) studied the pattern of new firm creation in Sweden for the period 1986–9. He also found a negative (but not significant) relation between these two variables. For their part, Reynolds *et al* (1991) arrived at a negative and significant correlation between an indicator of the unemployment rate (the proportion of the average revenue received from social security programs) and the regional rate of firm creation in the USA. The study was conducted using D&B data for the period 1982–6.

However, econometric studies using time series data tend to suggest a clear positive relationship between unemployment and new business formation (Harrison and Hart 1983; Storey 1991). This approach is interesting but raises many problems of data availability and consistency that limit its scope (Robson 1994).

We could conclude by saying that the vast majority of the cross-sectional studies does not support the hypothesis of a positive relation between the unemployment rate and the firm creation rate. On the contrary, the empirical results obtained reveal a negative correlation between these two variables. In order to assess the veritable relationship between them, it would perhaps be necessary to test the impact of a variation in unemployment insurance premiums. It is possible that the generosity of social programs inhibits the natural entrepreneurial propensity of people who have been laid off. The relative expected return from unemployment becomes higher than the expected return from self-employment (Knight 1921).

Impact of migration on the firm creation rate

In our opinion, migration variables constitute another group which can be associated with the 'push' model. Indeed, it is well-known that many immigrants are pushed toward entrepreneurship by problems of integration in their adopted society (Toulouse 1991). Even though this type of variable has been abundantly tested in the entrepreneurial literature (Chrisman *et al.* 1992), until now, no one seems to have associated it explicitly with the 'push' model. We have taken it upon ourselves to do so in this study.

Most authors have observed a strong positive correlation between immigration and the regional rate of firm creation.[4] It would seem, then, that the entrepreneurial propensity of immigrants is indeed stronger than that of the host population, for reasons which are probably attributable to integration difficulties.

Impact of economic turbulence on the firm creation rate

A third category of variables appears to be relevant in the context of this model: they are what one author has called variables of 'economic turbulence'

(Westhead 1989). As the name suggests, these variables attempt to reflect the general economic climate of a region by highlighting the broader trends in terms of company closings and loss of employment. This category lends a certain materiality to the factor of the threat of lay-offs or closings that were observed in the survey by questionnaire (Binks and Jennings 1986a; Storey 1982).

Generally, variables such as the number of company closings or resultant job losses are used to represent the concept of economic turbulence. It seems that a high rate of loss of employment is positively correlated to the rate of firm creation, at least in the UK (Storey and Jones 1987; Westhead 1989).

EMPIRICAL RESULTS

Overview of the methodology and principal results

Tests were performed for the following four dependent variables: DB0191, DB1291, DB3591 and CNT8692. To refine even further, we have added two new dependent variables: the number of companies registered with the CNT in 1986 per 1,000 inhabitants (CNT86) and the number of companies registered with the CNT in 1991, per 1,000 inhabitants (CNT91).

The explanatory variables were selected based on the conceptual framework of the push model; that is, negative forces which encourage entrepreneurship. We wanted to represent the three main types of variables which seemed best to conform to the findings of the literature; that is, the unemployment rate, migratory flow, and the number of company deregistrations. We then defined and tested a certain number of variants of these variables to determine which were the most significant. As expected, the most significant variables were found in the models with the highest R^2.

In order to highlight the impact of regional variations with respect to the firm creation rate, we conducted tests for four alternative groups of geographical clusters:

1 The Quebec census divisions (CD);
2 The Quebec census divisions plus the census subdivisions of the Montreal Urban Community (CD + CSD from MUC: this procedure permits division of the MUC – Montreal Urban Community – into clusters which correspond to the others);
3 The census metropolitan areas plus the Quebec census agglomeration (CMA + CA: this procedure makes it possible to obtain all regions having over 10,000 inhabitants);
4 The Quebec census divisions minus the census subdivisions included in the census metropolitan areas or census agglomerations (CD – CA + CMA: this procedure makes it possible to obtain the rural regions).

The tests showed that the best results are obtained using the dependent variables CNT86, CNT91, CNT8692. For the sake of simplicity, we have presented only these results, since they were the most significant (see Table 8.4).

Interpretation of the results

Our results, obtained by using OLS regressions, are presented in the following tables. Only the most significant results for each of the geographical groupings are discussed below. Other results are available on request. Because of the different number of observations and the different dependent variables used in the four regressions, it is impossible to use the R^2 as a criterion to determine which is the best regression. However, our model performed quite well with R^2, ranging from 0.36 to 0.70, a result generally considered excellent in the context of such a cross-section data set. Thus, it appears that the 'push' model is quite useful in predicting the rate of business creation across regions within the province of Quebec, whether across the whole territory or in urban and rural areas.

The role of unemployment

A look at the series of regressions (see Table 8.5) reveals that the unemployment rate prevailing in 1986 is negatively correlated to the rate of firm

Table 8.4 Independent variables used in the empirical tests

CITNC86	Percentage of non-Canadian citizens, 1986.
CNT86DH	Number of companies deregistered from the CNT bank in 1986, per 1,000 inhabitants.
CNT91DH	Number of companies deregistered from the CNT bank in 1991, per 1,000 inhabitants.
CNT8692DH	Average annual number of companies deregistered from the CNT bank over the period 1986–92, per 1,000 inhabitants.
MIGQ86	Percentage of migrants five years and older relocating within the province of Quebec in 1986.
MIGQ8186V	Variation in the percentage of migrants five years and older relocating within the province of Quebec between 1981 and 1986.
MIGC86	Percentage of migrants five years and older coming from other Canadian provinces in 1986.
MIGC8186V	Variation in the percentage of migrants five years and older coming from other Canadian provinces between 1981 and 1986.
MIGE86	Percentage of foreign immigrants five years and older from outside Canada in 1986.
MIGE8186V	Variation in the percentage of foreign immigrants five years and older from outside Canada between 1981 and 1986.
TCH86	Unemployment rate in 1986.
TCH8186V	Variation in the unemployment rate between 1981 and 1986.

creation in the different regions of Quebec over the 1986–92 period. The coefficient of unemployment is negative and statistically significant in all regressions, except for rural regions, where it is insignificant but still negative. This suggests that unemployment provides a negative incentive to create businesses. In the context of an analysis using data at an aggregate level, this result confirms the findings of other authors.[5]

This result is hardly surprising considering that the level of unemployment in a given area is more likely to reflect the state of the demand in that area than the incentive of unemployed individuals to create a business. There is a strong argument to support our belief that this is indeed the case. Had we compared unemployed workers' willingness to create a business across different regions of Quebec, we may have found the expected result. However, because the pool of potential entrepreneurs is dominated by individuals who do have a steady job, and because the incentives of these workers to become self-employed should normally be negatively related to the level of unemployment,[6] the overall effect of unemployment on the rate of entrepreneurship is very likely to be negative. In other words, the negative demand-side effect of unemployment on entrepreneurship may dominate and thus hide its positive supply-side effect, preventing us from observing the

Table 8.5 Regression analysis for CNT8692EH/OLS: geographical groupings I,II, III and IV

Independent Variables	I Census divisions (CD)	II CD and Montreal census subdivisions (CD and MUCs CSD)	III Census metro areas and census agglomerations (CMA and CA)	IV CD excluding CMA and CA (rural)
Constant	7.18333***	10.15622***	12.46971***	5.56220***
	(1.30454)	(1.42239)	(2.14754)	(1.37933)
TCH86	−12.24134***	−17.90165***	−36.30914***	−6.06961
	(4.74536)	(5.66509)	(9.72559)	(4.99726)
MIGQUE86	46.36321***	30.87269***	33.95204***	46.03308***
	(5.88756)	(6.02330)	(7.92410)	(7.15713)
MIGCAN86	−38.21129**	−40.30851**	−41.62847*	−34.76714
	(17.89095)	(17.45337)	(24.16285)	(28.78098)
MIGEXT86	177.521***	162.182***	207.352***	247.383**
	(49.62625)	(28.95657)	(50.07465)	(100.525)
Number of observations	90	117	31	78
R²	0.64366	0.53612	0.67539	0.47462
Adjusted R²	0.62690	0.51956	0.62545	0.44583

Notes:
* Significant at the 90 percent confidence level.
** Significant at the 95 percent confidence level.
*** Significant at the 99 percent confidence level.

phenomenon described by other researchers in the fields of entrepreneurship and economics.[7]

As Hamilton (1989) points out, it is possible that the relationship between unemployment and new firm formation may be non-linear. At low levels of unemployment, those who become unemployed recognize that market opportunities exist and are 'pulled' into starting their own firm; as unemployment continues to rise, these business opportunities diminish and formation rates fall.

However, in other regressions we included variations in the rate of unemployment as well as the rate of unemployment itself. These regressions are presented in Table 8.6. This was done so that the level of unemployment would capture the state of the demand in each region, and so that the variations in the level of unemployment would capture the supply-side response of newly unemployed workers to unemployment.

The results confirm our expectations. The coefficient of unemployment is still negative and significant in all four regressions, whereas the coefficient of the variations in unemployment is always positive and significant when the migration variables are excluded from the regressions. The fact that the results do not seem very robust to the inclusion of the migration variables may be due to the possibility that worker mobility and unemployment are

Table 8.6 Regression analysis for CNT8692EH/OLS: geographical groupings II and III including employment variations

Independent variables	II CD and MUC's CSD		III CMA and CA	
Constant	17.03640***	10.24537***	20.98086***	12.49496***
	(0.88859)	(1.42942)	(2.13165)	(1.88544)
TCH86	−39.94217***	−18.85900***	−66.35844***	−36.62457***
	(5.48982)	(−3.24849)	(15.65613)	(8.64047)
TCH8186VAR	7.83061***	1.81398	6.97292*	4.84520**
	(2.47320)	(2.31951)	(3.84073)	(2.25905)
MIGQUE86	–	29.56583***	–	30.89773***
		(6.26090)		(7.50201)
MIGCAN86	–	−39.06586**	–	−45.77435**
		(17.55577)		(20.51186)
MIGEXT86	–	154.635***	–	203.610***
		(30.57009)		(40.52009)
Number of observations	117	117	31	31
R^2	0.35941	0.53866	0.45376	0.70474
Adjusted R^2	0.34817	0.51788	0.41475	0.64569

Notes:
*   Significant at the 90 percent confidence level.
**   Significant at the 95 percent confidence level.
*** Significant at the 99 percent confidence level.

intrinsically linked phenomena, causing coefficient estimates to be relatively unstable. Nonetheless, overall these results suggest that, as expected by the theory, there is an entrepreneurial positive supply-side response of workers to unemployment. The effect of unemployment on entrepreneurship is complex. On the one hand, a high level of unemployment appears to signal that business opportunities are scarce. On the other hand, once we control for the level of unemployment, we find that the higher the number of workers joining the pool of unemployed individuals, the higher the incentive to start a business.

Finally, note that (Table 8.5) the coefficient of the unemployment variable in the urban regression is much larger than in the rural regression, suggesting that the negative impact of unemployment in urban areas is much more important than in rural areas. This may be attributable to the higher inter-regional proximity in urban areas, which makes it easier for an entrepreneur from a depressed region (with high unemployment) to locate his business in a booming region (with low unemployment). Through a case study of a few regions, further research should focus on understanding the different dynamics between urban and rural areas.

The role of mobility

The results also show that the composition of the population in the different regions is relatively important in explaining the distribution of the rate of entrepreneurship across the various regions. The three variables MIGQUE86, MIGCAN86 and MIGEXT86 allow us to divide immigration in each region into three components: local immigration (migrants from other parts of Quebec); national immigration (migrants from other provinces of Canada); and international immigration (migrants from other countries).

The results from Tables 8.5 and 8.6 indicate that the proportion of foreign immigrants (MIGEXT86) is positively correlated with the rate of business creation in regressions, confirming that the vitality of immigrant entrepreneurship often hypothesized in the literature; the results are strongly significant from a statistical point of view. Similarly, the proportion of the population in each region which is made up of individuals coming from another area within the province of Quebec (MIGQUE86) also has a positive impact on the rate of regional business creation. The coefficient of the variable is always positive and statistically different from zero in all four regressions. This shows the importance of inter-regional mobility in the process of firm creation. The relationship seems strongest in rural areas, which suggests the potential of individual mobility to foster regional economic development. Because the regressions control for the level of unemployment and because we used data on the composition of the population at the start of the period (i.e. in 1986), this result cannot be interpreted as a spurious correlation reflecting only the possibility that migrants would be attracted towards more entrepreneurial regions. The correct interpretation seems to be that, while migrants are probably attracted by prosperity, they also contribute to prosperity by eventually creating a firm in the region into which they have moved.

On the other hand, the proportion of immigrants coming to the province of Quebec from other provinces in Canada (MIGCAN86) has a negative impact on the rate of regional entrepreneurship. However, the coefficient of this variable is not statistically significant in the rural equation model. Therefore it seems that, overall, Canadians immigrating from other provinces do not do so with the intention of creating a business in the province of Quebec. It is surprising, however, that the coefficient of this variable is negative and statistically significant in most equations. One may think that most Canadians moving to Quebec from other provinces do not come to create a business but rather to occupy a corporate job (for example, a marketing vice-president at the Royal Bank in Toronto may be relocated in Montreal to become Quebec's regional marketing director). To explain the negative correlation between this variable and the rate of business creation, we conjecture that such people may be more likely to live in urban residential areas (suburbs of large cities), where businesses are less often located.

Finally, it is worth mentioning (although these results are not reported in the tables) that we did not detect any statistically significant impact of firm deregistrations (whether measured by CNT86DH, CNT91DH or CNT8692DH) on the rate of business creation for any of the four geographical groupings used in this study. We had hoped that a high rate of firm failure would have signalled a high rate of firm creation. We failed to capture the effect of turbulence on entrepreneurial activities. This may be due to the fact that deregistration is a poor proxy to measure economic turbulence. Let us note, however, that since the series was calculated from 1981 and 1986 figures, it might be interesting to test this hypothesis again when the more recent 1991 census data become available.

CONCLUSION

Our study clearly shows that the fundamental thesis of the push model, namely that unemployment has a positive impact on entrepreneurial activities, is empirically rejected in the province of Quebec when we fail to include variations in unemployment in the regressions. As several other studies have already shown,[8] we found that unemployment is negatively and significatively linked with the rate of regional business creation. The results hold for the period covering 1986–92 for most geographical groupings used in the analysis; one notable exception is rural areas, where unemployment does not seem to have an impact on business creation.

However, we must stress that 'push' and 'pull' models of new business formation cannot be treated in isolation. Unemployment may in fact be both a 'push' and a 'pull' surrogate variable in an essentially non-linear relationship (Hamilton 1989). It is possible that, within the context of an empirical study using aggregate cross-section data, unemployment captures the state of the demand in each area better than the supply-side response of unemployed individuals setting up businesses that they would not have set up otherwise (i.e. had they been securely employed in the first place). Indeed, most, if not all, studies corroborating such conclusions are regional, as in this chapter, that use cross-section aggregate data rather than individual data to examine this hypothesis.

We then included both the unemployment rate and variations in the unemployment rate as explanatory variables in our regressions. By using unemployment as a proxy for the state of the demand in the different geographical units, the variations in unemployment are more likely to capture the higher incentive of unemployed individuals to create businesses. Our results suggest that the inclusion of such variables helps to circumvent the difficulties encountered by several authors in identifying the expected effect of unemployment on entrepreneurship in empirical studies using aggregate cross-section data.

The other significant result of this chapter is the effect of the three types of immigration on the rate of entrepreneurship across regions. We found that both intra-provincial and international migration had a positive impact on business creation; the opposite result was found for inter-provincial migration (except in our experimental regression). Thus, immigration appears to be an excellent predictor of entrepreneurial activity. This result is consistent with that of other studies on immigrant entrepreneurship.

Our results have important implications for public policy, in particular policies regarding regional development and immigration. For instance, our study reveals that immigration is beneficial to business creation. If we believe, as many authors have shown,[9] that new firms are responsible for the creation of the majority of jobs, then the adoption of more liberal immigration policies would seem appropriate in order to reduce unemployment. This also appears to be an interesting way to promote regional development, especially in regions where unemployment is high. Seen in this perspective, aggressive programs targeting immigrant entrepreneurs, such as those of Canada, Australia and New Zealand, appear particularly useful.

A seemingly paradoxical policy, which is nonetheless in line with orthodox free market economics, is suggested by our results. In light of our findings concerning the impact of unemployment and mobility, it appears that regional development is not best achieved through the direct creation of jobs, but rather through the promotion of workers' mobility or through the removal of barriers to their mobility. Such a policy may appear paradoxical to some, given that it could lead to the exodus of workers from certain regions where the government is investing to foster development and create jobs. However, the government's costly effort is more likely to reduce workers' mobility and be detrimental to the development of other regions where they would have relocated at no cost to taxpayers. In the end, such a market-based regional development strategy would lead to a greater variance in income between the different regions, but probably to a higher average income.

Finally, we must underline certain limitations to our results, considerations that we will try to take into account in future works. First, as it has been said, push and pull models cannot be treated in isolation because unemployment may be at the same time a push and a pull factor. Consequently, we will have to test a combined version of the two models to see the real influence of unemployment on firm formation.

Second, as micro-level surveys, cross-sectional data analysis and time-series analysis do not provide consistent results in the literature, policy conclusions based on the results of only one methodological approach are likely to be flawed. This is why our research will have to extend to the other methodologies, and particularly to the time series analysis. New business formation is in practice a time-dependant process, not a static phenomenon.

Third, the analysis of new firm formation is an inherently inter-disciplinary phenomenon. Approaches which, for understandable reasons of data availability and variable specification, omit significant variable categories, as most econometric researches do, will always fail to produce satisfactory and comprehensive explanations.

Fourth, explanations of trends in the level of new business formation over time are likely to require different explanatory frameworks and model specifications than are required to account for the pattern of spatial variations in the phenomena. It is increasingly likely that unemployment-push models are an appropriate explanatory framework for the former but not for the latter.

ACKNOWLEDGEMENTS

The authors are grateful to Richard Harrison, Claire Leitch, Maureen McGuigan, Ian MacMillan, Rita McGrath and Atul Nerkar for very helpful comments.

NOTES

1　See Storey (1982); Binks and Jennings (1986a); Westhead (1989); Hamilton (1989).
2　We review and provide references for the pull model, the resource model, the contextual model and the network model in Roy *et al.* (1994).
3　See Schumpeter (1939); Oxenfeldt (1943); Dahmen (1970); and Johnson (1986)
4　See Schell and Davig (1981); Pennings (1982); Johannisson (1991); Bull and Winter (1991); Westhead and Moyes (1992); Chrisman *et al.* (1992).
5　The potential endogeneity of unemployment is not an issue here, since the unemployment figures are for 1986, whereas the dependant variable measures the rate of business creation for the 1986–92 period.
6　This is true because high unemployment signals a poor state of the demand (businesses are more likely to fail than usual). Therefore, high unemployment regions may not be optimal areas in which to create a new business. Second, given that

labour market conditions are more difficult for the unemployed when unemployment is widespread, employed workers would normally hesitate to leave their current jobs in order to become self-employed.

7 The more generous the unemployment benefits and other social programs aimed at unemployed workers, the more likely this will be the case (see Johannisson 1991). Since these programs are relatively generous in Quebec, one might expect the incentive of unemployed workers to start a business to be relatively small. This would also help to explain the relative dominance of the demand-side effect in the data. Another explanation may simply be that unemployment is inhibiting business creation by causing psychological stress, financial insecurity, or by reducing the borrowing capabilities of potential entrepreneurs.

8 Binks and Jennings (1986b; Johannisson (1991); and Reynold et al. (1991).

9 Birch (1979, 1987); Gudgin et al. (1979); Sweeney (1987); Kirchoff and Phillips (1988, 1991).

REFERENCES

Aldrich, H., Rosen, B. and Woodward, W. (1987) 'The impact of social networks on business foundation and profit: a longitudinal study', *Frontiers of Entrepreneurship Research*, Babson College Press.

Aydalot, P. (1986) 'The location of new firm creation', in D. Keeble and E. Wever (eds) *New Firms and Regional Development in Europe*, Beckenham: Croom Helm.

Banks, M.C. (1991) 'Location decisions of rural new ventures', *Frontiers of Entrepreneurship Research*, Babson College Press: 363–77.

Bannock, G. and Doran, A. (1978) *Small Firms in Cities: A Review of Recent Research*, London: Schell.

Barkham, R. (1992) 'Regional variations in entrepreneurship: some evidence from the United Kingdom', *Entrepreneurship and Regional Development* 3 (3): 225–44.

Beesley, M.E. and Hamilton, R.T. (1984) 'Small firms' seedbed and the concept of turbulence', *Journal of Industrial Economics* 23: 217–31.

Berry, B.J.L. (1973) *Growth Centers in the American Urban System*, Cambridge, MA: Ballinger.

Binks, M. and Jennings, A. (1986a) 'New firms as a source of industrial regeneration', in M. Scott et al. (eds) *Small Firms Growth and Development*, Aldershot: Gower.

—— (1986b) 'Small firms as a source of economic rejuvenation', in J. Curran et al. (eds) The Survival of the Small Firm, Aldershot: Gower.

Birch, D. (1979) *The Job Generation Process*, Cambridge, MA: MIT Program On Neighbourhood and Regional Change.

—— (1987) *Job Creation in America*, New York: The Free Press.

Bull, I. and Winter, F. (1991) 'Community differences in business births and growths', *Journal of Business Venturing* 6: 29–43.

Butler, J.E. and Hansen, G.S. (1991) 'Network evolution, entrepreneurial success, and regional development', *Entrepreneurship and Regional Development* 3 (1) 1–16.

Chrisman, J., Van Deusen, C. and Anyomi, S. (1992) 'Population growth and regional economy: an empirical analysis of business formation and job generation in the retail sector', *Entrepreneurship and Regional Development* 4 (4): 339–55.

Cooper, A.C. (1973) 'Technical entrepreneurship: what do we know?', *R&D Management* 3: 59–64.

Cross, M. (1981) *New Firm Formation and Regional Development*, Farnborough: Gower.

Dahmen, E. (1970) *Entrepreneurial Activity and the Development of Swedish Industry, 1919–1939*, Homewood, Il: Richard Irwin.

Florida, R.L. and Kenney, M. (1988) 'Venture capital, high technology, and regional development', *Regional Studies* 22: 33–48.

Foreman-Peck, J. (1984) *New Firm Formation and Industrial Change in the Interwar Economy*, University of Newcastle-upon-Tyne, Discussion Paper no. 80.

Fothergill, S. and Gudgin, G. (1982) *Unequal Growth: Urban and Regional Employment Change in the U.K.*, London: Heinemann.

Garofoli, G. (1992) 'New firm formation and local development 4 (2): 101–25.

Geroski, P.A. (1990) *Entry and Market Dynamics*, Oxford: Basil Blackwell.

Gibbs, J.P. and Poston, D.L. (1975) 'The division of labor: conceptualization and related measures', *Social Forces* 53: 468–76.

Gould, A. and Keeble, D. (1985) 'New firms and rural industrialization in East Anglia', in D.J. Storey (ed.) *Small Firms in Regional Economic Development*, Cambridge: Cambridge University Press.

Gudgin, G. (1978) *Industrial Location Processes and Regional Employment Growth*, Farnborough: Saxon House.

Gudgin, G., Brunskill, I. and Fothergill, S. (1979) 'New manufacturing firms in regional employment growth', *Center for Environmental Studies* 39.

Gudgin, G., Hart, M., Fagg, J., D'Arcy, E. and Keegan, R. (1989) *Job Generation and Manufacturing Industry 1973–86, A Comparison of Northern Ireland with the Republic of Ireland and the English Midlands*, Belfast: Northern Ireland Economic Research Centre.

Hamilton, R.T. (1989) 'Unemployment and business formation rates: reconciling time-series and cross-section evidence', *Environment and Planning A* 21: 249–55.

Harrisson, R.T. and Hart, M. (1983) 'Factors influencing new business formation: a case study of Northern Ireland', *Environment and Planning A* 15: 1395–1412.

Hoover, E.M. and Vernon, R. (1959) *Anatomy of a Metropolis*, Cambridge, MA: Harvard University Press.

Johnson, P. (1986) *New Firms: An Economic Perspective*, London: Allen & Unwin.

Johnson, P.S. and Cathcart, D.G. (1979) 'New manufacturing firms and regional development: some evidence from the northern region', *Regional Studies* 13: 269–80.

Johnson, P.S. and Darnell, A. (1976) *New Firm Formation in Great Britain*, WP-5, Durham: Department of Economics, University of Durham.

Johannisson, B. (1990) 'Community entrepreneurship: cases and conceptualization', *Entrepreneurship and Regional Development* 2: 71–88.

—— (1991) *Regional Patterns of New-Firm Formation: The Case of Sweden*, Vaxjo University, Sweden: Center for Small Business Development.

Keeble, D. (1990) 'Small firms, new firms and uneven regional development in the United Kingdom', *Area*: 234–45.

Kirchhoff, B. and Phillips, B. (1988) 'The effect of firm formation and growth on job creation in the United States', *Journal of Business Venturing* 3: 261–72.

—— (1991) 'Are small firms still creating new jobs', *Frontiers of Entrepreneurship Research*, Babson College Press: 335–49.

Knight, F.H. (1921) *Risk, Uncertainty and Profit*, Chicago: Chicago University Press.

Leone, R.A. and Struyk, R. (1976) 'The incubator hypothesis: evidence from five Smsa's', *Urban Studies* 13: 325–32.

Lloyd, P.E. and Mason, C.M. (1985) 'Spatial variation in new firm formation in the United Kingdom: comparative evidence from Merseyside, Greater Manchester and South Hampshire', in D.J. Storey (ed.) *Small Firms in Regional Economic Development*, Cambridge: Cambridge University Press.

Malecki, E. (1990) 'New firm formation in the USA: corporate structure, venture capital, and local environment', *Entrepreneurship and Regional Development* 2 (3): 247–66.

Marlow, S. and Storey, D. (1992) 'New firm foundation and unemployment: a note on research method', *International Small Business Journal* 10 (3): 62–7.

Mason, C.M. (1982) *New Manufacturing Firms in South Hampshire: Survey Results*, Southampton: Department of Geography, University of Southampton, no. 13.

—— (1992) 'New firm formation and growth', in P. Townroe and R. Martin (eds) *Regional Development in the 1990s: The British Isles in Transition*, London: Regional Studies Association and Jessica Kingsley Publishers.

Mason, C.M. and Harrison, R.T. (1990) 'Small firms: phoenix from the ashes?', in D. Pinder (ed.) *Western Europe: Challenge and Change*, London: Bellhaven Press.

Mussati, G. and Fumagalli, A. (1990) 'Survival, entrepreneurship, growth: which relationship? The Milanese area's case', in Proceedings of Rent-IV Research in Entrepreneurship 4th Workshop, Cologne, Germany.

O'Farrell, P.N. and Crouchley, R. (1985) 'An industrial and spatial analysis of new firm formation in Ireland', in D.J. Storey (ed.) *Small Firms in Regional Economic Development*, Cambridge: Cambridge University Press.

Oxenfeldt, A.R. (1943) *New Firms and Free Enterprise*, Washington DC: American Council on Public Affairs.

Pennings, J.M. (1982) 'Organizational birth frequencies: an empirical investigation', *Administrative Science Quarterly* 27 (1): 120–44.

Québec, Ministère des Communautés culturelles et de l'immigration. Direction générale des politiques et des programmes (1990) *Au Québec pour bâtir ensemble: un énoncé de politique en matière d'immigration et d'intégration*, Montréal: la Direction.

Reynolds, P., Miller, B. and Maki, W. (1991) 'Regional characteristics affecting new firm births', *Frontiers of Entrepreneurship Research*, Babson College Press: 378–90.

Riggs, F.W. (1964) Administration in Developing Countries, Boston, MA: Houghton Mifflin.

Robson, M.T. (1994) *Macroeconomic Factors in the Birth and Death of UK Firms: Evidence from Quarterly VAT Registrations*, paper presented to ESRC Conference, Ayr, Scotland.

Roy, G., Toulouse, J.M. and Vallée, L. (1994) *Regional Business Creation and 'Push' Factors: The Case of Quebec*, Quebec: Maclean Hunter Entrepreneurship Chair Working Paper, February.

Schell, D.W. (1983) 'Entrepreneurial activity: a comparison of three North Carolina communities', *Frontiers of Entrepreneurship Research*, Babson College Press: 495–507.

Schell, D.W. and Davig. W. (1981) 'The community infrastructure of entrepreneurship: a sociopolitical analysis', *Frontiers in Entrepreneurship Research*, Babson College Press: 563–90.

Schumpeter, J.A. (1939) *Business Cycles*, New York: McGraw Hill.

Shapiro, A. and Sokol, L. (1982) 'The social dimension of entrepreneurship', in C.A. Kent *et al.* (eds) *Encyclopedia of Entrepreneurship*, Englewood Cliffs, NJ: Prentice-Hall.

Statistiques Canada, Division des normes (1992) *Classification géographique type: CGT 1991*, Ottawa: la Division.

Storey, D.J. (1982) *Entrepreneurship and the New Firm*, London: Croom Helm.

—— (1985a) Manufacturing employment change in Northern England 1965–78: the role of small business', in D.J. Storey (ed.) *Small Firms in Regional Economic Development*, Cambridge: Cambridge University Press.

—— (1985b) 'The implications for policy', in D.J. Storey (ed.) *Small Firms in Regional Economic Development*, Cambridge: Cambridge University Press.

—— (1991) 'The birth of new firms – does unemployment matter? A review of the evidence', *Small Business Economics* 3: 167–78.

Storey, D.J. and Jones, A.M. (1987) 'New firm formation – a labour market approach to industrial entry', *Scottish Journal of Political Economy* 34: 37–51.

Sweeney, G.P. (1987) *Innovation, Entrepreneurs and Regional Development*, London: Frances Pinter.

Thompson, W. (1968) 'Internal and external factors in the development of urban economies', in H.S. Perloff and L. Wingo (eds) *Issues in Urban Economics*, Washington DC: John Hopkins Press.

Toulouse, J.M. (1991) 'Les immigrants et la création d'enterprises: test d'un modèle préliminaire auprès des chinois et des haïtiens', Hull: Actes du colloque national sur la régionalisation de l'immigration au Québec, 22 November 1991.

Vivarelli, M. (1991) 'The birth of new enterprises', *Small Business Economics* 3: 215–23.

Walton, J. (1977) *Elites and Economic Development*, Austin, TE: Institute of Latin American Studies, The University of Texas Press.

Westhead, P. (1989) 'A spatial analysis of new manufacturing firm formation in Wales, 1979–1983', *International Small Business Journal* 7: 44–68.

Westhead, P. and Moyes, T. (1992) 'Reflections on Thatcher's Britain: evidence from new production firm registration 1980–88', *Entrepreneurship and Regional Development* 4 (1): 21–56.

9

AN INVESTIGATION OF CONFLICT IN THE FRANCHISEE–FRANCHISOR RELATIONSHIPS

Findings of the pilot study

Steven Spinelli Jr and Sue Birley

Franchising has played a significant role in the development and expansion of businesses in the USA for many years. For example, the number of business format franchisors has grown from 909 in 1972 to over 3,000 in 1993 (*Entrepreneur Magazine*, January 1994) while, in the same period, individual outlets grew from 189,640 to over 570,000 (IFA 1991). In 1991, 540,000 franchised outlets had sales of over $750 billion, accounting for 35 percent of all retail sales (IFA 1991). A similar pattern has emerged in the UK, where a survey conducted by National Westminster Bank for the British Franchise Association in 1991 revealed 18,600 franchised outlets with sales of $4.8 billion, forecast to rise to over £10 billion by 1996. Reflecting this pattern, Stern and El-Ansary (1988) estimate that 10 percent of all retail sales in Europe are through franchised outlets. Indeed, the International Franchise Association estimates there are between 11,000 and 62,000 franchised outlets outside the USA and the UK and that sales generated will rise to $1 trillion by the year 2000 (IFA interview with Terrien Barnes, Director of Research, January 1993).

Key to the success of the franchise organizational form is the interdependent relationship between the two parties – the franchisor and the franchisee. Clearly, the nature of such a relationship gives rise to the potential for conflict. In this chapter we report the preliminary findings of a study of one British franchise, ServiceMaster, which asks the question: Does the economic and financial structure which defines the relationship between the franchisee and franchisor firms result in behaviour which is likely to exacerbate interorganizational conflict?

DEFINITIONS

The interorganizational form

Miller and Grossman (1986) described franchising as an organizational form structured by a long-term contract whereby the owner, producer, or distributor (franchisor) of a service or trade-marked product grants the non-exclusive rights to a distributor (franchisee) for the local distribution of the product or service. In return the franchisee pays an upfront fee and ongoing royalties and agrees to conform to quality standards (Justis and Judd 1989). In a later study, Achrol and Etzel (1990: 2) describe a franchise as 'an incentive distribution system for organizing individual firms pursuing their own rewards'. Taking this latter perspective of franchisor and franchisee firms being independently liable organizations, we prefer to describe the phenomenon as an interorganizational form. This is consistent with Stern and El-Ansary's (1988) definition of a marketing channel of distribution as sets of interdependent organizations in the process of making a product or service available for use or consumption. Channel structure refers to the nature of the firms involved in the channel, the nature and extent of their inter-related roles and the allocation of the channel's productive value.

Distribution of productive benefits

A key aspect of franchisee relationships is the central role of the trade mark (Caves and Murphy 1976) whereby the franchisee is cloaked in the identity of the trade mark but operates as a separate legal entity (Eaton and Joseph 1988). Thus, franchising is the establishment of a relationship between independent firms who share an intangible asset, customer goodwill, embodied in the trademark. The intangible asset is enhanced or diminished by the delivery of the product or service to the consumer, and the value of the asset is derived by capitalizing the stream of future earnings. The capitalization value is the basis for the franchise fee and royalty payment. The up front fee, generally termed a franchise fee, is usually paid at the time the licence agreement is executed. A royalty is a scheduled regular payment, calculated as a percentage of the total revenue generated by the franchisee firm. There is considerable variation in the magnitude of both types of fees (Sen 1991) but all are the apportionment of the value of the benefits derived from the shared intangible asset, the trade mark (Caves and Murphy 1976; Michael 1993).

Franchising types

Two distinct types of franchising are described by Dicke (1991). Product franchising was originally created by the makers of complex durable goods who found existing wholesalers either unable or unwilling to market their products. These manufacturers built their own distribution systems and franchises were created as alternatives to the high cost of company-owned outlets.

Product franchising is characterized by franchised dealers who concentrate on a company's product line and to some extent identify their business with that company (US Department of Commerce 1988). Product franchises include gas stations, car dealerships and soft-drink bottlers.

Business format franchising grew out of the concept of distribution channel development and control. It was formalized in the late 1950s by entrepreneurs who believed that the outlet itself could be a product (Dicke 1991). Initially the motivation was to enhance efficiency through minimizing cost (franchised outlet versus company-owned outlets) and later as a method of expanding revenue by prescribing detailed operational practices to protect and, ultimately, enhance the trade mark. Thus, franchising was used to create bilateral gains for channel members through vertical integration (Williamson 1991).

Business format franchising accompanies the trade mark and distribution rights with information on the production processes and delivery system. Inherent in this is the assumption that the information exchange will ensure the maintenance of the trade mark value (Caves and Murphy 1976). The value is then enhanced through the development and exploitation of economies of scale. Business format franchising usually includes a marketing plan, documented and enforced procedures, process assistance, and business development and innovation (Achrol and Etzel 1990). It is an entire way of doing business and is a more complex relationship than product franchising because the method by which the asset is to be shared is stipulated in the licence agreement (Dant *et al.* 1992). For example, the McDonald's franchisee must staff and market per the contractually agreed methods whereas the product franchisee, say the Pepsi bottling franchise, centres on the soft drink formula and the packaging of the product.

This complex channel system raises the question of coordination and control over the marketing functions (Simpson 1990). Each franchisee, as a downstream channel member, impacts the value of the intangible asset as the trademark becomes manifest in the delivery of the product to the consumer. Thus, the performance of each outlet has a pro-rata impact on the total income stream of the franchise system and specifically to the franchisor *vis-à-vis* royalty payments. Direct cost and benefits of individual performance are associated with agency concerns which ultimately affect the trade mark value (Jensen and Meckling 1976). Clearly, the relationship must necessarily be dynamic because no long-term contract can cover all contingencies (Boyle 1991). There is an interdependent effect of action taken by the parties either bilaterally or independently (Carney and Gedajlovic 1991). This is due to the continuing interaction between the franchisee and the franchisor involving general business discussion, feedback on marketing, and operations process adjustments. The level of interaction varies by franchise system but often exceeds the strictly interpreted contractual requirement (Dwyer *et al.* 1987; Jakki and Nevin 1990; Kaufmann and Stern 1988). This chapter is concerned with relationships within one business format franchise.

THEORY DEVELOPMENT

Since the body of literature in the field of franchising is still in the emergent stage, it has been necessary to draw upon perspectives from divergent sources. The resultant broad literature search, which included neoclassical economics, transaction cost economics, agency theory and conflict theory helped us to identify the issues and to operationalize the analysis.

Microeconomic structure and pricing behavior

Under a marginal cost scenario, total cost equals fixed cost for the franchisor. This occurs because the franchisor puts overhead in place prior to selling franchises for the purpose of establishing support systems. The total cost curve is parallel to the X axis. The franchisee's total cost equals variable plus fixed cost. The franchisee total cost curve is upward sloping and to the right. For both entities profit equals total revenue less total cost. Also, the profit maximizing price for both entities is the point at which marginal revenue equals marginal cost. For the franchisor $MC = 0$. $MR = 0$ where total revenue is maximized. Stated differently, the franchisor will desire to drive revenue higher with lower pricing until revenue is maximized. When a lower price no longer generates a sufficient increase in quantity to make up for the per unit reduction in price, price will be stabilized. With each unit increase in quantity of sales a marginal cost is incurred for the franchisee. With the same pricing equation of $MR = MC$ the franchisee will be willing to lower price until it equals marginal cost. Thus, an issue inherent in this organizational form is that franchisee $MC > 0$ while franchisor $MC = 0$ and therefore franchisee price $>$ franchisor price. These different perspectives towards the pricing of the individual product or service establish a basis for conflict in the relationship. The ways in which this conflict is likely to manifest itself are through marketing policies of promotion, new product development, market research, and local and national advertising, the usual focus of marketing effort in the business format franchise.

Transaction cost economics

While microeconomics anchors our approach to potential conflict, transaction cost economics allows a broader perspective by placing the principal burden of analysis on comparisons of the 'costs of running the economic system' (Arrow 1985: 48). The theory also embraces the assumption that the parties involved in the relationship are motivated by economic self-interest and will engage in opportunistic behavior to maximize their own position (Bergen *et al.* 1992). Whereas the firm is the basis for analysis in micro-economic theory, the transaction is the basic unit of analysis in transaction cost economics (Williamson 1975). In view of the nature of franchising, this would appear a more fruitful perspective to explore.

It is particularly relevant when we examine the basic dimensions on which the transactions differ and the implications of those differences for designing appropriate governance structures since central to the dimensional bound-aries in transaction cost analysis (TCA) is asset specificity (Williamson 1985). This appears uniquely to link TCA with the central theme in franchising, the sharing of an intangible asset, the trademark, and the particular issues of governance that arise from that sharing. Moreover, TCA is concerned with developing the most appropriate safeguards that best protect the transactions against the hazards of opportunism (Simpson 1991). The formal safeguard employed in franchising is the licence agreement which delineates the specific nature of common ownership and the behaviour between the parties in support of that asset.

> As economics expands beyond its central core of price theory, and its central concern with quantities of commodities and money, we observe in it . . . a shift from a highly quantitative analysis, in which equilib-rium at the margin plays a central role, to a much more qualitative institutional analysis, in which discreet structural alternatives are compared.
>
> (Simon 1979: 6–7)

Thus, transaction cost economics moves beyond the marginal analysis involving efficient allocation of resources to what Williamson (1991) describes as 'discreet structural alternatives'.

Williamson (1975) notes that the critical differences in organizational form and governance mode centre on the frequency, uncertainty and degree of asset specificity in supplying a good or service in a transaction where asset specificity is defined as 'the degree to which an asset can be redeployed to alternative uses and by alternative users without sacrifice of productive value'. It can be distinguished in six ways:

- site specificity;
- physical asset specificity;
- human asset specificity;
- brand name capital;
- general assets dedicated to a specific customer;
- temporal specificity: site specificity which requires on-site human assets.

Taking these dimensions, the franchise company stakes its future on the shared development of brand name capital since continued investment in reputation and brand name assets is critical to competitive advantage and success (Klein and Leffer 1983; Shapiro 1983). This may also be crucial for debt acquisition. Intangible, firm-specific assets can form a basis of security for the lender (Balakrishnan and Fox 1993). Temporal and site specificity, in varying degrees are also integral to the franchise organizational form (Mundstock 1991). Human and physical asset specificity may be important to franchise success and dedicated assets generally are not as important. Clearly, there are a number of dimensions over which the brand name asset is specified. Achrol and Etzel (1990) point out that the franchisee perception of franchisor support of standardization is important to the level of conflict in the franchisee–franchisor relationship. Franchisor support services, sometimes contractually obligated, address a number of the dimensions delineated in the transaction cost approach to asset specificity. We submit that franchisor support of standardization is, in fact, a key aspect of brand name capital. This allows us some insight to the particular areas for conflict in franchising – the contractually obligated services.

Conflict literature

In 1985, Pondy reviewed his seminal work on conflict in commercial organizations (Pondy 1967) and proposed a revised 'pure conflict system model', based on the principle of continual, often managed, conflict. In this model, exhortations of organizational harmony are simply strategies employed to control both a conflictual organizational environment and the outcomes of conflict.

The current literature on conflict clearly follows Pondy's new perspective as a persistent organizational reality (Brett et al. 1990; Merrill and Thomas 1992; Witteman 1992). Brett et al. (1990) studied conflict as a phenomenon which affects both inter and intra-organizational relationships. Retha Price (1991) specifically investigated channel conflict. She concluded that management style in conflict resolution had an effect on the optimal organizational form. Because conflict resolution entailed interpersonal skills and interorganizational negotiation, both formal and informal channel structures were important. Price's (1991) thinking is expanded by Merrill and Thomas (1992) who studied organizational management styles. Relational strengths in an organization, especially personal and informal relational characteristics, greatly impact organizational design.

Magrath and Hardy (1989) developed a strategic paradigm for predicting manufacturer–reseller conflict. They found that conflict in this distribution channel stems from key goal variables such as differences in marketing (including target customer and product lines), the specific design of the channel and interpersonal relations. Levels of conflict were associated with the specificity of channel relations and the corresponding monitoring activities. If the parties to the channel relationship understood mutual expectations, responsibilities and commitments and these issues were monitored, conflict levels would be expected to be lower.

THIS RESEARCH

The literature described above has given us sufficient reason to conclude that there is the potential for conflict in the franchise relationship based in the differences in the microeconomic structures of the franchisor and franchisee firms. Moreover, it has allowed us to identify areas of conflictual behavior which are likely to result from these structural differences in the firms. Therefore, this research traces the process of creation, management and exit of the relationship and asks the following questions:

1 The perceived contract: What are the goals particular to the relationship between the franchisor and the franchisee?
2 The primary source of potential conflict: How satisfied are the franchisees with the services supplied by the franchisor?
3 The value which the franchisee places on the relationship as reflected in the trade mark: What is the franchisee's perception of the cost of leaving the franchise arrangement?
4 The manifestation of conflict: What is the apparent level of hostility of the franchisee towards the franchisor?

METHODOLOGY

Data collected

Three instruments were drawn from the literature in order to explore the above propositions:

1 Achrol and Etzel (1990) – a study of franchisee–franchisor relations – goal definition constructs and franchisor services.
2 Ping (1990) – a study of perceived exit costs in a wholesaler–retailer relationship – measurement of exit costs by substituting franchisor for wholesaler and franchisee for retailer.
3 Kaufmann and Stern (1988) – a study of perceived hostility in a wholesaler–retailer relationship – the hostility or conflict construct. The hostility construct is developed from Macneil's (1974) Relational Exchange Theory as specifically applied in a questionnaire used by Kaufmann and Stern to measure conflict in buyer–seller relationships.

Sample

ServiceMaster is a home and office cleaning franchise which was started in the USA in 1952 and which has operated a semi-autonomous business in the UK since 1973. There are 181 franchisees in the UK, operating 300 'territories'. We obtained an introduction to the company by an executive of their commercial bank. The franchisor agreed to cooperate in the study by supplying a mailing list and writing a letter of introduction which voiced support for the project. This gained us several advantages. First, we had an up-to-date specialized list. Second, we increased the potential value to the franchisee by adding the interest of the commercial bank (the bank's name appears in both the introductory letter from the managing director and our cover letter). Thus, with the support of the franchisor, the questionnaire was mailed to all franchisees during May and June 1993. Adopting Dillman's (1978) methodology, 52 responses were received, representing a 30.5 percent response rate. The characteristics of the franchisees and their franchises are shown in table 9.1

FINDINGS

Goals

Achrol and Etzel (1990) developed four goals which may describe the franchisor–franchisee relationship (see Table 9.2). Respondents were asked to respond to each statement on a scale 1 (not important) to 5 (very important). As expected, the majority of franchisees viewed all the statements to be of some importance and, relatively speaking, the goal of quality assurance the most important. However, a significant minority would appear to be unconcerned with developing and improving relationships with their franchisor. This finding varies somewhat from Achrol and Etzel (1990) study where relationship building was the conclusive finding. If this significant minority is evident in other companies as we continue our research they may provide important and richer insights into the causes of conflict in the franchise system.

Table 9.1 The characteristics of the franchisee and their firm

	Mean	*SD*	*Range*
The franchisee			
Year franchise agreement signed	1984–5	6 years	1991–1976
Number of years in current job	6.1	5.6	1–21
Number of years in franchising	6.7	6.0	1–25
Number of outlets currently operated	1.4	0.7	1–4*
The franchise			
Sales (y/e December 1992)	£143,950	£2,845	£25k–£4.25m
Annual fixed expenditure per outlet	£22,740	£1,386	£5k–£90k
Variable expenses per unit per £ of sales	30.1%	4.49%	10%–70%
Profit margin per unit	23.7%	4.37%	1%–40%
Promotion expenses per £ sales	3.7%	1.24%	1%–15%

Note:
*67 percent of respondents operated only one outlet, and 27 percent only two

Franchisor services

In order to explore the possible reasons for the perception of the relationship described above, Table 9.3 shows the list developed by Achrol and Etzel (1990) to ascertain the franchisees perspective of the importance of the services provided by the franchisor. As can be seen from Table 9.3, the overall pattern is as would be expected in such a dependent relationship with all the services except one, that of advice on inventory control, scoring a mean value greater than the neutral score of 3. Overall, and interestingly in view of the focus of this research, the three most important would appear to be procedural and trade mark oriented rather than oriented towards aspects of directly adding sales volume:

1 Resolving disagreements and complaints quickly, eagerly and fairly (4.36).
2 Clearly defined procedures for operating the franchise (4.15).
3 Programs and procedures for training employees (4.13).

These findings are somewhat consistent with Achrol and Etzel (1991) but with far less emphasis on the relational issues and greater emphasis on operational concerns.

Services may be very important but if they are not delivered to the satisfaction of the franchisee we would expect to see a high level of dissatisfaction. Therefore, we also probed the franchisee's perception of their adequacy. Only six of the eighteen services score an overall mean which is greater than three:

1 Provision of standardized equipment (4.25).
2 To act as a supplier of products (3.94).
3 Access to franchisor management (3.67).
4 Clearly defined procedures for operating the franchise (3.60).
5 Developing new products and services (3.40).
6 Programs and procedures for training employees (3.15).

We used the Wilcoxon Signed Ranks Test to measure the direction and magnitude of the difference between importance and adequacy within paired variables (Table 9.3), thus asking the question: Is there a significant difference between the importance of each franchisor support service and the adequacy with which it is delivered?

In only two of the eighteen support services were importance and adequacy congruent. Moreover, importance exceeded adequacy in all areas except the supply of equipment and the supply of products from the franchisor to the franchisee. As Achrol and Etzel (1990) did not measure adequacy we have no comparative data. However, there is prime facie evidence to suggest that there is clear dissatisfaction as to the relationship between the two parties. Additionally, although the overall importance of the marketing functions are ranked low, their perceived adequacy is significantly lower (Table 9.3). This would accord with the conclusion of Achrol and Etzel (1990) who also found

Table 9.2 Relative importance of franchisor–franchisee relationship goals

	Mean score*	SD
At this point in time, developing a more cooperative relationship with your franchisor is relatively . . .	3.42	1.19
Compared with other goals, given current business conditions, improving communications and information sharing between franchisee and franchisor is . . .	3.85	1.18
Relative to other goals, at this time better coordinated franchisee–franchisor quality assurance is . . .	3.92	0.99
Weighted against other goals, strengthening the mutual commitment between your franchisor and you is . . .	3.75	0.95

Note:
* Score 1 = not important; score 5 = very important

Table 9.3 Franchisor services importance and adequacy

	Mean scores		Standard deviation		Z score	SL-2
	Importance	Adequacy	Importance	Adequacy		tailed
Training	4.135	3.154	1.067	1.017	−4.1404	0.0000
Accounting	3.885	2.365	1.096	1.010	−4.4685	0.0000
General management	3.923	2.615	1.064	1.013	−4.4451	0.0000
Credit	3.365	2.442	1.237	1.274	−3.3422	0.0008
Financial management	3.731	2.288	1.031	1.073	−4.7515	0.0000
New products	4.096	3.404	0.934	1.176	−4.1571	0.0000
Promotion	4.000	2.827	1.029	1.248	−4.5698	0.0000
National advertising	3.962	1.981	1.154	1.000	−5.5122	0.0000
Marketing information	3.808	2.365	1.172	1.138	−4.9014	0.0000
Local advertising	3.308	1.827	1.307	1.024	−4.9959	0.0000
Contact	3.923	3.673	0.904	1.184	−1.2341	0.2172
Equipment	3.885	4.250	0.832	0.813	−2.6033	0.0092
Supplies	3.923	3.942	0.882	0.998	−0.3429	0.7317
Problem solving	3.808	2.846	1.121	1.144	−4.1307	0.0000
Inventory	2.808	2.308	1.067	1.112	−2.2931	0.0218
Operations	4.154	3.596	0.802	1.112	−2.9944	0.0027
Fairness	4.365	2.865	0.687	1.299	−5.4091	0.0000
New territories	2.885	2.327	1.745	1.424	−3.0857	0.0020

marketing to be of low importance and recommended a higher level of sharing of marketing information as a solution to this perceived problem.

Exit costs

Clearly, if the franchisor is unhappy with the services provided by the franchisee, one option is to withdraw from the relationship. However, such a decision would incur a number of costs. To explore the franchisee's perception of these switching and exit costs we used a construct developed by Ping (1990).

Table 9.4 lists the statements ranked by the mean score. From this, it would seem that the franchisees appear to understand both the role and value of the trade mark and its components and the ease with which fixed assets can be redeployed. This is consistent with the Transaction Cost paradigm. However, mean values can mask bi-modal distributions. Therefore, the frequencies for each score are also shown. Our caution is important. There are clear bi-modal distributions in three areas:

1 Store conversion costs on exit.
2 Lost customer goodwill on exit.
3 Costs of modifying the operating procedures on exit.

The issues of goodwill and operating procedures clearly reflect trade mark values concerns. Therefore, it is surprising to see the level of disagreement on these issues. Similarly, on the surface, store cost conversion would cause less concern although the role and intricacy of signage on buildings and equipment in many franchises may explain the group concerned with this expense. Nevertheless, this result does indicate a need for further analysis. Overall, however, there is clear evidence that franchisees consider the exit costs to be high. Alternately stated, they appear to understand the value of the franchise.

Clearly, it is likely that the greater the variance in franchisee valuation versus the PDV formula the greater the increase in the conflict measure construct. The value of the franchise from the perspective of the franchisee is the incremental income stream generated by the trade mark. This is calculated on a net present value basis. The franchisor calculates the value of the trade mark in the establishment of the franchise fee and royalty. In the franchise studied in this research the royalty fee was 7.5 percent and the franchise fee was £25,000. Based on the reported revenues in the survey and a 20 percent discount rate, the incremental value of the franchise trade mark was calculated to range from –£10.000 to £100,000. However, in the questionnaire, only twenty of the fifty-two respondents listed a market value for the trade mark. Thirteen franchisees who left a blank answer to this question were subsequently telephoned. One franchisee did not understand the question and twelve simply could not estimate a trade mark value. For those

Table 9.4 Exit and switching costs

	Scores*					Mean	SD
	Disagree				Agree		
	1	2	3	4	5		
If I left the franchisor, I would spend a lot of effort converting the store	22	7	7	12	1	2.24	1.4
If I left the franchisor I would have to spend a lot of time, money and effort to set up alternate suppliers	8	7	11	19	7	3.19	1.3
Terminating my licence agreement would involve considerable legal expense	2	1	7	19	23	4.15	1.0
Terminating my licence agreement would cost my company time, money and customer goodwill	10	6	4	9	23	3.56	1.6
The costs involved in exiting the franchise relationship would probably be high	1	9	11	18	13	3.65	1.1
I have personally invested a lot of time and effort in the relationship with the franchisor	7	9	14	17	5	3.01	1.2
A lot of the company's energy, time and effort have gone into building and maintaining the relationship with the franchisor	6	5	26	11	4	3.04	1.0
Much of the company's investment with the franchisor is unique to the relationship	8	5	7	14	17	3.53	1.4
Terminating my licence agreement will increase my marketing budget	2	5	6	20	19	3.94	1.1
Ending my relationship with the franchisor will increase my training costs	5	5	6	16	20	3.79	1.3
Ending my relationship with the franchisor will require modification of the operating procedures	10	12	9	6	15	3.08	1.5

Note:
*Alpha = 0.7298

twenty respondents who did estimate the value of the trade mark there was a £32,233 negative variance per franchisee firm with the net present value of the franchise fee and royalty payments.

Conflict

The results presented above give support to the view that there is potential for conflict within the franchisor–franchisee relationship. They have also indicated the areas of possible conflict. Therefore, the final part of the study utilized Kaufmann and Stern's (1988) constructs to ascertain whether there was explicit evidence of hostility from the franchisee towards the franchisor. Table 9.5 shows the four hostility scales and the mean scores for this study (alpha = 0.7). Generally, these results suggest a low level of hostility from franchisees towards franchisor. Moreover, the alpha is acceptable. Therefore, two of the scales were recoded to measure hostility in the same direction for all scales (score of 1 indicating very low hostility and 5 very high hostility).

The mean hostility score is 2.52 (SD = 0.9) indicating that, overall, there is no real hostility. However, examining the results in more detail, we find the following pattern:

- 56 percent score less than 3 and are labelled 'satisfied';
- 29 percent score 3 and are labelled 'ambivalent';
- 15 percent score more than 3 and are labelled 'angry'.

CONCLUSION

Clearly, the results of this study are specific to one franchise, ServiceMaster, and it is possible that we would obtain different results from, say, a fast food franchise. Therefore, our design for the main study includes cohorts of franchises from a variety of industry franchises. The results described here encourage us both to continue with our study and to analyze the inter-relations in these data in more detail.

Developing franchisee–franchisor relations is a dynamic, long-term process. In this chapter, we have shown clear theoretical and empirical evidence of the potential for conflict in this relationship. However, our pilot study gives only tentative support for the proposition that the microeconomic structural differences in the franchisee and franchisor firms result in marketing and new store development that leads to hostility. Indeed, the data suggest that franchisees consider the marketing services which they receive to be both

Table 9.5 Measures of hostility from franchisee to franchisor

	Mean*	SD
Our organization feels the same way about the franchisor before and after any dispute	2.63	1.3
Our organization has retained anger towards the franchisor because of past disputes	2.25	1.3
If it was up to me we would not be part of the franchise system any longer	1.69	1.1
If I was the franchisor I would act in the same way as the franchisor does now	3.10	1.3

Note:
*Score 1 = disagree; score 5 = agree

unimportant and inadequate. This evidence leads us to conclude that marketing may well be the focus of behavioral effects due to structural differences between the two parties but that it is manifest through the franchisee viewing the marketing activities of the franchisor as contradictory to their own needs and, therefore, discounted.

There is a higher level of support for the proposition that the trade mark value is understood as the primary linkage between the franchisee and the franchisor. However, the maintenance of the trade mark is seen as occurring in the standardization of the systems, not in the marketing functions. Thus, the franchisee would appear to be saying that the franchisor is good at developing an operating system that is proven and which, therefore, reduces franchisee risk. This, in turn, enhances the value of the franchise by allowing the franchisee to apply a lower discount rate to the income stream.

Given that an important historical and theoretical reason for franchising is the economy of scale in marketing, there seems to be a dramatic opportunity to enhance the franchisor–franchisee relationship by addressing the specific nature of perceived inadequacy in marketing as viewed by these franchisees. It is logical to assume that if the franchisor could induce a high level of recognition of the importance of marketing in the franchisee hierarchy of goals, relational and trade mark gains could ensue.

The tentative 'peace' in the relationship, as revealed by the conflict construct, may hinge on the day-to-day perception of adequacy in operational and training issues and is supported by franchisee understanding of exit costs. The tentative nature of the lack of conflict in the relationship is supported by the general lack of ability of the franchisee to quantify the values of the trade mark and by the specific undervaluation when quantified. Additional, the bi-modal distribution of expectations of exit costs may reveal a segment of the population financially prepared to disrupt the relationship if events were to pose such an option.

REFERENCES

Achrol, R.S. and Etzel, M.J. (1990) *Enhancing the Effectiveness of the Franchise Systems: Franchisee Goals and Franchisor Services*, The George Washington University and the University of Notre Dame, Babson Research Conference 1992.

Arrow, K.J. (1985) 'The economics of agency', in J. Pratt and R. Zeckhauser (eds) *Principals and Agents: The Structure of Business*, Boston: Harvard Business School Press.

Balakrishnan, S. and Fox, I. (193) 'Asset specificity, firm heterogeneity and capital structure', *Strategic Management Journal* 14: 3–16.

Bergen, M., Dutta, S. and Walker, O.C. (1992), 'Agency relationships in marketing: a review of the implications and applications of agency and related theories', *Journal of Marketing* 56, July: 1–24.

Brett, J.M. Goldberg, S.B. and Ury, W.L. (1990) 'Designing systems for resolving disputes in organizations', *The American Psychologists* 45 (2), February: 162.

British Franchise Association (1992) *1991 NatWest/BFA Franchise Survey*, London: Howarth.

Carney, M. and Gedajlovic, E. (1991) 'Vertical integration and the franchise systems: agency theory and resource explanations', *Strategic Management Journal* 12: 572–86.

Caves, R. E. and Murphy, W.F. (1976) 'Franchising: firms, markets, and intangible assets', *Southern Economics Journal*, 42: 572–86.

Dant, R.P., Wortzel, L.H. and Subramanian, M. (1992) 'Exploring the relationship between autonomy and dependence in franchise channels of distribution', in Boston University *Frontiers of Entrepreneurship 1992*, Boston: Boston University.

Dicke, T.S. (1991) *Franchising in the American Economy, 1840–1980*, PhD dissertation, Ohio State University.

Dillman, D.A. (1978) *Mail and Telephone Surveys*, New York: John Wiley.

Dwyer, F.R., Schurr, P. and Oh, S. (1987) 'Developing buyer–seller relationships', *Journal of Marketing*, 51, April: 11–27.

Eaton, M.M. and Joseph, R.T. (1988) *Antitrust Issues in Franchising*, presented at the American Bar Association's Fundamentals of Franchising Program.

Entrepreneur Magazine (1994) *15th Annual Franchise 500*, January: 170–219.

International Franchise Association (IFA) and Horwath International (1991) *Franchising in the Economy 1990* Evans City, PA: IFA Publications.

Jakki, M. and Nevin, J.R. (1990) 'Communication strategies in marketing channels: a theoretical perspective', *Journal of Marketing* 54 (4), November: 36–51.

Jensen, M.C. and Meckling, W.H. (1976) 'Theory of the firm: management behavior, agency costs and ownership structure', *Journal of Financial Economics* 3, October: 360–95.

Justis R.A. and Judd, R. (1989) *Franchising*, Cincinnati, OH: Southwest Publishing Co.

Kaufmann, P.J. and Stern, L. (1988) 'Relational exchange norms, perceptions of unfairness and retained hostility in commercial litigation', *Journal of Conflict Resolution* September.

Klein, B. and Leffer, K. (1983) 'The role of price guaranteeing quality', *Journal of Political Economy* November: 659–86.

Macneil, I.R. (1974) 'The many futures of contract', *Southern California Law Review* 47: 691–816.

Magrath, A.J. and Hardy, K.G. (1989) 'A strategic paradigm for predicting manufacturer–reseller conflict', *European Journal of Marketing* 23 (2): 945–108.

Merrill, C. and Thomas, C.K. (1992) 'Organizational conflict management as disputing process: the social escalation', *Human Communications Research* 18 (3): 400–14.

Michael, S.C. (1993) 'Why franchising works: an analysis of property rights and organizational form shares', presented at the 1993 Babson Conference on Entrepreneurial Research.

Miller, A.R. and Grossman, T.L. (1990) *Business Law*, Glenview: Scott Foresman.

Mundstock, G. (1991) 'Franchises, intangible capital and assets', *National Tax Journal* 43 (3), September: 299–305.

Ping, R.A. (1990) *Responses to Dissatisfaction in Buyer Seller Relationships: Exit, Voice, Aggression, Loyalty, and Neglect*, doctoral dissertation, University of Cincinnati.

Pondy, L.R. (1967) 'Organizational conflict: concepts and models', *Administrative Science Quarterly* 12, September: 296–320.

Pondy, L. (1985) 'Overview of organizational conflict: concepts and models by Louis R. Pondy: reflections on organizational conflict', *Journal of Organizational Behaviour* 13 (3), May: 255–61.

Price, R. (1991) 'An investigation of path–goal leadership theory in marketing channels', *Journal of Retailing* 67 (3), Fall: 339–61.

Sen, K.C. (1991) *The Use of Initial Fees and Royalties in Business Format Franchising*, PhD thesis, Washington University.

Shapiro, C. (1983) 'Premiums for high quality returns to reputation', *Quarterly Journal of Economics* November: 659–86.

Simon, H. (1979) 'From substantive to procedural rationality, in F. Hahn and M. Hollis (eds) *Philosophy and Economic Theory*, Oxford: Oxford University Press.

Simpson, J.T. (1991), *An Empirical Investigation of the Impact of Governance of Marketing Channels of Distribution*, PhD thesis, University of Michigan.

Stern, L.W. and El-Ansary, A. (1988) *Marketing Channels*, Engelwood Cliffs, NJ: Prentice Hall.

US Department of Commerce (1988) *Franchising in the Economy*, Washington DC: USGPO.

Williamson, O.E. (1975) *Markets, Hierarchies Analysis and Anti-trust Implications*, New York: Free Press.

—— (1985) *The Economic Institutions of Capitalism*, New York, NY: The Free Press.

—— (1991) 'Comparative economic organization: the analysis of discreet structural alternatives', *Administrative Science Quarterly* 36: 269–96.

Witteman, H. (1992) 'Analyzing personal conflict: nature and awareness, type of initiating event, situational perception and management style', *Western Journal of Communication* 56 (3), Summer: 248–80.

APPENDIX I

MEASURING ENTREPRENEURSHIP OVER TIME

William B. Gartner and Scott A. Shane

ABSTRACT

This article is a review of three measurement issues that impact the study of entrepreneurship over time:

1 Level of analysis differences between firms and individuals.
2 Differences between rate and stock measures.
3 The effects of choosing particular time frames on subsequent analytical results.

Based on a theory that views entrepreneurship as depending on ownership rights (Hawley 1907), this paper develops a longitudinal measure of entrepreneurship in the USA – the number of organizations per capita. The problems and advantages of using a measure based on organizations per capita as an indicator of entrepreneurship is examined.

Understanding how and what is being measured in studies of changes in entrepreneurship over time, is an important issue for academic researchers and public policy-makers. For example, is entrepreneurship increasing in the USA? If entrepreneurship is increasing, is this trend comparable to any previous time periods, or is the current increase in entrepreneurship a new or unique social phenomenon? What influences changes in entrepreneurship over time? The choice of certain measures of entrepreneurship are likely to influence the answers to these questions.

Levels of analysis

Studies of entrepreneurship focus on either individual level activity (e.g. self-employment) or on firm level activity (e.g. new incorporations). Self-employment research focuses on individuals who employ themselves, that is, individuals who report wages, but not wages paid to them by other individuals or organizations. In most studies of the self-employed, firm founders would, therefore, be classified as wage earners, and not as entrepreneurs. New firm research focuses on the rate of the new firm entrants, typically measured as new incorporations, so such businesses as proprietorships or partnerships will not be counted.

Rates and stocks

A rate is a change from one state to another (e.g. the number of people who become self-employed for a specific year, or the number of new firms created for a specific year), while a stock specifies a particular level (e.g. much like a stock of inventory), such as the number of self-employed, or a particular number of firms, for a specific time period. It is important to recognize that entry into business does not necessarily guarantee remaining in business. For example, while the number of people who become self-employed may increase for a specific year, the number of people who remain self-employed may actually decrease if more of the self-employed fail to remain in business than those that enter. The stock of the self-employed can decrease if the outflow of self-employed is greater than the inflow. For those persons interested in whether entrepreneurial activity results in wealth creation (either individually or societally), the realization that entry into business may not lead to a sustainable business (and therefore no creation of wealth) should be a signal that measuring rates of business formation and self-employment may not be appropriate for this type of research.

Time frame

The factors that drive changes in the rate of entrepreneurship are not likely to be manifest over short time periods. Changes in values, attitudes, technology, government regulations, world economic and social changes have a significant influence on changes in entrepreneurship over time. Studies that have measured entrepreneurship over recent time periods are, therefore, likely to miss the influence of these variables.

We introduce a measure of entrepreneurship (organizations per capita) based on a theory of entrepreneurship as ownership. This measure shows the stock of organizations in the US economy over time (from 1857 to 1992). The problems and advantages of using a measure based on organizations per capita as an indicator of entrepreneurship is examined. We conclude with some suggestions for improving entrepreneurship research by recognizing the limitations of particular longitudinal entrepreneurship measures and by challenging the field to seek convergent validity among measures.

APPENDIX II

NEED AND ISSUES ON VENTURE BUSINESS SUPPORT IN JAPAN

Shuichi Matsuda and Itaru Shirakura

ABSTRACT

The Japanese style management in the traditional major corporations has gradually been changing and a decaying phenomenon of the management characteristics has occurred. It is a matter of urgency to support venture businesses to replace the traditional major corporations. This paper presents the social, institutional and other issues including those involving the corporation itself of how to support venture businesses in Japan and clarifies the direction of those solutions through the comparison of venture businesses in the USA and Japan.

Many researchers have undertaken comparisons on a worldwide basis of venture businesses entrepreneurs and venture capital, presenting the characteristics of each nation (Gibb 1993; MacMillan 1993). It is to be regretted, however, that regarding Japan, after World War II, papers dealing with such comparisons are all but non-existent. This is due to the number of researchers specializing in this field being limited in number (Kurokawa 1992; Matsuda 1991). By clarifying the changes currently taking place in the economic environment of Japan and studying the needs for a system of support for venture businesses together with the issues involved, the characteristics of the situation concerning venture businesses will be presented. This paper will be dealing with the following factors.

1 Characteristics of Japanese style management inherent in the traditional major corporations and its decaying phenomenon.
2 Downfall of major corporations and the importance of venture businesses to support the rapidly aging society and to bear the load for the coming generations.
3 Comparison of growth industries as viewed from over-the-counter market in the USA and Japan and presentation of the characteristics of Japanese venture businesses through a comparison of a breakdown of industry types listed in the over-the-counter market.
4 Social, institutional and other issues including those involving the corporation itself in order to support Japanese venture businesses in the future.

APPENDIX III

RISK PERCEPTIONS OF ENTREPRENEURS

John W. Mullins and David Forlani

ABSTRACT

An exploratory study of thirty-four founders of rapidly growing firms was conducted to investigate antecedents of entrepreneurs' perceptions of new venture risk and potential. Drawing on theories of risky decision-making in the economics and behavioral decision theory literatures, the experimental study tested four hypotheses:

H1 The greater the variability in predicted outcomes of a proposed new venture, the greater will be its perceived risk.

H2 The greater the magnitude of a proposed new venture's largest potential loss, the greater will be its perceived risk.

H3 The less the variability in predicted outcomes of a proposed new venture, the greater will be its perceived potential.

H4 The greater the magnitude of a proposed new venture's largest potential gain, the greater will be its perceived potential.

Hypotheses H1, H2 and H4 were supported, while H3 was not. The results of our study indicate that both the variability perspective (Fisher and Hall 1969) and the hazard perspective (March and Shapira 1987) are meaningful to entrepreneurs in their assessment of the risks associated with new ventures. Greater variability and greater hazard led to perceptions of higher new venture risks. For new venture potential, however, while greater possible gains led to perceptions of higher potential, variability in the likelihood of such gains had no effect. Apparently, higher probabilities of deviation from the target outcome tend to be discounted when considering upsides (potential), but not for downsides (risk).

Together, the results have implications for the presentation of sensitivity analyses in fund-raising efforts, analyses which entrepreneurs often develop to assess the likely outcomes of proposed ventures under different scenarios. Since such analyses call attention to possible variability in future outcomes, their use is likely to increase the perceived risk associated with the venture.

181

In our study, the presentation of four ventures having equal expected values led to perceptions of widely ranging risk, but much less difference in potential. In typical sensitivity analyses which provide best case, worst case and most likely case scenarios, it may be that the best and worst case scenarios offset each other as to perceptions of potential, but that the implied variability in anticipated returns increases the perception of risk, thereby detracting from the attractiveness of the overall proposal. Thus, the presentation of sensitivity analyses may tend to raise perceptions of risk but not potential, something which entrepreneurs seeking funding are loath to do. Downplaying of such analyses may therefore be advised in the process of seeking capital for new ventures.

References available on request.

INDEX

183